To. Mel Saunders, an old work colleague.

THE WHITE HORSE SHOW
A Village Charity

With all best wishes

THE WHITE HORSE SHOW
A Village Charity

Brian J Tilling

ATHENA PRESS
LONDON

THE WHITE HORSE SHOW
A Village Charity
Copyright © Brian J Tilling 2007

All Rights Reserved

No part of this book may be reproduced in any form
by photocopying or by any electronic or mechanical means,
including information storage or retrieval systems,
without permission in writing from both the copyright
owner and the publisher of this book.

ISBN 10-digit: 1 84748 007 1
ISBN 13-digit: 978 1 84748 007 1

First Published 2007 by
ATHENA PRESS
Queen's House, 2 Holly Road
Twickenham TW1 4EG
United Kingdom

Printed for Athena Press

Acknowledgments

I offer my most grateful thanks to the following people, without whose help and kindness I would never have achieved this work:

To Mr J Seagrove for designing the cover of this book, the enhancement of old photographs and entering its entirety on to a CD for the publishers.

To Mrs Lynn Seagrove for various photographs of White Horse Shows, and the photograph of the floodlit St Mary's Church at Uffington.

To Mrs J Shorten for the photograph of St Mary's Church and Tom Brown's School.

To Mr W Mitchell and Mr D Kelsey, MBE, for photographs and information contained within.

To Col. A J Bateman, OBE for his support and valued advice at all times over a considerable period of time.

I am indebted to Mrs Joan Little, widow of the late John E Little, whose encouragement and memories made the whole thing possible. Most grateful thanks.

Thanks to John Gibbons Studios, The Shambles, Lower Common, Uffington, Oxfordshire, for permission to use his copyrighted photographs of the 2005 White Horse Show.

Finally, thanks go to the White Horse Show trustees and the White Horse Show Committee for their cooperation in the publication of this book.

The History and Origin of the Uffington White Horse Show

I moved away from Uffington in April of this year after being a founding member of the White Horse Show Committee in 1972. When I am on some of my frequent visits back to the old village, quite a number of people still stop and ask me different things about the show and its origin and its aims. So for the purpose of any interested people I will try to set out in the following the origin and aims of that project.

But first I must go back in time to early 1919, when the Old Village Hall was erected at the Top Corner. For those who don't know, this is at the junction of High Street and Broad Street. The Old Village Hall was in fact a redundant Nissen hut from the First World War. How did Uffington get this? Quite simply, it was through the generosity of the servicemen returning home after their demob in late 1918 or early 1919. Instead of accepting the monies that had been collected around the village to welcome them home they decided to purchase the said Nissen hut from the War Department at a cheap rate. My grandfather and father were amongst many others involved, and this information, of course, came from them. This village hall served the village well under the management of the Parish Council until 1958 and 1959, when its age began to cause severe maintenance problems. The main and most serious problem was that the underfloor cross-carrying timbers became rotten and unsafe. After an examination and written report by a local architect, at least a third of the floor was condemned as unsafe and taken out of use. After a considerable amount of deliberation by the Parish Council and other organisations, it was decided that there were insufficient funds in the village hall accounts to carry out such repairs. With this in mind the then Parish Council under the chairmanship of Mr Billy Packer decided to call an open public meeting in the village hall. This would enable all interested people to come along and give their views as to what could be done to keep a village hall in the village. The meeting was held in April 1960 and was well attended, with many suggestions for what could be done to maintain a hall for the use of local organisations. At the end of a very long, and at times a very heated, meeting, on the suggestion of the chairman it was decided to form a committee of willing people to raise money to build a new village hall. The people who were willing to undertake this mammoth task were as follows: Mr and Mrs M Conners, Mrs J Reed, Mrs E Adams, Mr W Mitchell, and Mr B Tilling. The committee was to be run under the auspices of the Parish Council, who in turn would lend to the committee a sum of £5 until they could raise enough money to return the same.

These people met at the home of Mr Mitchell on the following Monday night to discuss ways to start this task. At that meeting we decided to call ourselves the Village Hall Building Fund Committee; the chairman would be Mr W Mitchell. To start the money-raising we would organise a bingo game every Saturday evening, and on alternate Thursday evenings would run a whist drive. Thus, on the Saturday evening following our first meeting, we were up and running.

Our first attempt at money-raising proved a great success and made what was then a fantastic profit of over £15. At our next meeting on the following Monday evening we decided to return the £5 we had received from the Parish Council. At that time this gave us a great feeling of satisfaction; we were now on the way to a new village hall, despite the usual snide remarks that kept coming through to us – 'They will never make it.' Our bingo and whist drives were continuing to make money, and it was decided that when the new football season commenced in August we would endeavour to run a football sweepstake to raise further funds. I was appointed promoter to run sweepstakes and draws for the Village Hall Building Fund, for the purpose of keeping within the law. First I had to apply to the Faringdon Rural District Council for a licence to run any such thing. The auditor of my accounts, which had to be submitted to the Faringdon Rural District Council every three months, was Mrs Betty Packford from Woolstone.

Uffington Old Village Hall

At the commencement of the 1960–61 football season we started our football sweepstake with a set of 420 tickets selling at 6d. each, paying out £5 for the highest score and four IOUs at 2s.6d. each. This proved to be very popular with the public. After a run of six weeks I decided to increase the size of the ticket set to 620 and pay out eight IOUs at 5s. Again these proved popular and with the help of people working at Harwel, Shrivenham and Didcot we were able to sell all the tickets nearly every week. During this time we were also running Derby and Grand National sweepstakes as well as a grand Christmas draw. These efforts went well throughout the 1960–61 and 1961–62 football seasons. The 1962–63 season also started well, but unfortunately our luck was about to come to an abrupt end in January 1963. This was due to the very bad weather that came then; no matter how much we tried after the weather cleared and football started again, we were unable to get this on the run as we did before. Since we had started, until our luck turned sour, we had raised the fantastic sum at that time of nearly £3,000.

White Horse Hill as photographed during a helicopter trip

At this time we had still not found any volunteers for the posts of secretary or treasurer to the Building Fund Committee. So Bill Mitchell continued to take notes at our meetings. For the first two years he also undertook to do the banking of funds that we were raising. At this time we persuaded Mr Hugh Arbuthnot to take care of this side of things for us. Being a retired banker he also produced balance sheets, which kept the Parish Council happy.

Still being as determined as ever not to give in to all the knockers, we pressed on with the bingo and whist drives together with the Christmas draws and Derby and Grand National sweepstakes. But in 1971 we had to admit that the monies that we were raising were no more than just holding our bank account at inflation level, which in real terms meant we were at a standstill and getting nowhere. In spite of this our committee still confirmed to the Parish Council and its new chairman that we were going to try and resolve the matter by enlarging our committee by co-opting more volunteer members.

At our next meeting Mr Mitchell suggested that we make an approach to Mr John Little to see if he had any suggestions that he could offer us, as by now we were beginning to really struggle to hold our own against the rising inflation. Mr Mitchell undertook to make this approach and said he would report back at our next meeting. We did not have to wait that long for our answer, as Mr Mitchell informed us that Mr Little had in fact agreed to come to our next meeting on what he had described as a fact-finding mission. John, as he became affectionately known to us in the future, was quite impressed with the progress we had made to date with the enormous task we had been set to achieve. He thus promised to go away and come back to our next meeting with some more ideas on raising the capital we required.

The next meeting, with John in attendance, proved to be another turning point for the three villages of Uffington, Woolstone and Baulking. John proposed at this meeting very wide-ranging changes in the whole way in which we approached our task. To start with he said that a new village hall would in itself be beneficial to all three villages, therefore perhaps we could co-opt more members from Woolstone and Baulking, if they were approached with this in mind. He also thought it would be of benefit to put in one great money-raising project each year, but to still carry on with our other functions. The committee immediately accepted John's proposals without exceptions. Following this John undertook to approach people from Baulking and Woolstone to join us. He also stated that he would give money-raising some more thought and report back at our next meeting in a fortnight's time.

As promised, John reported back at our next meeting, and some report it was! He had certainly done his homework. On the co-opting of new members to represent Baulking he had obtained Mr Jack Jeeves; to represent Woolstone were Mr Hugh Shorten and Colonel Harry Hopkinson. We were most grateful to John for the trouble that he had gone to in gaining this extra help that we were going to need in the very near future. John informed us he had given the money-raising side a great deal of thought and requested that we all meet at his home at the Pantiles on the following Monday evening to meet the new members. At this meeting he would also give us a detailed rundown of money-raising. We all agreed on this move, as we knew what a great job John had done in running the Flower Festival in the three villages in 1964. This festival in itself had raised enough money to carry out urgent repairs to the roof of Uffington Church, which had been leaking very badly.

On meeting at the Pantiles the following Monday evening we were all introduced to each other. Then John got down to explaining his idea of the way forward in our money-raising efforts. As 1972 was the 150th anniversary of the birth of Thomas Hughes, John suggested that we run a large event in the village to celebrate that fact. We could use the three days over the August bank holiday in 1972 to achieve that aim. After a very long discussion on what could be organised over those three days, we were all unanimous that we must attempt the project. John then said that, as we would need the approval of the Parish Council to use different facilities within the village, an open meeting under the auspices of the Parish Council would be the best way forward. He then stated he would make the approach to the Parish Council chairman and report back to us as soon as a decision was forthcoming. True to John's ways it was not long before we were summoned to another meeting at the Pantiles.

At that meeting we were informed by John that he had been successful in persuading the Parish Council to call an open public meeting in the village hall that could be attended by villagers from the three villages. This meeting would be chaired by the Parish Council chairman, Mr Philip Burgess. We then went into another very long discussion on tactics that we could adopt at that meeting. In general, John would lead with a free hand on our behalf.

The evening of the meeting arrived in due course. The village hall was full to capacity, bearing in mind that a part of the floor was marked KEEP OFF, FLOOR UNSAFE. Some of us decided nevertheless to sit on this area, knowing full well that we would not suddenly disappear down in a hole never to be seen again. Prior to the meeting some rumours had been started round the village by the preachers of doom that at long last the Building Fund Committee were giving up, having realised that they could not achieve the task they had been set some eleven years before. On opening the meeting the chairman Mr P Burgess gave a brief explanation to the public present of why the meeting was taking place. He said that the meeting had been called in response to a request from Mr J Little regarding a function that he wanted to run in the village. He then asked Mr Little if he would like to address the meeting. Mr Little replied that he would be willing to explain what he had in mind. He thus explained that he would like to organise a three-day event in the village to celebrate the 150th anniversary of the birth of Thomas Hughes. All the proceeds from this event would be going to the fund for a new village hall. But, before he could make any real start on this project, he would have to have a working capital of money to hand. He then proposed that the Village Hall Building Fund Committee and the Parish Council both donate £100 each to allow this project to start.

The chairman Mr Burgess then asked Mr Mitchell if his committee would have any objection to the proposal that Mr Little had made. Mr Mitchell was quick to reply that he was certain that the Building Fund would be only too pleased to subscribe their share of the funds, providing the Parish Council would also provide their share. With this, the Parish Council went into a very close huddle to discuss their position. After a few minutes the chairman said that they could not provide any money as such from the public fund, as there were insufficient funds in that account. But all was not lost as they did have £100 which had been left to the village in the will of the late Mrs W Wyatt, the widow of the last farmer to rent Manor Farm from the former Craven Estate. This money was to be used towards building a new village hall.

This of course caused a considerable number of comments and questions from us members of the Building Fund Committee present. We were not against this money being used to ensure that the proposed event got started by Mr Little, but were angry that we had not been informed of this legacy, and we would be asking more questions concerning that in the future. Therefore, in the true light of day, the Building Fund Committee would be funding the whole exercise. This point was put to the meeting and accepted by the vast majority of those present.

Mr Little then thanked those present for their time and trouble in attending the meeting, and said that if anyone could spare any time to assist in the project they should let him know, as he would be grateful. On closing the meeting the chairman, Mr P Burgess, thanked all those present for their input to the debate that had taken place and offered his services to Mr Little.

At the next meeting of the Building Fund Committee, John gave us a brilliant update on his project. He informed us that he had a very good response from volunteers coming forward to help with the event. He had in fact been able to form a separate committee to run that event. This committee was: chairman, Mr J Little; secretary, Mrs I Curzon; assistant secretary, Mrs J Little; treasurer, Mr P Burgess; assistant treasurer, Mr W Mitchell. Other members of the committee were: Mr D Witts (vice-chairman), Mr B Mattingley, Mr J Mowland, Mr D Ross, Mr H Shorten, Mr R Liddiard, Mr M Birks, and the press officer Mr Jack Lofton. John had also been successful in obtaining Sir John Betjeman CBE as president, and Professor Stuart Piggott as vice-president.

His list of patrons was also formidable, as follows: the Earl of Craven; the chairman of the Berkshire County Council; the County Councillor Shrivenham Division; the Lord of the Manor of Uffington; the Rt Hon. Airey Neave, DSO, MC, MP; Captain T L Lonsdale; David Astor Esq.; the Hon. Robert Boscawen, MC, MP; the Rt Hon. John Fraser, MP; the Rt Hon. Marcus Lipton, MP; the Rt Hon. G R Strauss, MP; the mayor of Chester; the president of Newbury Field Club; the principal of the Working Men's College (London); Alexander Macmillan Esq.; the headmaster of Ruthin School (Wales); the headmaster of Twyford School (Hampshire).

The First Show – 1972

As has been previously said, the August bank holiday weekend of 1972 would be the date for this event to take place. It was agreed that the event would be called the Tom Brown's Festival. This would be in recognition of the birth of Thomas Hughes, the author, 150 years before in the village of Uffington. On John's advice it was also decided that the full Building Fund Committee would not be recorded as members of the Festival Committee. This was because we were in the process of becoming a charitable trust, and it was thought at that time this would contravene the terms of the forthcoming charity. This thought was later proved to be wrong. But this did not stop the whole Building Fund Committee being involved and helping with the festival.

John's determination paid off in the end, and the Thomas Hughes Memorial Trust was formed and duly registered with the charity commissioners as a charitable trust to build the new village hall. By doing this John had relieved us of any tax liability that we would have incurred if we were not a registered charitable trust. Plans were now advancing for the organisation of events that were going to be included in the 1972 festival.

The field that was going to be used as the main showground was the old recreation ground. For the benefit of people not knowing where this was, it was the field in front of the White Horse Housing Estate. This of course is now occupied by the new village hall, Craven Common and the Jubilee Field. This was possible at the time by the kind permission of Mr Bob Spence the farmer.

The festival programme was as follows:

In Tom Brown's School: an exhibition of Thomas Hughes – books, letters, paintings and nineteenth-century bygones. In the village school: an antiques fair. In the old recreation ground: rural crafts, pottery, thatching, glass blowing, wine making, honey making, wood carving, beaten pewter work, steam model railway (rides for children), produce stall, cake stall, candy stall, Thomas Hughes souvenirs, i.e. pottery, pens and books, knitted gifts, toys etc., trade fair, buy-a-brick for the new hall. There were also special Post Office hand stamps and commemorative envelopes (available over the three days). All this was running over the three days.

On Sunday from 2 p.m. to 5 p.m.: there was a nineteenth-century cricket match (played to the rules and dress of the period). In the village hall was the mummers play: first performance at 6 p.m., second performance at 7 p.m. The mummers play was introduced by Charles Bailey. The cast was as follows: Father Christmas – William Mitchell; King George – Jack Jeeves; Starcher – Charles Russ; Doctor – Robert Iles; Mrs Vinney – Adrian Packford; Beelzebub – David Coxhead; Jack – Ernie Packford. The last time the mummers play was performed was in 1951, during the Festival of Britain.

On Monday from 11 a.m.–midnight: parade of historic cars to the village field and judging. At 2 p.m., past time revels and games (*It's a Knockout*, 1857-style) organised and presented by the Faringdon Round Table. The teams taking part were from local organisations.

Event 1 – The Uffington Steeplechase

Event 2 – The Mini-Marathon, Heat 1

Event 3 – Chasing the Cheese

Event 4 – The Mini-Marathon, Heat 2

Event 5 – The Whistle Race

Event 6 – The Mini-Marathon, Heat 3

Event 7 – The Three-Sack Race

Event 8 – The Mini-Marathon, Heat 4

Event 9 – The Punt Race

Event 10 – The Mini-Marathon, Heat 5

Event 11 – The Mud Scrum

Event 12 – The Mini-Marathon, Heat 6

Event 13 – Water Stocks

Event 14 – The Mini-Marathon, Heat 7

Event 15 – The Wheel-Barrow Race

Village Hall – mummers play – first performance 6 p.m., second performance 7 p.m.

In the field from 8 p.m. until midnight – roasting of lamb and barbeque.

Also on Monday afternoon the special one-day Post Office hand stamp of mail from the show field was transported to Faringdon by stage coach. This went well until it rounded the bend in Fernham on its way to Faringdon. Then – alas! – the stage coach was surrounded by highwaymen who had been laying in wait at the Woodman Inn. This was organised by the late former landlord of the Woodman, Mr John Lane, who was at that time a generous supporter of the show. However, after some strong language and a little more delay, the mail eventually reached Faringdon, with the stage coach returning to the show field. Every person that made the trip fully enjoyed the experience without too much worry about the highwaymen.

Prior to the show on 20 August, the Tom Brown's Gymkhana was held at Church Farm in Baulking, by kind permission of Mr Ron Liddiard. The organisation of this event was carried out by Mr J Chambers and his daughter Ann.

Events to follow these, still raising money for the new village hall, included the 9 September screening at 8 p.m. of the film *Tom Brown's Schooldays*, starring John Howard Davies as Tom and Robert Newton as Dr Arnold. This was shown at the Lefroy Lecture Theatre RMCS, Shrivenham by kind permission of the commanding officer.

It was, of course, the film star John Howard Davies who declared the weekend events officially open.

On 8 October at 7.30 p.m. a recital was held in St Mary's Church, Uffington. The soloist was Mr Charles Corp, tenor, who received the gold medal for solo singing at the Guildhall School of Music and Drama. He was accompanied by William Allen Humpherson, FRCO, LRAM, BDS, organist and choirmaster at the military church of St Alban, Larkhill Garrison, Wiltshire.

As can be seen from this, John's organising ability had been working in overdrive. One thing became clear to all of us – a colossal amount of work needed to be done to prepare for this weekend event to take place. Not forgetting that just as much would want doing afterwards to clear up. But from this mammoth task the White Horse Show was born. After everything had been completed regarding this event, even more serious thinking was going to be needed to plan the way forward.

Hand-made toys, 1972

It was generally agreed at the wash-up meeting after this weekend event that a three-day event was too much to ask for. However, in general terms, if we were going to achieve our aim of having a new hall then we could not afford to let events of this type drop. We all decided to go away from this meeting and give this problem serious thought and come back to the next meeting with our views for going forward. John then gave a good report on the financial rewards from the effort that had been put into the festival. Although he could not give a final figure for the profit it would be well in excess of £2,000. This gave us all a great feeling of satisfaction and proved beyond any shadow of doubt that John's tactic of holding one big effort each year was the correct one. The next meeting was scheduled to take place at John's home, the Pantiles, in one month's time.

At our next meeting a great deal of thought was given to different ideas on the show for 1973, the final decision being that it would be a one-day event on the Monday bank holiday in August. It would also be held in the same field as the 1972 show. Mr J Chambers and his daughter Ann had kindly agreed to hold another gymkhana the week before this at Church Farm in Baulking, again by kind permission of Mr Ron Liddiard.

The committee had now opted to become the White Horse Show Committee for the purpose of raising funds to finance the Thomas Hughes Memorial Trust. The committee was made up as follows: chairman, Mr J Little; vice-chairman, Col. H Hopkinson; secretary, Mrs J Little; treasurer, Mr H Shorten; historic cars, steam traction etc., Mr W Mattingley; rural craft and trade, Mr D Witts; showground organisers, Mr B Tilling, Mr W Mitchell and Mr M Connors. It was at this meeting that Mr Hugh Shorten announced that a most extremely kind donation had been offered to our cause by Professor and Mrs Seton-Lloyd of Woolstone. They had offered to donate the old school at Woolstone to be sold, with the profits of the sale going to our funds for a new village hall. As can be appreciated, the whole committee was stunned by this great act of generosity by Professor and Mrs Seton-Lloyd. It was then decided that Mr Hugh Shorten would liaise with Professor and Mrs Seton-Lloyd concerning this generous gift. This Hugh did with great skill and tact, overcoming problems on the way to the eventual sale. At long last we could see our goal being achieved; but the money-raising had to carry on, for obvious reasons. It was also decided that Mr Ware-Cornish, the architect from Woolstone, should be approached for advice on the design and structure for a new village hall that would also be complementary to older buildings within the village. John and Hugh would arrange to meet Mr Ware-Cornish for a discussion with this in mind and report back in due course.

In the meantime it had been decided that the present site of the village hall would be unsuitable for the new hall. The County Council and the police had both objected to the site, as it would be too close to the junction of High Street and Broad Street. It was as a result of this predicament that the Parish Council was forced to start negotiations with various parties for a new site. The new chairman of the Parish Council, Mr Saunders-Price (proprietor of Nortons stores), was leading the way on this subject. We could not go into the business of purchasing land because it would have been outside the original terms of the Old Village Hall Building Fund Committee remit, which was set back at the public meeting in 1960.

1973

At this time it was decided to take up John's advice and apply to the Charity Commission to register our charity as the Thomas Hughes Memorial Trust. The deed of the trust was to be to build a new village hall. While all these things were going on, plans for the 1973 show still had to be made and events booked. As it was only a one-day event it would not be held in the same complex as 1972. This time we were also to be without the publicity of Thomas Hughes, so we were going to try and make it an old-time country show. We had found out by a kind of feedback from the public that, in running shows of this nature, publicity was of paramount importance. To achieve this we had to get the advertising started in good time; to this end the events had to be booked before posters could be printed. One good thing in our favour was that we still had the services of Jack Loften, who was a reporter on the *Swindon Evening Advertiser* and also the local weekend papers. Mrs Joan Little, John's wife, had agreed to become the show secretary. These Littles must have been gluttons for punishment, but how grateful we were. The buy-a-brick campaign was going to be an ongoing thing. The names of all the contributors were recorded in a book which would be placed in the foundations of the new hall, a second copy being preserved in the hall. This again was being run by Hugh Shorten and Col. Harry Hopkinson. Some of the souvenirs left from the previous year would also be on sale again. Some of the other exhibits in the marquees were to be: a display of GWR relics by Mr D Castle of Wantage; a sale of plants by Mr F Painter; a pottery-making demonstration by Pauline Thompson and Trevor Chaplin from East Hendred, glass blowing by Mr P Williams, Stanford in the Vale. There was also cooper craft by Angus Clark, Faringdon; soft toys, Mrs M Tilling, Uffington; blacksmith and forge, Mr Anthony Robinson, Mortimer, Berkshire. One of the oldest working exhibits to be at the show was a set of steam gallopers.

Many of the elder members of the community suddenly returned to their childhood days and the steam gallopers did a roaring trade. They were also very popular with the young as well. Music was provided by a model organ from Stroud, in Gloucestershire, owned by Mr David Dando.

In April 1973 we received from the Charity Commission the confirmation that we were an official registered charitable trust. We were to be known, as per our request, as the Thomas Hughes Memorial Trust, with terms of reference as per our deed. Capt. Lonsdale of Kingston Lisle readily agreed to become a patron. The trustees were Mr J Chambers, Mr Franklin, Professor Seton-Lloyd and the Rev. Jim Tillyard. We were also grateful that Mrs Marion Wallis had offered to carry out the duties as secretary of the trust. At the wash-up meeting for this show we, as a committee, had to admit again that we had not got the programme right. The first show we ran for three days and we found that far too strenuous and taxing on our resources; but by cutting back to a one-day show we had gone too far the other way. We had prepared and arranged the field, which had been just as much work as the previous year, but had only used it for one day.

Thus, we decided to go away and think about what would be best suited for the 1974 show. On top of this we had to find another site in order for this to be a possibility anyway. Another thing to be taken into account was the problem of car parking, which had caused us great problems this year. The police had also made their position quite clear: they were not happy with the parking this time. Therefore, they would want to be kept in the picture over parking in the future. We had recognised that the parking for the last two years on the old village green had been insufficient, and this was one area we were going to have to improve on. Also raised at this meeting by our secretary Mrs Marion Wallace was the fact that she had been approached by a prominent member of the local Women's Institute, who had claimed that, to date, they had not received any thanks for the money they had raised and donated to our cause. Hugh quickly admitted that he was to blame for this serious mistake and that he would personally go to the next WI meeting and render his apologies in person. The committee were very grateful to Hugh for his offer; after all, we were very grateful for the excellent financial help that these ladies had given us and felt we could do with a lot more spirit like this from other sources. As always there was a lighter side to the more serious things that cropped up from time to time. There had to be, as it was the one thing that kept us going through the bad times. The fun thing at this time was that I proposed that Hugh not only apologise for our oversight, but offer his services to the WI and become their president. But, typical of his sense of humour, Hugh thought that he would have to decline the post of president of these wonderful ladies due entirely to the workload that he already had. At our next meeting Hugh reported back with the outcome of his attendance at the WI meeting, which in his words had gone very well. He had apologised for our shortcomings and received in return from these wonderful ladies a firm commitment that they would continue to help us to the best of their ability. After that meeting I said to Hugh that I thought that he was a very brave man to enter into the lions' den without a thought for his own safety, after which I always addressed Hugh as 'The Pres'. Even when he phoned me after this he introduced himself by saying, 'This is "The Pres".' This name stuck with him until he sadly passed away. Both he and his wife Joy always saw the funny side of life.

Whilst all the happenings of the last two shows were taking place, Mr Saunders Price and the Parish Council had been in negotiations over the building of Craven Common with Mr Bob Spence. The outcome of these talks resulted in Mr Spence making a gift to the parish of what is now termed the Jubilee Field, and Mr Spence receiving the old village green in return. I know that the rights and wrongs of this deal still come up in discussions in the village now. But, as far as the Thomas Hughes Trust and the Old Village Hall Building Fund Committee are concerned, I can categorically state that we were not involved in these negotiations at all. This was a purely Parish Council matter. I did personally question the Parish Council chairman at the time we were told of the deal, particularly concerning the public footpaths. I was assured that the deal did not affect the right of the public to use these footpaths as they had done over the past years.

Given this assurance, my own feeling was that the village had got a very good deal. At the time, however, there were people in the village who turned very spiteful towards our cause – this we were to find out in the very near future. But I am happy to say that the majority of parishioners were very pleased with the result; after all, this deal had given the village a site for the new village hall.

While all this was in progress Mr Ware-Cornish, the architect, had produced a full plan for a new hall, which all members of the trust, together with members of the old Building Fund Committee, found very pleasing. All points raised by the committee and the trust had been taken into account. It was then decided to seek a meeting with the Parish Council to discuss the next step of the project. The meeting with the council was very cordial and correct. In fact, we seemed to have a council of very grateful councillors. At the end of this meeting it was decided that the trust and Building Fund Committee should go away and decide where we stood on the financial side. This we carried out to the best of our abilities. We took a great deal of advice from a very experienced person working in the building trade, who dealt with contracts and costing. That person was no other than one of our own members, Mr Hugh Shorten. He advised us to go out to seek estimates for this work, as inflation was starting to increase at a frightening rate. As could be expected we took his advice without hesitation and went down that road. Alas, our jubilation was only to be short-lived! One of the parish councillors had obtained the signatures of nine members of the parish to call a further open parish meeting to discuss an alternative village hall plan. As can well be appreciated, the mood of all the people who had struggled for thirteen years to raise the funds for this project turned to real anger. That a parish councillor could sit in a meeting with us and say nothing against our project then go away and stir up trouble in this fashion we found unbelievable. I will not at this time name the guilty person, but it is something that will stick in my mind for ever.

Prior to this undesirable meeting we as a committee had to call a gathering of our own members to try and counteract this setback at such short notice. When we had our meeting we had a rough sketch plan of the alternative hall that had caused all the trouble. To only have this in front of us while trying to defend our position was in no way going to improve our anger. We thus had to demand a proper plan, which gave measurements and all the relevant information that we required, to compare it with the Ware-Cornish plan. With reluctance this was supplied, after a further delay. When you bear in mind the roaring inflation that was taking place at this time, our extreme anger will be appreciated. We then discussed the alterative plan. On the night of the open meeting Mr Hugh Shorten would deal with the building technicalities that would be raised. Colonel Harry Hopkinson would take all the general questions and for the most part would be the spokesman for our group.

On the night of the dreaded meeting the village hall was again packed to capacity. On opening the meeting the parish chairman gave a brief rundown as to why the meeting had been called; he then handed over to the councillor who had requested the meeting. As this person stood and tried to speak, pandemonium broke out. One of the nine signatories jumped to their feet and made it clear to all present that they and three more had been duped into signing the petition for calling the meeting. For the next ten minutes or so a lot of anger was let loose, but, full credit to them, none of our committee took any part in the farce. When the chairman did finally regain order the meeting carried on, although with very heated exchanges. One thing that I must add is that our two main representatives, Hugh and Harry, were cool and brilliant under, at times, extreme provocation. The villages of Uffington, Woolstone and Baulking have a lot to thank these two men for; note that there will be more thanks to them later. The final outcome of the meeting was that, due to a sizable grant that was forthcoming from the County Council, the final decision of which hall would be adopted was to be made by an independent body of arbitrators. This body would consist of architects nominated by the County Council. They in turn would report back to the Parish Council; but no time limit could be put on receiving that report. We needed this like a hole in the head. Already running on a very tight budget, with inflation getting worse all the time, we were left to wonder whether we would get a new hall in the end. One thing was for certain, we were not going to let the spiteful knockers win. To see that this did not happen we had to listen again to our three wise men – John, Hugh and Harry – and get on with the jobs we had in hand, such as planning the 1974 show.

1974

We again thought about the duration of the 1974 show and came to the conclusion that it would be a two-day event. We thought that we could handle this, within reason. The new site for the show would be in the Fawler Road sports field. This had been cleared by the trustees of the Craven Field. I must add that this field had been donated to the village as a sports field by the family of Lord Craven. We had also had the kind permission of Mr Jim Matthews to use his field on the opposite side of the road for car parks. At least we could go on planning this show – not to forget the past bitter setback, but to put it in the back of our minds. The most worrying problem concerning this show would be the provision of toilets; in the past we had had the use of the facilities at the Old Village Hall. This year we had to build our own. This was not the easiest of tasks, but one we were to overcome by the start of the show. We received more entries for this show than ever before, and on the day everything but the weather was going well. The Saturday had been very wet; we took the decision to delay the erecting of the marquees until the Sunday morning, when we would meet at the field at 6 a.m. What fools we were: it was blowing a gale. But, not to be beaten, we got going with a great deal of help from exhibitors who had camped overnight. Assisted by a vintage tractor we achieved our goal, although the public were entering the show as we erected the third and last marquee. New attractions at this show included a welly-wanging contest – in plain English, a £10 prize went to the person who could throw a wellington boot the farthest. This was run by Mr Ron Liddiard, who, with his rendering of the Berkshire dialect, had everybody that heard him in stitches of laughter. This also paid off with a handsome profit for the show.

For the first time we had skydiving by the Robins. This was a team of seven RAF personnel from Abingdon who were ranked as the best in the country at that time. In fact, they had just come second in the European championship. In reality, Doug Peacock who was in the team was European champion; and also in the team was Alison Jones, the female European champion. When the time came, in the afternoon of the Monday, a very strong wind was still blowing and it was thought doubtful by the ground marker, who had come by road from Abingdon, whether it would be possible for them to jump in such a wind. But, true to form, we heard by radio link that they were taking off from Abingdon in their de Havilland Rapide aircraft to make the attempt.

Just after the aircraft appeared over the show field, the team informed the ground controller that they were going to climb to the required height. When they had achieved that height they would then come over the landing marker to drop their direction and distance marker. This device would have a radio signal within it to give the team a distance measurement from where the ground marker had landed. On this information a decision would be made on whether it was possible to jump or not. Sure enough, the aircraft came over and dropped the marker; this disappeared from our view in a north-easterly direction in no time at all. It left those on the ground in no doubt that there would be no skydiving in this wind.

But we were proved to be wrong. We received a message from the team leader, Doug Peacock, that the marker they had dropped had in fact travelled just over three miles. On this information it was far too windy to use the flat chutes, but, because of the size of the waiting crowd, they would use ordinary parachutes and do their best. This information was relayed to the waiting crowd. The aircraft were nearly out of sight in a south-westerly direction beyond Woolstone Hill when we saw the parachutes leave the aircraft. To everybody's amazement they had jumped and were drifting at a great rate in our direction. We were asking ourselves then how close were they going to get to the marker, with all the odds stacked against them. We soon had the answer: just one member, John Holey, landed by the marker on the football pitch. Alison Jones landed in the next field, not far from high-tension electricity cables. Doug Peacock and two more landed on the opposite side of the road in the car park, with the other two just over the hedge on the opposite side of the show field to Alison

Jones. Needless to say, they were all praised for their bravery in jumping in such weather conditions. When talking to the team afterwards we learned that they had actually left the aircraft just over three miles from the show field, at 3,700 ft. With this in mind, coupled with the adverse wind condition, what an achievement it was to get as close as they did. After being brave enough to jump in these conditions, we on the committee were thankful to see them all down safe.

The team, after looking round the show and meeting the chairman, promised to come back to the show the next year to perform again. I was lucky enough to get my programme autographed by the whole team. This is now one of quite a few souvenirs of the many White Horse Shows that I helped with.

After this show was over we found that we had hopefully got the duration of our shows about right, and decided that the two-day event was the right way forward. Having then announced that we had created the basis for a very big profit, which could not be finalised until a later date, the treasurer Mr Hugh Shorten then told us that he did have some good news for us – but also some very bad tidings as well.

First, the good news was that the independent body of architects had found in our favour with regards to the new village hall and had favoured the Ware-Cornish plan. This had been the opinion of the committee all the time, as we had heard that the alternative plan had apparently been drawn up not by an architect, but by a marine engineer. This decision of course delighted the committee wholeheartedly – we had been right from the start.

The next news was the bad news; this could not have been any worse. It was that, the whole time it had taken for the open meeting to take place and the independent board of architects to report back, inflation had overtaken us. Inflation, of course, had to be added to the original prices that Hugh had obtained on the estimates for building the new hall. We had therefore gone forward in leaps and bounds in raising money for this project only for some very spiteful person to snatch the rug out from under our feet. To say that the committee was angry is very much an understatement; we just sat there absolutely seething. It was left to the three wise men, John, Hugh and Harry, to calm us all down in the end. I must add at this point that I do not apologise for referring to these three as 'the wise men'; they had so many times in the past put the cooling effect on some of the anger of myself and others. Without them we would have let go in frustration at the unnecessary setbacks we had received over the last fourteen years; instead we sat down and listened intently to the suggestions that were being discussed as to the best way out of the predicament that we had been plunged into. At that point it was decided to go away and cool off, to do some rational thinking yet again on the best way forward, without disclosing any thoughts we might have to anyone outside the committee. We would therefore meet again in one week to put any ideas forward.

That week seemed to really have flown by when we all sat down to see where we could go. We were in for a very big shock when John opened the meeting. He said he had a statement he wanted to make, but first we had to undertake two conditions for him to make that statement. Those two conditions were: that what was going to be said would stay in the confines of the committee in the foreseeable future, and was to be accepted without being recorded in any minutes. Knowing John as we did, we all gave our assurances to his satisfaction on this matter. When John made his statement it became all too clear why he wanted it kept in complete privacy. What it amounted to was that John, Hugh and Harry were going to stand as guarantors on the strength of the White Horse Show to enable us to carry on with the plans to build a new hall. To ensure their acceptance for this they had to face the enormous task of re-mortgaging their houses; but they were prepared to do exactly this without hesitation. To think that these three families could do this on the strength of the White Horse Show, together with the trust they must have had in the other committee members, is virtually unbelievable. One thing is certain; the committee had the greatest of respect for these three families, and vowed never ever to let them down. It was on that promise that the entire committee's determination was founded – the White Horse Show would continue until the new hall had been built and all debts cleared, come what may. With all this cleared it was decided to go into detail concerning the building estimates that had been received by the committee.

This of course was gone through by Hugh, who explained different details and their meanings. It must be understood by all: this was a very exciting time for all of the committee members and could never have happened if the extremely generous offer had not been made at the start of this meeting.

When the meeting broke up it had been decided that, at our next meeting, Hugh would have gone back through all the estimates to place before us the shortlist, so we would not get too bogged down with small details. It was at this time that I had a duty to do, so as not to cause any future animosity in the letting of contract to build the new hall. I therefore handed to John, our chairman, a letter that stated I was forgoing my right to take part in any discussions regarding the letting of contracts, as one of the building contractors, namely H J Knapp & Sons, was owned by a close relative of my mother. With the past animosity we had had I was not prepared to go down that road. John then informed the rest of the committee of my intentions regarding this issue. This came as a surprise to them, but my decision was accepted unanimously. I thus took no further part in any discussions whatsoever on this subject, but was kept informed by the minutes.

I have given more thought to the naming of the parish councillor who deceived us as a committee by calling the open meeting regarding the design of the new hall, and have decided that I must after all name this person on a point of principle. If I carry on without doing so some people will be able to trace back to the Parish Council of that time, and then we could be into the guessing game to find someone to blame. I do not wish to go down that road either, because the wrong person may be blamed. The one and only person was Mrs P Arbuthnot, who at that time was in dispute with the Vale planning authority, plus anyone else in the village that did not agree with her, concerning the building of Craven Common. Unfortunately, we that were trying to achieve a new hall were caught in the crossfire. Trying to build a new hall on the same field as Craven Common put us right in the line of fire. I may add at this time that the marine engineer who came up with the alterative plan for a new hall was no other than a close friend of that parish councillor.

On 22 February 1974 Mrs Arbuthnot again found fault with the trust and made an application to see the full report of the independent board of architects. Obviously she was still very annoyed that she had not won the argument. At our next meeting we gave her request short shrift; we were not prepared to delay any further the building of the new hall. This was for two reasons: first and foremost it would not have been right to do so as inflation was far too rampant; and secondly it would not have been fair to the public of the three villages that had supported us from the start.

The meeting regarding the letting of contracts for the building of the new hall was held, and I again reiterate that I was not present at the meeting. On receiving the minutes for the same I was glad that I took the line I did, as H J Knapp & Sons had been awarded the contract.

To be able to get this under way, economies had to be made to keep inside a very strict budget. First the east-end section, which was to have housed the stage and changing rooms, was to be left until a later date. Everyone agreed that a stage was needed, so to facilitate this a folding drop-down stage was designed. The other main budget-saving move was made by forfeiting the wood-block floor for a temporary one until the funds became available afterward.

At this stage I think it only right to say that the award of grant aid of £6,875 was due largely to the pressure and help of the Rt Hon. Airey Neave MP and Rt Hon. Douglas Hurd MP. Without their help I doubt whether we would have obtained that amount. This was awarded to our project on 28 June 1974. It was also at this time that we were able to offer our sincere congratulations to Harry on his promotion from colonel to brigadier.

On 10 January 1975, at last, work started on the new village hall. The committee at our January meeting offered Hugh Shorten our grateful thanks in appreciation of his planning and considerable forethought for bringing this project to the start of fruition. Other good news on the night was that we had got a further grant of £13,750 – this was from the Department of Education and Science. This brought our total assets to £27,874 as at 9 January 1975.

In April 1975 the increase in building workers wages would affect us as well as the cost of materials and plants, which would increase our costs by a further £2,800. This would be a case of 'grin and bear it'. At least we were up and running; after fifteen years' hard work we finally had something to show for it.

1975

While all these things were taking place, the 1975 show was very much still in the minds of the committee. It was again to be held in the Craven Sports Field. So heavy was the workload and commitment needed to keep abreast of things that nearly all of the committee were trying to cover two or more jobs at the same time. I had the good fortune to obtain the services of Mr Alton Bailey to assist me in the preparation of the show field and car-parking fields. As the police had again criticised us on the subject of traffic control on the highway, it was decided to have at least two gateways into the car-parking field. It was at this point that I decided that two days before the show and two days after away from my employment on annual leave was not going to give me sufficient time to fulfil my commitment to the show. It was from this year, 1975, that I committed to take two weeks' annual leave from my employment; one week before the show to build the showground and one week after to dismantle it and clear up.

This was going to be our fourth show and we were beginning to build a reputation on the quality and the value of the entertainment that it contained. The entrance fee for this year's show was going to remain 40p for adults and 20p for children, with local senior citizens having free entry. It was gratifying to know that we were getting the right results for our efforts, and were going in the right direction to keep the show going. I think it also right to remind people that all the local organisations that were running stalls at our shows were also making quite a lot of money as well.

Some of the attractions at this years show were as follows. Doug Peacock had confirmed that the Robbins Freefall Parachute Team were coming again on the Monday; with better weather they would give a better account of themselves. The band of the Royal Gurkha Rifles had also confirmed to Harry that they would attend to give two performances on the Monday. Other attractions were to consist of demonstrations by a cooper, thatcher, blacksmith and an apiarist showing working bees in a transparent hive comb. There would also be lace making, spinning and weaving. Vintage and veteran cars would also be in attendance, as would be veteran stationary engines. We had also been promised two steam rollers and two steam traction engines. Additional music would be played by a vintage fairground organ. Children's amusements would again be supplied by Mr Jeff Harwood from Goldaming in Surrey.

The somewhat indifferent weather on the Sunday of the show, this being very heavy showers, probably kept the attendance down on that day. But on the Monday there were smiles on the faces of the committee members, as the sun was shining and the public turned up in their droves. We experienced no problems with traffic build-up on the road, as Harry had taken over the organising of the car park personnel; with his organising ability it went like clockwork.

A late event that we thought received a very good reception was Tim Weaving giving a sheepdog demonstration. At the end of his run he received good applause from the spectators. His border collie also enjoyed the fuss made of her by the children after the demonstration. This was one event that we decided we had to follow up for further shows; likewise the parade of the Old Berks foxhounds was also appreciated as part of a country show. Doug Peacock was pleased with the Robins Freefall Parachute Team: all seven members of the team landed in perfect line just behind the marker cross in the centre of the football pitch, and this from 4,000 ft. In conversation with the team afterwards I learned that Doug Peacock had in fact come first in the European Championship. Not to be outdone, Alison Jones had also won the women's section. With everything else going off well, and later when a profit of £1,300 was announced, we were very pleased with our efforts. The only problem was that certain members of the cricket club were quite annoyed that there was an indentation on the very perimeter of the outfield. With these same members now laying down restrictions on the use of the sports field, it left me to wonder how long we would be able to run the show under these circumstances. Nevertheless, it was decided that we had no alternative but to try and see what we could achieve in the same place for the 1976 show.

But, before the committee had this headache to get past, we had the pleasure of the official opening of the new hall to organise, and we were determined that this was a pleasure we were not going to miss.

The official opening was scheduled for Saturday 29 November 1975 at 3 p.m. First, a management committee had to be formed for the running of the new hall. This was achieved by inviting each organisation in the villages to nominate a representative to attend a joint meeting with the trust, with a view to forming such a body.

The representatives of the organisations were as follows: Children's Play Area, Mrs D Mace; Guides and Brownies, Mrs J Mitchell; Mothers' Union, Mrs M Seymour; Parochial Church Council, Miss K Bafern; Scouts and Cubs, Mr A Shand; Toc H, Mr G Packford; Uffington Boys' Football Club, Mr A Bailey; Uffington Senior Football Club, Mr P White; Women's Institute, Mrs Nettle; Young Wives, Mrs A Pottinger; Youth Club, Mr D Capelin; Uffington School Fellowship did not wish to be represented.

After some discussion the above representatives agreed to form the management committee. They duly elected Mr Alec Shand to become their chairman, which he accepted. Mr Shand then went on to explain that he proposed to call that committee 'The Community Association' and register them as a charitable trust for the same purpose as we had done ourselves.

With this necessity completed we could then carry on with the final programme for the opening ceremony. The official opening was going to be performed by Mrs L Ackroyd (née Hughes), great-grandniece of Thomas Hughes. She would be accompanied by her sister, Miss Nancy Hughes. Mr and Mrs Witts had volunteered to put on a country supper in the evening at £1.25 each, with any profit going to the Community Association. This was readily accepted and Mr and Mrs Witts were thanked for their offer.

In the meantime, Mr Alton Bailey and Mr Pete White were

going round the villages door to door collecting donations of cash to purchase chairs for the new hall. The response to their endeavours was a terrific success, and when the chairs are used in the hall we should always be grateful to Alton and Pete. It was suggested by John that the new hall be called The Thomas Hughes Memorial Hall. This was accepted by all, in view of the work and thought that John had put into this project. This name was to be displayed on the outside wall of the new hall in wrought-iron lettering made by Mr M Richings, the local smithy-farrier.

Stone commemorating opening of new village hall

The afternoon of the official opening finally arrived, with everything taking place as planned. The new hall was full to capacity when Mrs Laddie Ackroyd was introduced by Mr Derek Witts, who was our MC for the afternoon of events. Mrs Ackroyd stated how proud she was to have been invited to open our new hall, and how the late Thomas Hughes would have also approved of having his name carried by such a fine and fitting hall, blending into the surrounding area in the village of his birth. The hall was then blessed by the Reverend Jim Tillyard on behalf of St Mary's Church. Mr Jack Mildenhall then followed on behalf of the congregational chapel for the same purpose. The keys of the Thomas Hughes Memorial Hall were then officially handed over to Mr Alec Shand, Chairman of the Community Association, by the chairman of the Thomas Hughes Trust, Mr Bill Mitchell. At this point I felt that we had reached the massive target that we had been set way back in 1960. We realised of course that we still had a great responsibility to the three people who had re-mortgaged their homes to make this afternoon's celebrations possible. To mark the opening of the hall the long-standing and long-suffering original chairman of the Old Village Hall Building Fund Committee, Mr Bill Mitchell, had the task of planting a young ash tree. This duty he duly carried out by the boundary hedge opposite the main door of the hall. It was thought at that time that this tree would stand as a reminder of the afternoon's events for some years to come. It just goes to prove how wrong a committee can be, even with the best intentions. It stood for quite a few years through all winds and weathers until one day the wind became too much for it to bear. This strong wind split the top fork of the tree; it was then attacked by two vandals from Craven Common armed with a chainsaw. More about this at a later date.

After these events of the programme we were able to wander round and meet some of the public who had came to witness these celebrations. The first person to approach me and offer his congratulations was Mr Billy Packer. Mr Packer had been, of course, the Parish Council chairman at the time we had undertaken the giant task of raising the money to build this new hall. In all fairness to him, whenever he met any of the old committee after the public meeting that he chaired, he always made time to enquire about our progress. This showed that he was a very genuine person, really interested in the progress that we were making. After a very firm handshake together with a pat on the back, he said how thrilled he was that we had achieved our aim in spite of all the knockers who had said over the fifteen years that we would never get to what this afternoon was all about. His genuineness and kind words meant a great deal to me, and certainly made my part of the task worthwhile. Another feeling of satisfaction that it gave me was in the reality of replacing a facility that both my father and grandfather had played their part in giving to the village some fifty-six years earlier.

1976

With these celebrations over it was back to the headaches of planning the 1976 show. We had already been informed by the cricket club that no steam engines or other heavy machinery must encroach on any part of the cricket field whatsoever. This put a stop to having any steam at the 1976 show, as well as creating much extra work. We now had to unload all weighty material on or by the football pitch, then move that material to the top part of the field by car and trailer, only going on to the outer part of the outfield of the cricket pitch in extreme cases. This restriction, of course, had to be strictly adhered to during the clearance of the field after the show. On top of this we had to fence off the wicket square with fence posts and chestnut paling to stop any member of the general public from walking on that square.

This extra work was all we needed to keep our spirits up. However, in the meantime, Mr Pete White and his wife Angela had offered to organise a heavy horse show to be a part of the show on the Monday; this was of course accepted with open arms. With the restrictions on the sports field it was impossible to hold that event in the same field. We thus approached Mr Jim Mildenhall to seek his permission to hold the heavy horse show in his small field adjacent to his farm. Being an old-time farmer he was only to glad to oblige. As for the access to his field, he was only too pleased to let us make another gateway into the field wide enough for large horse boxes to gain entry. The other problem to face us with this site for the heavy horses was the public access from the main show field to the horse arena. Once again, Jim was only too pleased to let us cut a piece out of the parting hedge between the show field and his, providing we re-fenced it to be cattle-proof after the show. This of course we undertook to do. It was also decided that we would site the beer marquee at the top end of this field also; this was being run by the now deceased John Lane, the landlord of the Woodman Inn in

Fernham. The same entrance then could be the way in for the dray when delivering to the beer marquee, thus avoiding the need to cross the cricket pitch.

We seemed at last to have got over most of the problems, but with a somewhat increased workload, which we hoped that we could cope with.

Some of the attractions to take part in this show were as follows. There was a demonstration of aerobatic flying by radio-controlled aircraft by Mr M Atkinson of Wallingford Model Centre. Also, there was a penny-farthing cycle display by Mr E Webber of Taunton, who had already appeared on television. Again by popular demand there was a working sheepdog demonstration by Mr Tim Weaving of Kingston Bagpuize, with his registered border collie bitch, Jean. There was a parade of historic cars; a demonstration of kite flying; an Army team display by the Duke of Edinburgh's Royal Regiment. Blackbird Leys Gymnasts, a team of young women Olympic gymnasts who competed in national competitions, performed. There was a parade of the Old Berks hounds; 'Genie of the Flames' was a daring display by Mr M Gardner of Bodicote, Oxfordshire, as seen on television. BBC Radio Oxford would be broadcasting from the showground throughout the show.

Inside attractions included honey making by Mr W Mattingley of Uffington; plants and produce, Mr F Painter of Uffington; gemstone jewellery, Mr and Mrs D Creech, Fivehead, Somerset; lace making and tatting, Mrs J Bartlett and Mrs N D Wiseman, Sparsholt, Winchester; canal ware, James of Newbury; tiki stones, Iris Radway, Cheltenham; soft toys, Mrs M Tilling, Uffington; model fairground by Mr Joe Scutts, Swindon.

Refreshments were organised and provided by Uffington, Baulking and Woolstone Young Wives and Mothers Union.

The heavy horse show had drawn entries from far and wide, including Portsmouth, Basingstoke, Kidderminster, Salisbury, Woodland St Mary, Wheatley, Thatcham, Aylesbury, Faringdon, Reading and Wantage. Thankfully, the 1976 show proved to be very popular, with the crowds rolling in. On the Sunday a couple from Birmingham reported to the secretary's caravan that they had lost a ring, inquiring if it had been handed in at that time: it had not. But, last thing that evening, it was in fact handed in to the show secretary. To everybody's amazement the same couple enjoyed the show so much that, on the Sunday, they came all the way back to Uffington a second time and heard the appeal for them on the Monday, thus enjoying a reunion with their ring. With the popularity of the heavy horses we had to open a second field for car parking, thanks again to the kind permission of Mr Jim Matthews. This did not cause too many problems.

The fact still remained that all the committee were rather shattered on the Monday evening when the show was over; nevertheless, we were very pleased that we had had such a good turnout. As many committee members as possible would be working evenings to clear up after the show. I myself would be doing as much as I could all the week, as I was on annual leave from my employment with British Rail. The first task would be to reinstate the boundary between Craven Field and Mr Jim Mildenhall's field. But first we got as much material out through that gap as soon as possible, to save the trouble of getting it in small lots to the bottom of Craven Field. The fence was erected to Jim's satisfaction on the Wednesday following the show. All the straw bales had to be got to the bottom of Craven Field for loading back on to farm trailers and returning to Mr Bracey and Mr J Mathews. The total clearing of the field took just over a week to achieve; therefore, we decided we must try to do one of two things in future – that is, to attempt to get more help or cut down on the workload.

The most pleasing thing about this show was the success of the heavy horse section, and this was reflected in the profit margin, showing £3,000. With better planning, who knew our potential on this front?

Unfortunately, the site for the 1977 show was again to be Craven Sports Field in the Fawler Road. I had had a long talk with our chairman John over this site and about my complete disgust at the attitude of certain members of the cricket club. To me their attitude was completely incompatible with the good of the village, which I was forced to explain to them in no uncertain terms. After all, the football club could not have been more helpful, and yet if it had not have been for the football club using the field after the generosity of Lord Craven's gift to the village, we would not have had the field anyway. The terms of the gift were quite clear – the field had to be used for a sports field and if it was not used within a set time, the gift became null and void. Therefore, the thanks for that must go to the football club, because as well as being the only people to use the field they were also the only people to do any work on it.

1977

It was decided at our first meeting for the planning for the 1977 show that we would reluctantly have to increase the admission charges; they would be as follows: adults 50p, OAPs and children 20p, and local senior citizens would still be granted free entry.

A presentation was made to our retiring treasurer, Mr Hugh Shorten, by the show chairman, Mr John Little. The gift of an onyx desk set was greatly appreciated by Hugh. He also stated that he had appreciated the cooperation that was always forthcoming from the committee.

The post of treasurer had been filled by Mr Peter Erskine, who said that he was looking forward to working in close harmony with the rest of the committee.

It was reported that extra marquee space would be required, as there was a flood of extra trade stands confirming their booking for the show. Also, extra stationary engines were also booking in, forty so far, which was also way up on last year. Radio Oxford had also confirmed that they would be broadcasting from the showground over the two days of the show.

Dick Fawcett had agreed to signpost the way to the show from as far away as the M4 junction by Swindon, and from the M4 junction by Newbury. Also, he would be signposting it from Oxford in that direction.

I had arranged with Mr Jim Mildenhall for the use of his field under the same terms as last year. The committee had agreed to meet at Craven Field on Saturday 13 August at 10.30 a.m. I made a late arrival at this meeting, as I had been on night work, but was able to confirm to the rest of the committee that my request for annual leave of two weeks had been granted, so I would be available for a week each side of the show.

Again at this meeting, the same members of the cricket club were making their presence felt for all the same petty reasons. But, this time, most of the committee could see that an intolerable situation was going to develop if we had to use this field any more after this show. The Air Training Corps from Wantage were in attendance to hear the car-parking arrangements, as they had undertaken to help with them over the two days of the show. They would, of course, be earning some money for their cause.

Some of the attractions over the two days were: historic car rally, stationary engine display, Punch and Judy show by Johnny Chuckles of Radio Oxford fame, Duke of Edinburgh Royal Regiment Display Team, display of aerobatic flying by radio-controlled aircraft, Royal Army Ordnance Corps Combat Team, glass blowing, White Horse novelties, gemstone jewellery, horseshoe jewellery, model making, papier mâché models, enamelling, wrought ironwork, police dog-handling team demonstration, and Apex trampoline act. Also, there was the heavy horse show, together with their parade and the exemption dog show.

The crowds certainly turned out again for this show, with a profit of some £5,000 to our cause. But, sorry to say, there were still some very *sour grapes* around.

These sour grapes were in the form of straw bales to be moved from the field. A lot of rain after the show made these bales very wet and heavy. When I went down to the field nine days after the show in the evening, to my utter disgust I found John and his wife Joan trying to move some down towards the gate. I persuaded them that this was not a job for them to undertake, but I would see to the problem myself. But, hopefully, we would discuss this item at our next meeting. We were left with no alternative, so, with a small trailer on the back of my car, the next evening we recovered all the bales left in the field.

In the course of this operation we were confronted by our dearest friends from the bat and ball brigade. What followed was a very heated discussion on the state of the cricket field boundary mark. A tractor-wheel mark had been left encroaching at least six inches on to the outfield. In the kindest way possible I explained that there was a shovel in the boot of my car if they cared to borrow it. This they of course declined, not knowing the handle from the blade, as I had supposed. I had no choice left but to offer them both a kiss and a cuddle; they also turned this down and left, much to my disappointment.

At the end of our next meeting John made it quite plain to all members that he was not prepared to hold the 1978 show in Craven Field. He also stated that he had already approached a local farmer with proposals to hire a thirty-acre field for the 1978 show. This was music to my ears, as I could not have been involved with another show on that site. This in itself would have been a complete setback to the commitment that I had made to the shows until John, Harry and Hugh had been fully repaid for their generosity. But, thankfully, this was now not going to happen, although I would always remember the aggravation that we had received in that field when trying to help the village as a whole. Witnessing John and Joan struggling with those wet and heavy bales, watched by young and fit men, was the last straw. I know that very few people realised that John's health was failing, but it was, and there was no excuse for that type of selfish attitude by anyone whatsoever.

The good news that transpired from the 1977 show was that the profit margin from it had in fact discharged our responsibility from the debt that we owed to John, Harry and Hugh. It still does not discharge the gratitude that the three villages owe to these three generous people, although, to be fair, very few people knew anything whatsoever of this undertaking. With some of the rubbish that I have been asked about the show I thought it was about time the truth was told of the commitment these brave people made.

1978

With all of these things out of the way we could at last get on with the organisation of the 1978 show. The new site for this show was to be the forty-acre field known locally as Stutt Field; that is to say, the field opposite the fox cover at the bottom of the station road. This was by kind permission of the Lonsdale Estates. It was decided that we would have to make two extra gateways for access. This was because a part of this field would be required for car parking.

This year also saw the combining of the gymkhana with the White Horse Show. This was made possible by the kind permission of Mr Underwood, who had granted us the use of his field adjacent to the main show field. The gymkhana would be held on the Sunday of the show and would be run and organised by Miss Ann Chambers. Although there would be another big workload for the field sub-committee, it would be a more relaxed and pleasurable experience than the last two years.

This year was the centenary of the British Shire Horse Society and as our heavy horse section was a member of that society, it was also suggested that we should mark that event with a special Post Office hand stamp from the show. The Post Office was approached concerning this and readily agreed to the idea. A special hand stamp was designed by Mrs Seton-Lloyd from Woolstone; it was accepted by the Post Office, but the show would have to run this event under their supervision.

With the extra trade stands that were booking for this 1978 show, it was decided that additional marquees would be required. The marquee hire would now consist of one seventy-by-forty, four sixty-by-thirty, one twenty-by-twelve, and two twelve-by-twelve. Also, extra room would have to be allocated to the stationary engines and vintage and veteran cars. With all the extra bookings coming in, it looked at this early stage that this show would be a record one.

With the arena events that were being confirmed it gave us as a committee great confidence that it would certainly be a big success. The star event would be Dick Chipperfield's Racing Camels. The jockeys for this event were organised for the professionals by Richard Pitman and for the disc jockeys by Radio Oxford. Each team would consist of four jockeys.

Additional car parking space was again by kind permission of Mr J Matthews. The Caravan Camping Club had reserved Mr J Mildenhall's field in the Station Road and we could possibly deal with around 400 people attending the show.

The bad news for the committee was that, with John's health obviously failing, he had broken the news to us that this would be his last show as chairman, and Joan's last as secretary. They would of course be still available for advice, with John volunteering himself for the printing. They made it quite plain that the pressure they had been in over the last two years in Craven Field had taken its toll on them. When John made this announcement it was received with great disappointment. Harry then addressed the meeting with well-earned praise to both John and his wife for all they had done – not only being responsible for the birth of the White Horse Show, but to all of the other things that they had been responsible for around the village of Uffington. He also said that there would always be a warm welcome for them at any time. Without hesitation I said that he could not get away quite as easily as that, and promptly proposed that he accept the post of president of the White Horse Show. This proposal was seconded by Harry, with John accepting. When the meeting ended, all the committee thanked John and Joan; these thanks were richly deserved, and all of us promised to keep the show and his good work going.

Some twelve months before this occurrence, John had discovered that the only foundation stone that Thomas Hughes had ever laid was going to become redundant. This foundation stone was in the wall of a cooperative building in Tower Hamlets in London. Being John, he thought that this would be a great showpiece to have within our new village hall. He therefore undertook to make the necessary inquiries as to how this could be achieved. He eventually contacted the owners of the building, and on meeting them duly explained the situation to them. The fact was that Thomas Hughes was born in Uffington, although he had been the MP for Tower Hamlets at the time of laying the foundation stone. It would be a very fine gesture if, now this building was going to be pulled down, that stone could be preserved back in the village of his birth. With a very fine new village hall named after him in Uffington what better place could there be? Whilst talking with the building owners, John was very surprised how cooperative they were. They were also in agreement that Uffington would be an excellent resting place for this stone. If, therefore, we were prepared to bear the cost of transport from London to Uffington, they would preserve it at the site until we removed it. Luck was with us in the fact that Mr Sid Warren from Baulking Grange had a roofing contract in London, and would bring the stone to Uffington on his lorry and place it by our new hall. When it arrived, John arranged for a stone mason to take it away, clean and trim the rough from it and return the stone to the hall. Luck again was with us, as we were able to have it re-sited in the Thomas Hughes Memorial Hall exactly one hundred years to the day after Thomas Hughes, QC, performed that duty at Tower Hamlets on 19 July 1879. John, not about to miss an opportunity like this, arranged for this to take place. John also thought that the person to ask to carry out this task was one of our main patrons. On being invited, Capt. T L Lonsdale of Kingston Lisle Park said that he would be very honoured to carry out this duty. It was also agreed with John and the rest of the committee that the original chairman, Mr W Mitchell of the old Building Fund Committee, should have a place of honour in these celebrations. This took place on the centenary of the first stone-laying, 19 July 1979.

At the next meeting, which was the last before the show, yet another blow came to us – Joan had been taken into hospital. The committee expressed their wishes for a quick recovery and a speedy return to our fold.

The committee also welcomed Mrs Lynda Chester, who had kindly stepped in to help out with the secretary's duties while Joan was away. It was reported that all the outside and inside stands had been booked, and that there was no more space available inside the marquees. Army Cadets had confirmed that they would be helping with the car parking. The exemption dog show with Mrs A Hopkinson, and St John Ambulances were confirmed both days.

Resiting of foundation stone. Capt. T L Lonsdale (left) and original chairman Mr W Mitchell

With this, the show had plenty on offer to the public again: freefall parachutes, a clay-pigeon shoot, a tug of war competition, tossing the caber, Army static displays, a steam traction engine for children's rides. The gymkhana would be on the Sunday, with the heavy horse show on the Monday.

With the weather holding fine once more for our show, we had the best crowds ever over the two days; yet again it had given us the greatest feeling of satisfaction so far. The profit turning in from this show was yet again another record, with the funds benefiting by just over £6,000.

1979

With the same fields and parking being declared for 1979, how could we fail to look for another bumper turnout? The main thing that we needed to try to avoid was turning the show into a carbon copy of the previous one. We, of course, kept the gymkhana running on the Sunday, 26 August, with the heavy horse show being a big draw on the Monday, 27 August. The rest of the time over the two days would be filled in to the best of our ability, in creating an interesting spectacle to appeal across as big a cross section of the public as possible. To do this is not an easy task by any means, but with every member of the committee bearing this in mind we were sure to come up with events that would fit into the budget.

It was agreed also for the 1979 show that entrance for the public would be: adults 70p, children and OAPs 30p. Local senior citizens would still have free admission; this was one policy that John had set at the three-day festival in 1972, and we wished for it to continue. The price of advertising in the programme was also to increase to £5 for a half page and £10 for a full page. With the cost of equipment hire also rising, it was forced on us to look very hard at the cost of hire of our trade stands. Although our stands were considered to be priced reasonably, we were forced into the position where we would have to increase the price to inside stands to £16, and outside stands to £14. With all these things decided and in place we all needed to stick to the respective budgets that were decided by the full committee.

Unfortunately, there had been some unease felt by at least two members of the full committee about the distribution of the funds. It had been made perfectly plain to them on two or three occasions that the funds raised at the shows must go into the Thomas Hughes Memorial Trust for distribution. From there they could only be donated to the new village hall, as the trust was the only body authorised and covered by the Charity

Commission. If this procedure was not carried out to the letter of the law then our total income at the shows could be taxed. With that tax being as high as 60%, the work and the worry would just not be worth the bother. This difficulty together with trying to finance the building of a small hall extension to the main hall did not make sense to the majority of the committee. Therefore, we were not prepared to alter the terms of the trust until it was right to do so. Although, with some of the searching questions coming from the charity commissioners about the terms of our charity and the position of finishing the new hall, I was left to wonder whether in fact somebody was trying to force the pace on winding up the Thomas Hughes Trust. Certainly it looked this way to me, and after talking with John and Harry one evening in the show field they were also becoming suspicious.

We had the pleasure of welcoming a new minute secretary for our future meetings, of the name Jim Ormerod. Although a man in poor health he decided that he would like to help the cause. He would not be able to do very much at the show for health reasons, but would be there to help where he could. To me this was the sign of a very keen person: someone who wanted to do his bit for the village even in poor health. There are not many people about like Jim today.

Joan had undertaken to run a grand draw over the two days of the show. The tickets for this would be on sale as soon as possible. We had also got yet another first for the show in the form of an aerobatics team for the Monday. The total Arena One events were as follows:

Sunday

13.00 Sheepdog Trials
13.30 Model Aircraft
14.00 Darts vs. Archery
14.30 Royal Scots Greys Pipe and Drum Band
15.00 Aerobatics
15.30 Caber Tossing
16.00 Sheepdog Trials

Monday

12.00 Vintage Cars and Motorcycles
13.45 St John Ambulance Brigade Band
14.15 Vintage Cars and Motorcycles
14.45 Tug of War
15.15 Vintage Cars and

16.30	Royal Scots Greys, Pipe and Drum Band		Motorcycles, Presentation of Prizes
17.00	Aerobatics	16.00	Parade of Old Berks Hunt
17.30	Vintage Cars Parade		
		16.30	Darts vs. Archery
		17.00	Tug of War, Final
		17.30	St John Ambulance Brigade Band

As well as this full programme in the main arena, the show field was full with interesting trade stands. Local crafts were giving demonstrations, and there were static displays by the army. Inside the marquees were more trade stands and model exhibitions. It was also pleasing to see extra local organisations taking the opportunity to raise funds for their own benefit.

We were to learn afterwards that the gymkhana and the heavy horse shows had also attracted record entries, which also gave their organisers a great feeling of satisfaction. At the final meeting of the 1979 show we were to learn that the profit was in excess of £7,000. This was combined with the feeling of great satisfaction that we had got the price increases about right with the rising cost of staging the show.

1980

One big headache now facing us was the site for the 1980 show. The present trend was that agriculture fields only became available to us for two years, when they were led down for grass. After the two years of grass is cropped they are then ploughed for cereal crops. Having been offered a forty-acre field by Mr Jim Matthews along the Knighton Crossing Road, we were in some doubt as to the feasibility of this site because of the narrowness of the road. We were thus awaiting a decision from the police and highways as to the possibility of using this site. After meeting our chairman at this site the news was not good. They would only permit the use of this site if we were prepared to turn the route into a one-way system. After a very lengthy discussion it was decided that the colossal cost of implementing such a system would be completely out of the question. We therefore had to start looking again for another field. In the meantime other decisions had to be made in preparation for the next show.

Mr Jim Ormerod had been ill and wished to resign; his resignation was reluctantly accepted, but Jim would remain on the committee. Mrs Trish Follows gallantly accepted the post of secretary, with the promise that every committee member would help her as much as possible. It was decided that the disaster fund be increased by another £2,000; this then would leave that fund at £5,000. Hopefully this would cover the cost should we experience a complete washout of the show. We had in the past enquired as to the cost of insurance against this risk, but the astronomical cost of such cover made it not worth the bother. It was again drawn to the attention of all committee members by the treasurer, Mr Peter Erskine, that the rules on income tax and the charity commission must be rigidly obeyed. Various events were being suggested for 1980, but would have to be held in abeyance until early in January or until a new site had been found.

At our January meeting my worst fears were confirmed. The

only site available for the 1980 show was the Craven Sports Field. I thus informed the chairman that my initial thoughts were that I would be resigning, as I was not prepared to put up with the aggravation that I received the last time we were in this field. The committee had to realise that, by building the show field, I was in this site for a whole week before the show, on annual leave. The week after the show was likewise: pulling it to pieces and packing it away, leaving it ready for the next time it was wanted. I did not want the committee to get the idea that I was fed up doing this; in fact the opposite applied, I enjoyed doing it. But I could find better ways of enjoying my annual leave than being in the field taking the aggravation that came my way the last time we were there. This statement caused quite a stir, with both John and Harry promising to come and talk this through with me. I said I would wait for the outcome of their talk. Possible events already in hand for the 1980 show included, an Army band and Army displays, JCB Contest, RAOC 'Wheelbarrows', a sheepdog demonstration and a fire brigade demonstration.

John and Harry came to see me one evening the following week, before they were due to meet with representatives of the sports and social club. John had already put Harry in the picture to some extent on the amount of petty aggravation that we had experienced from the same members of the cricket club when we used this site last. To be fair, Harry had not realised how bad it had been. But I explained that having the same two people stand and watch John and Joan struggling to move bales of straw the last time had been enough. Harry gave me his word that it would not happen again this time.

When Harry met with the members of the sports and social club he made it quite plain that if this type of behaviour happened this time he would personally call the show off. Knowing Harry's extreme integrity, I accepted his word on this subject and gave him my word that I would continue to carry out the showground work. I was informed afterwards that at that meeting Harry pulled no punches whatsoever, with the clear message that, if the White Horse Show fell through, then at the end of the day there would be no funds to distribute to any organisation. That also included the cricket club.

After that meeting at least we were able to get on and plan the field ready for the next show. Again at our next meeting the question was asked about tax on the show profits; again it was reiterated by our chairman that if the profits were not paid straight over to the trust they would be taxed at 60%. It was then made abundantly clear by nearly everybody present that they would not be willing to carry on under those circumstances.

The committee were, of course, conscious that the money that had been raised had not been spent by the village hall management. This was entirely due to the fact that they were waiting for further grant aid to build the extension to the hall. How they could proceed any differently nobody could tell. The other worrying thing that also came to light was that the income tax authority had been questioning Hugh again and giving him rather a hard time. True to form, Hugh had kept them away, but for how long we did not know. The puzzling thing was where they were getting their information from. At this stage I was not the only member of our committee becoming suspicious. We had said for a long time that as soon as the new extension was complete we would be prepared to wind up the Thomas Hughes Memorial Trust and then to form another trust to take its place.

With the acceptance of Craven Field for the 1980 show came another problem in the form of gaining access to Mr Bob Spence's field, which he had kindly consented for us to use for the gymkhana. Although this field was adjacent to Craven Field, he did not want his fences taken down or broken. This meant building a bridge over a ditch and barbed wire fence to connect the two fields. We got over this problem with the help of a considerable number of wooden pallets. We stacked them and interlaced each layer until there was sufficient width to walk over the ditch and fence. To make a firm finish we secured them firm with scaffold poles. Then, to make the steps smooth and trip-free, these were lined over with plywood got from a local scrap yard. When Harry came to the showground that evening he was really impressed. Of course, as always, there were the doom preachers who could see it all collapsing, trapping goodness knows how many members of the public beneath. But the majority of our committee were quite impressed. But the sacred square in the centre of Craven Field still had to be preserved. So we fenced it off with chestnut paling. As usual during this operation – with a fourteen-pound sledgehammer in use to drive the fence posts – the cricket club members were conspicuous by their absence. But, as usual, members of the football club were helpful with this task, as well as in constructing the bridge.

We also had another blow to our committee in the form of the resignation of Mr Pete White and his wife Angela. A great amount of thanks and gratitude were offered to this husband and wife by the committee for their hard work in setting up the heavy horse section. This was quickly followed by the resignation of Miss Ann Chambers, who had other commitments and would not be able to give sufficient time to the organisation of the gymkhana. The committee also thanked Ann for her past dedication to the cause of the show, and wished her all luck in the future.

The committee was extremely lucky in finding people so quickly in taking over these two very important rolls in the show committee. The heavy horse section was being taken over by Mr Barry Mills and his wife Dee; the whole of the committee pledged their help to this very brave couple in their task. Ann would be organising the gymkhana for this year, so a replacement for that duty must be found for next year.

The heavy horse show would, by kind permission of Mr Jim Mildenhall, be held in his field, as on the last occasion. He also gave his permission for a barbed-wire fence to be removed as a temporary measure to allow the very large heavy-horse boxes entry into the field. I would replace this fence when the show was over. With thirty-six entries in the heavy horse show, with still more to come in, it was very important that we could get these big boxes off the road really quickly to avoid traffic congestion. The last time we allowed this to happen it was chaos all round the village, together with all approach roads to the village. If we allowed this to happen we could lose custom to the show and not be very popular with the police. The costs of the show were rising all the time, and the cost of the policing was the one cost that was rising more than anything else, and was the one which we were going to have to sit down and see where we could make savings.

In the end, after all the hard work and turmoil, the show

turned out to be a very great success. With large crowds over the two days, the gate money reached a massive £13,409. Together with other income, the total income of the show reached yet another record of £19,416. Despite expenditure also reaching record highs it was still going to give us record profits of £10,886. This, of course, gave all the committee a great feeling of satisfaction. But with this feeling there also went a certain number of pitfalls in the form of the vulture brigade waiting around the corner ready to plead poverty on behalf of their organisations. With the Charity Commission hovering yet again in the background, it was something that we were going to have to work out. But with John, Harry and Hugh to advise us we were in a somewhat lucky position. Still being the treasurer of the Thomas Hughes Memorial Trust, it was something that Hugh has been watching very closely in the past months.

1981

In 1981 the new extension to the village hall was to get under way in the form of a smaller hall which could be used by separate organisations than those using the main hall. This project was also completed in 1981. This was just as well, because we had to face the inevitable fact that we would have to wind up the Thomas Hughes Memorial Trust and form another to take its place. The profits from the White Horse Show would have to be paid straight into a trust, or there would be no point in the running of the show. With the tax liabilities at 60%, people would just not be prepared to work to that sort of commitment. But the forming of the new trust did not go as easy as we first thought it might. The Charity Commission were being somewhat dogmatic with the wording of the charity document and about just what organisations were going to be the benefactors of the said trust. So, until such time as the new trust could be cleared by the charity commissioners, all funds would have to be deposited with the Thomas Hughes Memorial Trust. This would have to be a benefit to our golden goal – the Village Hall Management Committee.

The 1981 show also saw some more changes to the show committee: Mr John Clarke joined us to take over the organisation of the stationary engines, in place of Dick Fawcett, who had left the village. The one person who joined us this year who I was going to find a great help was the one and only Sid Warren; he had joined us to organise and run the gymkhana. I was soon to learn that there would not be another dull moment in the field when Sid was around.

The site for the 1981 show had been found, thanks to the kind permission of the Lonsdale Estates, with the car parking in the adjacent fields by kind permission of Mr J Matthews. These things never prove to be as simple as they sound; in this case there was the little problem of a fairly large brook that separated the car parks and the main show field, which the public would have to cross. The show field was brilliant; it was at the bottom of the Fawler Road and totalled fifty acres. This gave us the best leeway we had ever had in showground space. The gymkhana and heavy horse show could all be in the same field for the first time. This was going to make the planning of the arenas much easier than before. It would certainly be much more appealing to the general public, and this had to be beneficial to the profitability of the show overall.

The problem of joining the car parks and the show field by the building of a bridge for some reason landed at my feet. But, again, luck was on our side. British Rail had been carrying out repairs on an over-bridge on the length of track that I worked on, and by way of chance the main carrying timbers had been left on site. On making enquiries over the availability of these timbers I was promptly told that they were surplus to requirements. Provided that I could remove them from site at no cost I was welcome to have them. The two main bearing timbers were thirty feet long and twelve by twelve inches, which was just what we were looking for.

On discussing this with Sid we decided to meet at the site where the timbers were, along with Sid's lorry and some manpower. We would load the timbers up and transport them to site where they were required; here things started to go wrong. The manpower was very thin on the ground, being just Sid, his son and myself. But, not to be beaten, we kept lifting one end of the timber and blocking it up until it was just a little higher than the lorry bed. Sid's son would then carefully back the lorry just under the timber, enough to allow Sid and myself to lift the timber just a little. Each time the lorry reversed, until we had the timber in balance and were able to slide it right on the lorry. When we had repeated this all over again for the second timber I suppose we had proved a point to ourselves – at times like this nothing is impossible. But, when we eventually got the timber to the site where it was wanted, we decided to call it enough for that evening.

The following evening I started to build the bridge by laying the two large timbers across the brook; these then had to be dug down in the ground to sufficient depth to allow sleepers to be fastened crossways and still only be at ground level. When this was done, Sid and I returned to the railway to transport thirty-two plain sleepers to the bridge site. For the next two evenings I was fastening these sleepers firmly to the cross-timbers by means of twelve-inch spikes. The handrails at each side of the bridge consisted of tubular scaffold poles, to make sure that no member of the public could fall from the bridge. Chestnut paling was used to fasten this.

With this part of the site preparation completed, we could now get going on the marking out of the showground and building the arenas. With all the events being in the same field, this was easier than in past years. In fact, we had completed this task by the Thursday evening prior to the show. With Mr Alton Bailey making the post starters with an iron bar, on the Tuesday I thumped in 286 fence posts with a fourteen-pound sledgehammer. I think that this still stands as a record of post driving in one day by hand at a White Horse Show. At all the shows afterwards we were blessed with a tractor and hydraulic post driver. This was through the kindness of Mr Tony Coxhead. But, on the Friday evening, Harry noticed that we had been quite *lapsus memoriae* in erecting the flag pole and failing to put the flag in position. This caused no problem with Sid in attendance; he promptly got hold of the flag and shinned the thirty feet up the pole to place the flag in its rightful place at the top, at the same time giving everybody in earshot his own rendering of the English language. With all of us rolled up in laughter, we had not had this fun in the field before; we all knew then we were going to enjoy Sid's contribution to the show committee.

It had been decided that the entrance fee for this year would remain unchanged, but the trade stand charges would increase. They were to be as follows: stands inside marquees would be £23 per ten feet. Stands outside were £20 per ten feet.

The following was the programme of events:

Sunday 30 August 1981   Monday 31 August 1981

09.00 Gymkhana, Arena 3   10.00 Show Opens
12.00 Show Opens   11.00–17.00 Heavy Horse

12.30	Nautical Training Corps Band, Arena 1		Show, Arena 2
13.00	Model Aircraft, Arena 1	11.00	Nautical Training Corps Band, Arena 1
13.30	Katabatics Display (Aerobatics)	11.30	Model Aircraft, Arena 2
14.00	Sheepdog Trials, Arena 1; Dog Show, Arena 3	12.00	Vintage Car Tests, Arena 1
		13.45	Girls Marching Band, Arena 1
14.30	Tug of War Heats, Arena 2	14.15	Caber Tossing, Arena 1
14.30	Nautical Training Corps Band, Arena 1	14.45	New Forest Axemen, Arena 1
		15.15	Old Berks Hunt, Arena 1
15.00	Model Aircraft, Arena 1	15.30	Nautical Training Corps Band, Arena 1
15.30	Sheepdog Trials, Arena 1		
16.00	Katabatics Display	16.00	Historic Car Concourse, Arena 1
16.30	Tug of War Final, Arena 1	16.30	New Forest Axemen, Arena 1
17.00	Vintage Motorcycles, Arena 1	17.00	Car Awards, Arena 1
17.30	Nautical Training Corps Band, Arena 1	17.30	Girls Marching Band, Arena 1
18.00	Show Closes	18.00	Show Closes

The show was another great success, with ample room for the public to circulate with comfort and ease. With yet more craft stands inside and out there was plenty to keep everyone interested all day. Again we were finding that the greater number and diversity of events and craft stands and trade stands we could accommodate within the show, the greater the public support. This was reflected in the number of ticket sales over the two days: these amounted to 18,431. The profit for the two days was just short of £10,000. With figures like this everybody gets a tremendous feeling of satisfaction. On top of this, the organisations that would be the benefactors in the future, when the new trust was formed, were probably considering how they could at least give the White Horse Show Committee some help in the future.

The new trust being formed was signed and witnessed by the chairman of the White Horse Show Committee, Brigadier Hopkinson. The members of this trust were as follows: Mr V Boaler, Mr R Cummins, Mr J Matthews, Mr P Erskine, and Mr W Mitchell.

It was also agreed that the benefactors would be Anglican churches of Uffington, Woolstone and Baulking; Strict Baptist Church; Congregational Church; Uffington Parish Council (for special requirements only); Thomas Hughes Memorial Hall Community Association; Jubilee Field Committee; Craven Field Trust; Scouts; Guides; Brownies; Cubs; Thomas Hughes School; Uffington C. of E. School; The Royal British Legion and Toc H. This list could of course be increased, but only with the total agreement of the White Horse Show Committee, the trustees and of course the charity commissioners. It was also agreed that the trustees would recommend the distribution of funds to the White Horse Show Committee, who would then have the chance to discuss them before agreeing with the recommendation before these were made public. This, I believe, was the only fair way, because by adopting this channel it gave the people who were working hard on the maintenance of the show all year round some say at least in the distribution of the funds.

1982

1982 saw Mr Derek Kelsey join the committee to take responsibility for the organisation of the vintage and veteran cars, together with the motorcycles. This section of the show was beginning to gain a lot of popularity at this time, and it was thought that this could take over a main slot in the arena if and when required. It was also decided that we would need a second bridge over the brook, as the single bridge caused considerable congestion, with the public still wanting access to the show as other people were leaving. With this addition, one bridge could then be used as the entrance to the show with the other as the exit. The second bridge was constructed entirely with tubular scaffolding and scaffold planks; these were loaned by Mr Sid Warren, who also supervised the erection of this bridge. When the strength of this construction was put under question, Sid promptly jumped in his lorry and drove it over to prove that, if it was strong enough to take a lorry, it was certainly strong enough to bear pedestrians. With this point made we did not hear any more safety questions regarding the strength of our bridges. We also had a young lad by the name of Daniel Chester join us in helping to get the show site ready this year. That Daniel was still at school impressed our committee no end; here was a young lad who was prepared to help do work to raise funds for other organisations. Looking at this in the true light of day we were really pleased about it, because if the White Horse Show was to continue, it was the young that would enable it to do just that.

There were to be two new events at this 1982 show. These were parascending and lawnmower racing. The parascending could take place behind the marquees, where there would be plenty of room for the Range Rover to gain enough distance and speed to tow the parachute. This would enable the members of the public to gain sufficient height to parascend back down to ground.

The lawnmower racing would need an arena of its own for safety reasons; this would be marked by posts and rope, like all the other arenas. The racing circuit would be marked with bales of straw, with other bales of straw adding an extra guard around the whole arena. It was thought that these two extra attractions would again appeal to a so far untapped cross-section of the general public. On this score we would have to wait until after the show.

The disappointment of this show was that the secretary's husband, Mr Chris Follows, who was a private pilot for Vickers-Armstrongs, had got us on the shortlist for the Red Arrows – but alas it was not to be, as they had to perform at an RAF event elsewhere on that day. Being a military event, it of course had first priority. At first it was thought that Geoff Harwood would not be attending this year's show, but while preparing the site John turned up with the good news that he would be coming after all. This was great, as we were wondering where we would be able to get the entertainment and rides for the small children. This again was very important, because, if there was no amusement for the small children, were the parents going to attend? This being a family show we were committed to entertain all the family or lose custom. On the other hand, the aroma of Geoff's bacon and egg breakfast wafting across the showground first thing in the morning would be missed by all, not forgetting his keenness to supply mugs of freshly brewed tea.

On the serious side, Geoff was always very generous with his donations to the White Horse Show, besides his being one of the original events at the very first show. His attendance and generosity over those years has been a great credit to him. We knew now that we did not have any problems getting trade stands and the like to attend the show, but in the beginning we had terrible problems persuading these things to come. This shift also showed up in the sponsorship of different firms around the area. It was reflected also in the rural craft stands, which were giving demonstrations but were also taking orders for their merchandise.

This same balance was becoming attached to the tender of ice-cream sales. In the first onset Roger Cummins had reported that the Wall's tender for this year's contract was well down on last year. But Southern Counties had offered 25% of gross profits. On phoning Wall's to tell them they had not got the contract, they turned a somersault in their keenness to obtain it, thus offering a better deal than that of the year before. Naturally this was accepted by the committee; this went to prove that the show had now got bargaining power. But whatever we did we had to take great care not to abuse that power; if we did we may well have finished up on the losing side, as greed will not win friends anywhere.

When the days of the show arrived the weather was dry and bright, but on the Sunday afternoon we had to call on the help of Whitney Marquees, as one of the trade marquees, a sixty-by-thirty, had a nasty snag in the roof section, and with the wind gaining strength this was thought inadvisable. The staff of Whitney Marquees eventually arrived to carry out the necessary repairs. This they did by sticking a small patch over the tear; we did not think that this was a very strong repair and made our thoughts known to these people. We were assured in no uncertain terms that this would be sufficient and would last until the Tuesday, when they would be removing the marquees from the showground.

But, alas, on the Monday morning the wind had gained in strength; the result was that the roof of this marquee began to tear even more. Before anything could be done to stop it tearing further we had to evacuate the trade stands and public from the marquee. Before the Whitney staff could get to the showground the roof had completely shredded. There was no alternative but to remove this marquee. The only way in which we could now accommodate these stall holders was to erect the army thirty-by-twenty which we had borrowed from RMCS at Shrivenham to use for the gymkhana on the Sunday. This way we could at least accommodate some of these stalls under cover; the rest would be outside and would have to be compensated for their trouble.

After the show was over, discussions took place with Whitney Marquees regarding this failure, which they were held totally responsible for. In fairness to them, they settled amicably. Once again it showed that nobody wanted to lose the custom of the White Horse Show now.

The one good thing to come out of this tragedy was the inspiration that it gave to Geoff Harwood to write a book of songs. Geoff called this book *Songs of the Vale*. I have still got my copy now. Again, out of sheer kindness, Geoff gave a great number of copies of this song book to John to be sold, with the income going entirely to the White Horse Show account. There are two songs in this book that relates to the White Horse Show; they are 'The White Horse Wind', which refers to the shredding of the marquee, and the other is 'The Uffington Portable Loo', which refers to the sectional tin gents' toilet that we used at the shows in the early years.

During the early afternoon of the Monday we also had another spectacular first: our secretary's husband, Chris, who had the day off duty from flying for Vickers-Armstrongs, had indicated that the Red Arrows might appear over the showground. They would be flying between two military shows at which they were performing. Sure enough, at about two o'clock in the afternoon, with a considerable roar, they appeared from the south-east to drop down and give a very low-level fly-past over the showground, leaving their trails of red, white and blue smoke hanging over the show. This drew gasps of amazement from the crowd at the same time. The leader had been in contact with Chris beforehand, whom he knew from his time in the RAF. He had said that if they had the time and favourable weather he would try the fly-past because of the disappointment we had had in not getting a full performance.

The demonstration of autogyro flying was a very popular event throughout the entire show, with the public requesting a continuance of this type of demonstration some time in the future.

The lawnmower racing was another good attraction, which pulled a good number of spectators to the arena. A considerable number were keen to get round the machines and question the owners about this sport. I had spent a fair amount of time with these people before the show and was a little bit sceptical when told that the world speed record for a class-three mower at that time was 61 mph. Just to prove a point I was promptly told to get in my car and follow a mower of this class down the field and keep my eye on the speedometer. This I was quite prepared to do. The mower then set off, with me in hot pursuit. When we returned to their base I had to admit that he had on two occasions reached 54 mph, which I thought was some achievement. I have been told now that this record stands at 82 mph.

Lawnmower racing, 1982

The parascending was also very popular and had a very busy time, with the public keen to participate in this sport. I could also understand their interest in this, having tried it myself on the Saturday before the show and thought it a great experience.

Despite the bad luck with the shredded marquee, the show proved to be yet another great success. With just over 20,000 tickets sold on the gate over the two days, we had another bumper profit of just over £10,000. However, with expenses rising over the last couple of years, consideration would have to be given in relation to the entrance fee to the show, if the quality was to be maintained. To reduce the quality of the show would be pure folly, but extreme caution had to be used in raising the entrance charges, or we may, on the other hand, price ourselves out of the market and drive families away from the show. To keep attendances up families had to be the prime target in maintaining the feasibility of the show.

1983

Whilst all of this had been going on we had had a very smooth changeover from the Thomas Hughes Memorial Trust to the White Horse Show Trust. This again was mainly due to Hugh, Harry and John. However, to some of us it was a very sad day when the Thomas Hughes Memorial Trust closed down. This trust had stood us in good stead through some very turbulent and trying times; without its existence, and the guidance of the three wise men, I still doubt if the new hall would ever have come into being. I am still left to wonder to this day how many committee members would have resigned had we not agreed to change the trust. One person said that if we continued to pour money into the village hall, we would have mass resignations. I still believe that we could have made a strong case to the charity commissioners because the last section of the original hall plan had still not been built, due to rising costs at the time. I was not alone in this belief, but change we did; it thus remained that 1983 and another show had to be faced.

The first setback was, sadly, the resignation of Mr and Mrs Mills from the committee; we thus needed to find another organiser to take on the mammoth task of running the heavy horse show. We could not afford to let this section fall by the wayside: the loss of patronage from the public would be too great to stand.

The trust reported back to the full committee with their recommendations that we fund the following: Baulking Church, resurfacing walls – £805; Woolstone Church, resurfacing walls – £1,050; Tom Brown School, heating system – £425; Red Cross, local disabled and aged – £200. Uffington Primary School, resiting garage and sheds – £600; Uffington Church, towards heating system – £2,000. Craven Sports Field, towards drainage – £3,000; Tennis Club, towards court – £1,000; a new community bus was proposed by Mrs Lynda Chester, who had been in consultation with others to form a committee to run the bus for the benefit of the local community, whose public transport was virtually non-existent – £7,000.

The full White Horse Show Committee endorsed all these grants with pleasure, with grateful thanks to the Community Bus Committee, whose bus would be carrying on its side a sign saying: 'Donated by the White Horse Show Trust'. This would of course be a form of advertising to benefit the White Horse Show.

At a special ceremony on 12 February 1983 at the village hall, the local minibus keys were handed over to the secretary of the Community Bus Committee, Mrs Sharon Smith, by our chairman, Brigadier Harry Hopkinson. All the show committee present thought that this project was an exceptional one, as it was going to benefit everybody within the three villages. One of the regular services which the bus would run was to be to Faringdon on a Tuesday morning, so that people could get to the health centre for doctor and nurse appointments, with long enough in Faringdon to do some shopping if required.

Some of the most tragic news possible was to hit us at our meeting of 24 March when the vice-chairman Mr Roger Cummins announced the sudden death of our chairman, Brigadier Harry Hopkinson, from a fatal heart attack. The committee immediately rose and stood in silence as a mark of respect to our late chairman.

It was felt that it would have been Harry's wish that we got straight back to organising and running the next show. This was easy enough to say but it was going to take all our strength and determination to achieve just that.

In the meantime I had found a replacement to run the heavy horse show. Mrs Christine Keen had agreed to undertake this task, providing she had the necessary help from the committee. I was able to give Christine the firm promise that I would personally see that she had all the help that she needed. Both our secretary, Trish, and Christine had been over to see Barry and Dee Mills to pick up the relevant paperwork and contacts so that the changeover could go as smoothly as possible. It was also at this meeting that Bill Mattingley and Daniel Chester agreed to join the committee as full members, although they had both been workers before. It was also decided that the entrance fees to the 1983 show would have to rise and they would be as follows: adults £1.50, children and senior citizens 75p, although local pensioners would still be admitted free. The show site was to be in the same field as the last two years; again field organisation would be easier as it would be a follow-up type of arrangement when we had the arena events confirmed.

The vacancy of chairman and vice-chairman had to be filled for the smooth running of the committee to continue. This problem was resolved as follows: Mr Roger Cummins became chairman, with the post of vice-chairman going to Mr Barry Godsell. The whole committee pledged their support to Roger and Barry, realising what an act they had to follow. It was at this meeting that Mrs Betsy Matthews offered to run a rare-breed show, consisting of birds and animals that were under threat of becoming extinct. As we were predominantly a country show this offer was accepted with open arms. Again this was another attraction to yet another cross section of the public so far untapped. In the past the refreshment marquee had been run under the guidance of Mrs Jossie Drew, with the help coming from the Young Wives and the profits going to the show. But this year Mrs Drew requested that they donate all of their profits to the British Heart Foundation as a mark of respect to our late chairman, Brigadier Harry Hopkinson. The committee did not hesitate for a moment in agreeing with this gesture. Yet another new member joining us to keep the contact with the military ongoing was Colonel Tony Bateman. Tony was also to prove a great asset to the show as a whole over the coming years.

As the help in the car-parking fields over the last couple of years had been dwindling, we were looking for an answer to this problem, bearing in mind that, if traffic was wasting too much time getting into the show, then we could well lose custom. The police had also begun to express dissatisfaction with this matter, and thought that we must improve in this department quickly. Sid informed us that he had a contact with Grove Rugby Club, who carried out this type of work to boost their funds. Sid was asked to follow up this suggestion and report back. Sure enough, Sid invited the chairman of Grove Rugby Club to our next meeting. He wasted no time explaining that they would undertake the organisation of the car parking over the two days of the show. To enable them to achieve this they would be bringing twenty members of their club. Their terms were that all members would be supplied with dinner on both days and the cost would be £250. These terms were accepted by the committee as reasonable, because we were going to be able to keep the show traffic on the move. When informed of our intention to employ Grove Rugby Club for these duties, Inspector Griffiths of Thames Valley Police was a very happy man, giving Grove Rugby Club a very glowing report on their ability to carry out these duties.

Mrs Ann Hopkinson (Harry's widow) had over the past three years been running the exemption dog show on the Monday of the show, so we were wondering if this year we would have a dog show. But we should not have worried. True to the wonderful person she was, she sent a message to the chairman that she would still be available to carry on with this part of the show. On top of this she also offered her help in the refreshment marquee at other times over the show weekend. How could anyone not admire a person with this grit and determination to keep the show going forward?

The most worrying thing ever to confront me for any show happened at work in the early hours of the morning on the last day of July. A fifteen-foot piece of rail decided to land on the top of my left foot. Needless to say, weighing some 5 cwt, it did do a certain amount of damage. X-rays at Princess Margaret Hospital at Swindon confirmed that I had sustained three broken bones in the top of my foot. It left me wondering if I would be able to be of any use in preparing the show field for the 1983 show. But in one sense I suppose that I was lucky, in that they decided not to put my foot in plaster; instead they would strap it up and see how that went.

After more X-rays a fortnight later it was decided to leave it in heavy strapping. I was instructed to walk as much as possible on the heel of my foot, without putting any weight on my toes. But, with the heavy strapping, I had to cut a slipper open down the front to have anything on my foot at all. Being lucky enough to have an automatic car I was still able to get about a little, although with difficulty.

When the time came to start and prepare the field ready for the show I had just about started to get used to the handicap of a broken foot. The one benefit was that, being on the sick-list, I did not have to use any of my annual leave for this show. With the posts being driven in by Tony Coxhead with a tractor, and with help from Alton Bailey and Sid, we did achieve the task of preparing the show field. One evening when John came down the field he asked me what I had done to my foot. On being told I had three broken bones in my foot his reply was that I was a silly fool and must be mad to carry on like that. My reply was a very quick reminder to him of a statement that he had made back in 1972 while preparing for that show, when someone had asked him what qualifications were needed to be on the committee. His reply at that time was that you had to be completely mad. I thus told him I was at last meeting with the main requirements of being a member of the White Horse Show Committee. But, to be honest, I would not recommend this way of gaining that qualification to anybody.

Again the 1983 show proved to be another great success. The rare-breeds section proved to be a great attraction, particularly with the younger generation. In fact, that marquee drew crowds over the two days. The greatest interest was focused on the pig section, where there was a saddleback sow with nine very small piglets. If you wanted to view these you had to be prepared to stand and wait until you could get close enough to see them, and it was not all young children trying to lean over the hurdles to get a better view.

The pleasing thing again about this show was that over the two days just over 20,000 people attended, giving us a profit margin of just over £10,000. The committee was justifiably pleased with the result.

Great appreciation must also be given to Mrs Josie Drew, together with the Young Wives: they ensured that the British Heart Foundation benefited to the tune of £1,100. This was donated to the chairman of the Oxford branch at a special meeting in the sports and social club as a memorial to our late chairman, Brigadier Harry Hopkinson. Harry was a person who I will remember for the rest of my lifetime; I am sure that other members of the committee who worked with him will do likewise.

With this profit margin the trustees felt able to recommend the following grants to the full committee for approval: Woolstone Church, £500; White Horse Playgroup, £300; Uffington Memorial Hall Car Park, £1,000; Uffington Toc H, £400; British Red Cross, £250; Baulking Church, £1,000; St Mary's Church, Uffington, £1,000; Sports and Social Club, £3,000. With no objections being raised these grants were passed.

Trust beneficiary St Mary's Church, Uffington, at night

1984

A new site for the 1984 show had been offered by Mr Collin Nash at Kingston Lisle. This site was out on the Kingston Common Road farther away from the village than we had been before. It was agreed that we could not pick and choose which site we could have and that the only thing to do was to visit the site to see what extra work would be required to stage the show there. This we did and found that the area in question was as good as we could expect. The main thing noted was that, as there was only one gateway for access to the show field and car parking area, we would need to have permission from Mr C Nash to make another entrance to the site. This would entail cutting a gap in the hedge, erecting a five-bar gate, plus piping a ditch and backfilling. We would not know the answer to these problems until we had had a site meeting with Mr Nash and Inspector Griffiths of Thames Valley Police. But hopefully we would have answers to hand by the next meeting.

At the following meeting it had been agreed by the parties involved that it was all right to make the extra entrance to the site, which was a relief. The headache left was what sort of bridge we were going to have to go over the ditch, as the agent for the landowner from whom Mr Nash rented the land did not really want to have it piped and filled in. It was decided to leave this problem until later and to really think about how this could be best done.

At this meeting it was also noted that the great service Mrs Josie Drew had given to the White Horse Show – in the organisation of the refreshment marquee over the years – had come to an end. A letter of appreciation would be sent along those lines. Mrs Stella Mattingley and Mrs Ann Smith had agreed to take on this task, again with the help of other members of the Young Wives. Proceeds of the refreshments this year would go to the church and to a charity so far unspecified, to be decided when the time came.

A full programme of events had already been booked, the timetable of which was as follows:

Sunday 26 August	Monday 27 August
09.00 Gymkhana, Arena 2	10.00 Show Opens
12.00 Main Show Opens	11.00–17.00 Heavy Horse, Arena 2
12.30 Fiesta Band, Arena 1	12.00 Jo-Jo the Clown, Arena 4
13.00 Sea Cadets Display, Arena 1	12.30 Royal Marines Band, Arena 1
13.30 Sheep Dog Demo, Arena 1	13.00 Circus Variety, Arena 1
13.30 Lawnmower Racing, 1st Race, Arena 5	13.30 Lawnmower Racing, 1st Race, Arena 5
14.00 Circus Variety, Arena 1	14.00 Auto Gyro Display, Arena 1
14.30 Lawnmower Demo Race, Arena 1	14.30 Lawnmower Demo Race, Arena 1
14.30 Dog Show, Arena 3	15.00 British Driving Society, Arena 1
14.30 Tug of War, Arena 4	15.30 Old Berks Hounds, Arena 1
15.00 Freefall Paras, Arena 1	16.00 Historic Cars, Arena 1
15.30 Sheepdog Demo, Arena 1	16.30 Aerobatics, Arena 1
16.00 Historic Motorcycles, Arena 1	16.45 British Drive Society, Arena 1
16.30 Aerobatics, Arena 1	17.00 Circus Variety, Arena 1
16.45 Sea Cadets Display, Arena 1	17.30 Royal Marines Band, Arena 1
17.15 Circus Variety, Arena 1	18.00 Show Closes
17.45 Fiesta Band, Arena 1	
18.15 Show Closes	

The 1984 show would always be known by the people preparing the site as the show of the transparent loo. When anybody asks if any show stood out to me in the preparation, this one always brings back fond memories for two or three different reasons. The first of these was the problem of the second entrance. Not being able to fill the ditch for the second gateway gave us a real headache, as we did not have the material to build a bridge with. The only way past this was to hire a 'Bailey bridge' and crane, and bridge the ditch in this way – keeping the cost down by doing the work ourselves. This was achieved on the Saturday morning prior to the show. Although our workforce was thin on the ground we were quite pleased with ourselves – to think we could do such amazing things to keep the show on the road. That Saturday morning the task was started and completed in five hours.

Another problem we had was that the main show field could only be accessed through the car-parking field. The parting hedge between the two fields was in an extremely poor state, causing us a severe security problem. The only cure for this was to practically install barbed wire as a defence against the general public. Again, this was achieved during the week leading up to the show. Yet another problem was that, after the 1983 show, the portable gents' toilet that Mr Geoff Harwood had dedicated a song to had gone missing. Who, may I ask, would want a second-hand corrugated-iron well-used gents' loo? I wonder if they had a sale for it. The mind just boggles at the depth some people will stoop to.

However the biggest laugh we had getting the 1984 show ready was as a result of the missing loo. Sid had volunteered to put this problem right by erecting another one on site before the show. Sid, as he had promised, came to the field with some good tall posts. On ascertaining the best position for the gents' loo he erected the posts ready to put the screen round the next day. Sure enough, next day Sid arrived armed with a good staple gun and a couple of rolls of new hessian to complete the job. He thus set about stapling the hessian around the posts. The only fault being that when the sun was shining you could see the silhouettes of anybody inside. This, of course, caused numerous comments from nearly everybody present, including Sid, who made some humorous comments of his own that had us all in stitches of laughter for the next half-hour. It was times like this that made the running of the White Horse Show the pleasure that it was. But, true to Sid's commitment, he returned on the Saturday before the show with tarpaulin to obliterate the transparent loo. The time between erecting this loo with hessian and the final skin of tarpaulin caused great fun, another reason why Sid was such a great asset to the show committee. This was going to be demonstrated yet again during the show itself.

The car-park marshalling was again being undertaken by Grove Rugby Club, and no problems were expected in this section of the show. This proved to be correct, as no traffic problems occurred on the roads leading to the show, although the traffic was very heavy and the show again well supported. The only problem experienced was at the horse-box entrance to the show. This was because, if there were any more than two people with a horse box or in a car following a box, they were expected to pay for entry to the show. But, unfortunately, some were just barging past without doing so, and this got back to Sid's ears. Being the organiser of the gymkhana he decided that he would go on to the gate in question and sort the problem out. It was not long before mayhem broke out on this gate, but, being Sid, he stuck rigidly to the rules. He would not compromise with the entry forms that had been sent out to prospective entrants to the gymkhana. In the end there was only one winner and that was Sid. I do not think that anyone else on the committee would have been strong enough to have stood the flak that was thrown at him as Sid did. But it proved once again what a great asset to the show committee Mr Sid Warren was. We also learned during the show that this was to be the site for next year's show, as Mr Colin Nash had been in attendance. It was during the show that I had a long talk with Mr Colin Nash over an incident that had happened some years before when he was out hunting on the local favourite – the one and only Baulking Green. It was close to this site that Mr Nash had been watched by them damned railwaymen chasing his hounds while riding on Baulking Green. He had headed towards a five-bar gate to jump and so keep up with the pack, but the old Green had different ideas and headed for a huge hedge. Unable to stop him, poor Colin had to just hang on and hope for the best. On the railway embankment we had a perfect view of the Green as he cleared the hedge with at least a foot to spare, with Colin still on board. When the hunt came back along the road later we had a few words with Colin and he confirmed it was not his intention to jump the hedge. It had just happened and there was virtually nothing he could do about it but to just hang on. He also confirmed that he was not actually in the saddle when the Green landed on the other side, but was still in the stirrups; what a painful experience it was when he came back down in the saddle!

Back on the subject of the White Horse Show, Colin did say that he would make an approach to the landowners regarding the ditch where we had had to hire the Bailey bridge, as he personally could see no problem in using large pipes and backfilling the ditch. However, he would let us know what the situation was in good time for next year. As regards to the barbed wire we had erected in the parting hedge between the two fields, we could leave it there ready for the following year.

It was also at this stage that we learned that for tax purposes we did not have to move show sites every two years. Since we had started to run the shows we had been under the false impression that, if we did not move every two years, the land we were using would be reclassified and be taxed as a show site. Thus the local farmers would be almost certain not to give us permission to use their fields. Apparently this only came into force when permanent fixtures were left on site, and of course we cleared our sites after every show, leaving us clear of this legislation.

The overall profit of the show was another great success, with gate money amounting to £19,126, leaving us with £8,500 profit. Needless to say, the whole of the committee were pleased. But we were all still aware that we must keep expenses down wherever possible.

As a result of this successful show the following grants were proposed to the full committee by the trustees and approved: Woolstone Church, restoration of west wall of church – £1,500; Uffington Sports and Social Club, floodlighting and reseeding – £1,400; Uffington Church, bells and tower restoration – £1,500; Uffington Scouts, canoes and roof rack – £500; Uffington Guides, patrol tent – £500; Uffington School, photocopier – £900; community minibus, mud flaps and roof rack – £300; Baulking Church, internal repairs – £800. This totalled £7,400 in grants, which must have meant another good year's work had been done. Also, everyone must bear in mind that all the local organisations that had attended the show had in one way or another also made a fairly good profit over the two days. On top of this the newly formed tennis club had earned good money in the litter-picking operation after the show.

The most serious complaint that we had was from the farmer of Colliers Farm at Baulking, and this one could have been very serious and dangerous. It was concerning the Marlborough Aerobatics; whilst they were performing their display they had got very close to the buildings on the farm. To make matters even worse, they had just started the afternoon milking session and the noise from the aircraft scared the cows very badly, which could have proved very nasty to the men carrying out this task. But, again, the luck was on our side and nobody got injured in any way. But this was one very important thing that we had to get right next time by the proper information being passed on to the aerobatics team. We could not afford the same mistake again.

1985

The refreshment marquee for the 1985 show was going to be run by Mrs Stella Mattingley and Mrs Kath Larkin from Fernham, and again was going to be making independent grants to other charities, as in 1984 and 1983. As the Girl Guides were very good in assisting with the refreshment marquee, they would do so again this year as in 1984, although it of course curtailed their ability to run their own money-raising event at the show. The committee promised to bear this point in mind in the future. As far as the entrance fee into the 1985 show was concerned, it was agreed with great reluctance that this would have to be raised again to match the ever-increasing cost of running the show. It was therefore decided that the entrance fee would be: adults £1.70, children and OAPs 80p, with local OAPs still being admitted free of charge. However, they needed to make their status known to the person on the gate, as that person might be a complete stranger and not know that they were a local OAP.

The programme of events for 1985 was also going to be very attractive and hopefully a good crowd puller. But, before the show could take place, there was more work to do in the showground preparation. Permission had now been given to pipe the ditch and backfill with hardcore. Eighteen-inch concrete pipes were available from the sports field and again Sid was available with his lorry to transport these to the site.

It was decided that this task would be undertaken on a Saturday morning a fortnight before the show was due to take place. Unfortunately, as usual, the workforce was somewhat short on the ground when the time came to carry out this work, but somehow we did manage to roll the pipes into the ditch in just the right place, so luck was with us again. During the week leading up to the show my luck was certainly right in. We were going to be having a helicopter at the show for the public to have rides in if they wished. On the Wednesday afternoon I was in the field on my own when the helicopter arrived to make their inspection of the site as to its suitability for such an event. I showed the crew the place that had been allocated for them to operate from and they were not too happy with the position. However, after moving one or two things, we were able to get a larger site for them, and with this they were very pleased. So much so that they offered to take me up for a short trip; this offer I could not refuse and climbed on board. To my amazement we went off in the direction of Reading. On the outskirts of Reading we turned and took in Oxford and back over Faringdon and White Horse Hill. The only drawback was that I did not have my camera with me, but I did thank them for their kindness, which I certainly appreciated very much.

The 1985 show was also the first time that I had a crack at driving a racing lawnmower, and what an experience that was. I certainly appreciated the smoothness of the car-park field and was amazed at the amount of throttle that was available; but, needless to say, with my stomach up in the air and two yards behind me it was not very comfortable. Not a sport that I think I would take up, although the people who do participate contribute quite a lot of money to charity. As far as the show was concerned they drew a considerable amount of people to watch them when they were racing.

Arena events for 1985:

Sunday 25 August

09.00 Gymkhana, Arena 2
13.30 Lawnmower Racing, Arena 5
13.30 Sheepdog Demonstration, Arena 1
13.45 Wild West Show, Arena 4
14.00 The Band of Royal Warwick Corps of Drums, Arena 1
14.30 Lawnmower Demo

Monday 26 August

11.00 Heavy Horse Show, Arena 2
12.00 British Carriage Driving Society, Arena 1
13.45 Cumberland Giants, Arena 1
13.45 Wild West Show, Arena 4
14.15 Lawnmower Demo Race, Arena 1
14.45 Band of Royal

	Race, Arena 1		Greenjackets, Arena 1
14.30	Dog Show, Arena 3	15.15	Old Berks Hunt, Arena 1
15.00	Cumberland Giants, Arena 1	15.45	British Carriage Driving Society, Arena 1
15.30	Sheepdog Demonstration, Arena 1	16.00	Cumberland Giants, Arena 4
15.45	Wild West Show, Arena 4	16.15	Vintage Cars and Fire Engines, Arena 1
16.00	Vintage Motorcycles, Arena 1	16.30	Marlborough Aerobatic Team
16.30	Marlborough Aerobatic Team	17.00	Wild West Show, Arena 4
17.00	Cumberland Giants, Arena 1	17.30	Band of Royal Greenjackets, Arena 1
17.30	Band of Warwick Corps of Drums, Arena 1	18.00	Show Closes
18.00	Show Closes		

As can be seen from this programme of events, we were still trying to attract as big a cross section of the general public as possible. The 1985 show still proved to have a few good laughs in its preparation, including the erection again of the transparent loo, although the transparency had of course been eliminated. There was the erection of the Army marquee, which we were borrowing from the Royal Military College of Science at Shrivenham each year. When it came to use it this year it was wanted for the refreshment side of the gymkhana, so Sid decided that he would organise this task with the helpers he had to hand. Being the leader he was he did not wish to be too long about putting it up, as he wanted to use it himself the same evening.

I myself was with Tony Coxhead and the tractor and post-driver at the top of the field and we could hear Sid giving his orders quite plainly, together with some of his comments as well. All of a sudden pandemonium broke out where the marquee was being erected. On looking down the field in that direction we could see that the marquee had collapsed down on top of the erecters. On arriving at the scene of the marquee the language could only be described as somewhat foreign, to put it mildly, but after it had been put up and completed everybody had a real good laugh. It was times like this that made the preparation of the show a pleasure to take part in; it certainly gave me a feeling of satisfaction that we had achieved our aim.

The 1985 show also proved to be another good profit-making event. The overall profit was £8,700, but before we could start to distribute these profits we would have to decide how much we were going to increase the disaster fund to. This disaster fund had to be maintained to be able to pay the costs should we have a complete 'washout' over the two days of any show, so we would still have enough to start the next show going again.

To give some idea as to the income and costs of running such an event as the White Horse Show, I will show just some of the income and expenditure for the 1985 show, and it must be understood that this is only a brief rundown. Income: trade stands brought in £3,800, ice cream selling rights £600, soft toys £200, sale of souvenirs £600, sale of programmes £450, dollar helicopters £300, gate takings £19,400. Expenditure (again only a brief of the total): Warwick Corps of Drums £200, aerobatic display £1,500, Band of the Royal Green Jackets £900, Cumberland Giants £700, heavy horses £1,330, electrical services to show field £1,100, Grove Rugby Club for car-parking duty £500, hire of marquees £3,000, hire of loos £1,300, police services £700, insurance £500, publicity and advertising £500.

As can be seen from this very brief set of figures, it had now become a very complex and intricate business to run the White Horse Show. At the last meeting of the 1985 show, Mr Roger Cummins expressed his wish that he would like to relinquish the post of chairman for the 1986 show, but would remain on the committee. This was accepted with reluctance by the committee, as Roger had served us well since the tragedy of the death of Harry. He had had a hard act to follow, but had performed it with brilliance. The committee were then unanimous in electing Mr Barry Godsell to fill the post of chairman. Barry had been with us for a number of years now and was well known and liked by the rest of us. Mr Alton Bailey had also tendered his resignation of the committee because he was moving away from the village.

Alton was thanked for his great contribution to the show and its causes over many years. As previously touched on, the committee also decided at this meeting to increase the disaster fund to £14,000 to safeguard ourselves from facing any shortfall in the meeting of expenses from future shows, and, as far as possible, to ensure their continuance. At this stage we had still not found a site for the 1986 show, and there were a considerable number of rumours going round that there would not be a show in 1986. It was decided that we must put a stop to the preachers of doom as quickly as possible, thus we took up space in the surrounding local press areas to deny these rumours.

1986

At our first meeting in January for the 1986 show we were able to breathe a little easier as a site had been found for the 1986 show. Mr Bracey, the farmer of Baulking Grange Farm, had kindly given his permission for the use of his field opposite the Kingston Lisle turn at the bottom of Baulking Fields. Quite a lot of work would have to be undertaken to make this a suitable site, and it was only to be for one year. This was because it was due to be ploughed for crop change in the autumn of that year. So, in between carrying out work on the site for the 1986 show, we were going to have to be hunting for a site for the 1987 show.

One thing we were at least getting used to by this time was dealing with three shows at the same time. I suppose that, as the shows increased in size, it was inevitable that this would happen. Whilst working on the next show we had to think about the following year, because it was getting difficult to book star attractions unless you were booking in good time, so this problem made sense. Also, some of the accounts of the previous year were running into the next year before they were settled. But somehow the committee were able to tolerate and accommodate this situation. However, back to the 1986 show.

On examination of the new site it was noted that another entrance would be required to the show site, to enable us to get the cars clear of the road and into the site. Also, the only way to keep things moving smoothly would be to take the entrance fees directly from the cars as they came into the site, before they were able to park. This would have to be achieved by fencing a large catchment area off with the pay booths; this needed to be wide enough to accommodate a car. Just how many booths would be required would have to be decided when the gate helpers had been worked out later on. All the gateways would need hardcore tipped in them as soon as possible. An extra field for additional car parking had been kindly authorised by Mr Ron Liddiard. As we were having a different firm operating the helicopters this year, a separate site meeting with their representative would have to be arranged, as we were certain that we would not be able to accommodate them in the main show field. But, thanks to Mr Jim Reade, who had kindly said we could use his small field next to our main show field, we were certain we could overcome this problem. On approaching the Fullers earth processing site owners, they readily agreed to allow access through their site to enable the back-up crew and their facilities for the helicopter joyrides. We could also use this for any emergencies that might come during the show.

Shire horse mare and foal, 1986

We were also to learn, with a great deal of reluctance, that Sid would not be with us for much longer, and certainly wouldn't be available to run the gymkhana this year. Both Sid and Tony had for some time been looking for someone to take over the organisation of this side of the show, but had been unsuccessful. We thus decided that we would, with great reluctance, have to forgo this piece of the show. This was a great pity, after seeing the amount of enjoyment that had been generated from this in the past. It was also one of the attractions that actually commenced with the first show in 1972, but took place on a different day, at a different site, becoming a part of the main show in 1979. I think by this time everyone on the committee could see that the health of our president was failing fast, but, true to his grit and determination, John would not give in and it was plain to see that he would always be a part of the White Horse Show.

We were still experiencing a fair few problems with trying to fit everything into the new site. This was, of course, always something of a headache when moving on to a new site. But, with the car parking being in the same field and the pay booths having to be well inside the three entrances to leave a large catchment area, this seemed to be the most difficult site to date. In fact I had lost count of the number of times that Daniel and I had been to the site in the last six weeks before the show. It ended with some very blunt talking and language with some members of our committee before the final site plan was accepted. When the time came to prepare the site for the show I was extremely grateful for the assistance of Mr Tony Coxhead with the tractor and post driver. The extra posts needed for the separation of the car parking from the show site together with the extra needed on the pay booths and catchment area was considerable. I believe this year we used nearly 400 posts; some task this would have been with a sledgehammer. However, at the show weekend, all the problems had been overcome. Thamesdown Helicopters had been and agreed that the separate field that had been kindly lent by Mr Jim Reade was fine. A very full programme of events was planned, as follows:

Sunday 24 August

12.00 Cricklade Town Band
13.30 Young Farmers
14.00 The Charlies
       (Trampoline Act)
14.30 Freefall Parachutes

Monday 25 August

11.00 British Driving Society
12.00 Cricklade Town Band
13.30 Young Farmers
14.00 Clowns International
14.30 Freefall Parachutes

15.00	Wasps Motorcycle Display Team	15.00	Band of The Scots Guards
15.30	Young Farmers	15.30	Wasps Motorcycle Display Team
16.00	Vintage Motorcycles Parade	16.00	Old Berks Hunt
16.30	Toyota Aerobatics	16.00	British Driving Society In Horse Arena
17.00	The Charlies	16.15	Vintage Cars Parade
17.30	Cricklade Town Band	16.30	Toyota Aerobatics
18.00	Show Closes	17.00	Clowns International
		17.30	Band of The Scots Guards
		18.00	Show Closes

The Heavy Horse Show would be taking place on the Monday commencing at 11.00. Also, on both days the Dixieland Rebels, the Morris Men and Johnny Chuckles with his Punch and Judy show would be performing at various times in Arena 3, at times advertised in that arena.

The weather forecast for the Monday of the show was rather grim; in fact a completely wet day was forecast. I think that the public had certainly taken the advice of the forecasters, as on the Sunday we were pushed to the limits on the gates trying to keep the road clear. I spent a full five hours inside the catchment area directing cars up to the different pay booths. Eventually we were able to open three extra booths, and with seven open we were able to relax a little, snatching a quick cup of tea in between times. But the crowds certainly turned up for the show, and when it was time to close for the day it was obvious to all concerned that it was the best attendance that we had ever had on the Sunday.

But, alas, it was to be a different story for the Monday; unfortunately the forecast of the weather on the Monday proved to be correct. To say it rained all day would be an understatement; at times the sky just opened and it fell down in buckets. But fortunately quite a few hardy stalwarts still turned up. In spite of the weather, the full programme of events was completed, much to our surprise. The most distressing thing about the whole show was the health of our president John. We all noticed over the entire show how John had stopped in the secretary's caravan and how very tired he looked. His wife Joan made very frequent visits to check on him and was obviously very worried as to his well-being. But, this being a White Horse Show, there was no way that John was going to be anywhere else but at that show. After all, the show was John's brainchild, and what an innovation it turned out to be. The one good thing about the 1986 show was that despite the weather we still made a profit of £1,500. This was very pleasing to the committee after the near washout of the Monday. In the past we had always tried to break even with the income from the Sunday, leaving the Monday income as the overall profit for all the hard work that had been put in over the previous twelve months.

Clearing up after the show this year was quite a trying experience after all the rain. To get in and out of the field with trailer-loads of equipment was a very awkward manoeuvre. If you used the same track too often you just became bogged down, which meant you had to unload, get unstuck and on to firm ground, and then reload. After a couple of days the language became unprintable, but after a week of frayed tempers we did eventually achieve our goal. I think that this still holds the record for the worst show we ever had to clear up after. I was extremely glad when Saturday 6 September arrived so that I could get away on holiday. But it was while I was away that I learned of the sad death of our president and founder, John Little. Although I knew of his very poor health and that he was deteriorating fast it was still very hard to accept that he had died. Uffington had lost an exceptionally fine gentleman. He had done more for the village than any other person that I had known in my lifetime, and that was fifty-three years at that time. John had worked untiringly for the church, created the museum, and when he came forward to create the White Horse Show for the village of Uffington the help the community received was endless. I therefore hope that the people of the three villages will never forget the legacy left by John Egram Little.

At our November meeting the tragic loss of John was still very much in the forefront of our minds. But it was a tragedy that we would have to overcome, if only to make sure that the legacy of John carried on. To make things somewhat more difficult, four resignations from the committee were received. They were: Mrs Ann Hopkinson from the running of the dog show; Mr John Clarke, who had been organising the stationary engines; Mrs Betsy Matthews from the rare breeds and poultry show. The other big blow to us was the resignation of our very efficient secretary, Mrs Trish Follows, who unfortunately for us was leaving the area. She had been very helpful at all times to anyone on the committee needing her help.

The committee thanked all four for their service to the cause of the show and wished them luck in the future. It was also decided to give a chance to the people of Shellingford and Kingston Lisle to join us in the show project by widening the trust to encompass both villages. In doing so we would increase the amount of labour to prepare the show sites. After all, this was the area where we were always short of help in leading up to the show. But, after exploratory talks on a fact-finding basis with people from those villages, it was decided to remain as we were. Another problem to be faced was the fact that a new site was required for 1987. We had a few sites in our view but whether any would come to bear fruit would have to wait to be seen at our next meeting. In the meantime, Mrs Greta Cummins agreed to take on the secretarial duties for the 1987 show; after standing by Roger through his time as chairman and now taking on these duties she proved a very brave person.

1987

At the January 1987 meeting a new site had been found and confirmed for the 1987 show. The site would be in the Fawler Road in fields belonging to Sir Adrian Swire, next to Craven Field. Some of the committee were dubious as to whether this site would be large enough for the show, but were to get a fair shock when they finally visited the site. It was therefore decided that myself and Daniel would walk the new site and report back to the next meeting. A fair amount of booking had already been undertaken for the next show. Southern Counties had already offered £1,200 for the rights on the sale of ice cream. Events already confirmed included the Marlborough Aerobatics and the Royal Green Jackets freefall parachutes for both days. Mr Martyn Elliot had kindly agreed to take over the organisation of the dog show and Mr Charles Philo was going to run the stationary engines. So, once again, everything was up and running. The only headache that now seemed to be left for the field-sub was to try and fit everything in place. We had the usual goodwill from the football club in their offer of the football pitch for the use of the heavy horse show, which we accepted without hesitation. It would mean removal of a post and wire fence to give access to this part of the show, but that would only be a minor task, as the main public entry to the whole show would probably have to be through this corner of the sports field anyway. After meeting the police with a rundown of the site and car-parking arrangements we would know more on what overall workload would be involved with our new site.

The meeting with Inspector Griffiths of Thames Valley Police regarding the car parking and the entrances and exits to both the car parks and main show fields went really well. The only request that Inspector Griffiths made was for an extra entrance to the car park for traffic coming from the Kingston Lisle direction, so as to avoid crossing traffic. The car parking was again by kind permission of Mr Jim Matthews on the opposite side of the road to the show field. He readily agreed to the gateway alteration, thus alleviating another headache for the field sub-committee.

A new attraction for this show was to be clay-pigeon shooting; the site problem for this attraction was overcome by the kind permission of Mr D Parrott, who let us overshoot his field at the top of the sports field. The only attraction not to be included this year would be the rare breeds and poultry, as nobody could be found to run this part of the show. Come the show we had found room for everything, despite the doubts that some of the committee had earlier on. This success was due mainly to the cooperation of the football club in accommodating the heavy horses on the football pitch. We were always aware that the horses wanted quite a large area for their arena, as the parking for the horse boxes and equipment needed to be adjacent to their preparation area. With the weather fine and a good forecast over the weekend we were hoping for a good turnout to make up for the disappointment of last year. We certainly had a good full programme of events, which we hoped the public would enjoy. The entrance fee had been increased to try once again to keep pace with rising costs, and would be: adults £2, children and senior citizens £1, with local senior citizens going in free.

Some of the attractions were as follows: Sunday 12 p.m. to 6 p.m. Exemption Dog Show at 2.30 p.m., Sheepdog Demonstration, Tug-of-War, Historic Motorcycles, Warwick Corps of Drums, Clowns International, Morris Dancers.

Monday 10 a.m. to 6 p.m. Heavy Horse Show all day, Giant Sumo Wrestlers, Old Berks Hunt Parade, Band of the Royal Scots Dragoon Guards, British Driving Society, Historic Motor Cars, Royal Green Jacket Freefall Parachute Team.

Both days: Marlborough Aerobatics Display Team, Lawnmower Racing, Historic Fire Engines and Military Vehicles, Stationary Engines, Cricklade Town Band, Thamesdown Helicopters Joyrides, Dixie Rebels Western Show, Clay Pigeon Shoot, Johnny Chuckles Magic & Punch and Judy Show, Motorcycle Star Riders, The Duke of Edinburgh's Royal Regiment Regimental Information Team, The Royal Artillery Main Display Team, Funfair, Sideshows, Inflated Funcastles,

Coconut Shies, Roundabouts, Art Exhibition. Over 200 Trade and Craft Stands in Marquees and in the open air, including Embroidery, Knitwear, Jewellery, Flowercraft, Glassblowing, Engraving, Pottery, Ceramics, Pokerwork, Horncraft, Basketry, Leathercraft, Nurseryman, Bee-keeping, Painting, Books, Bric-a-brac, Painted Porcelain and Woodware, Fully Licensed Bar, open all day, Free Car Parking.

Shire horses and wagons, 1987

The 1987 show would also be known after a loo; in fact this was the year of the flaming loo. This was the year when we thought that, to help things out, we would add an extra gents' loo by building one with straw bales. But, unfortunately, a lunatic full of beer decided that it was rather cold and tried to warm himself by setting fire to the loo. To say it caused chaos is very much an understatement. The first fire engine to arrive at the scene was an RAF tender; it looked good until it was discovered that it had no water. After a considerable number of red faces the fire was extinguished with hand-held extinguishers from one of the historic fire engines. It was discovered afterwards that the RAF tender had arrived at the show empty and should have been filled with water on the day of the show, but no one told the RAF crew when they left Abingdon to attend the show. Personally, if it had been left to me I would have left the drunken yobbo inside; it could have done one of two things – either sobered him up or roast him – and I certainly would not have worried which.

At about 2 p.m. on the Monday, our treasurer, Mr Peter Erskine, came round to the secretary's caravan with the great news that we had passed the record takings on the gate at 1 p.m. The only problem with this was that, although we were a registered charity, we could therefore end up paying tax, which was something else we would have to try and find a way around. One thing was certain – if anybody could, Peter would. Mrs Stella Mattingley and Mrs Kath Larkin, who had again run a very successful refreshment marquee, also reported record profits of £1,350. With all the very hard work that went into this project it was no more than fully deserved. This sum, as already declared before the show, would be split as follows: £650 each to the Prospect Foundation and the Princess Margaret Scanner Appeal and £50 to the Uffington Afternoon Club.

The overall profit of the 1987 show was of course a record, and stood at £15,600. The official attendance stood at 18,400 tickets sold at the gate over the two days. It was therefore decided to raise the disaster fund to £18,000 as a back up for the show should any disaster take place. The final meeting of the 1987 show was also a sad occasion because it was to be the last meeting for Mrs Joan Little, who was moving away from the area. Our chairman made a presentation to Joan and thanked her for all her hard work, interest and involvement during her sixteen years with the show committee. The rest of us assured her that the thanks that we all owed to her late husband John for the numerous tasks that he undertook around our village would never be forgotten, in particular the pioneering of the White Horse Show.

Another resignation that we would have to overcome was that of the secretary, Mrs Greta Cummins, due to family commitments. We were also warned that it might be to our advantage if we began to look for someone else to organise the craft and trade stands in the near future.

Mrs Sue Philo volunteered to become secretary for the 1988 show. Her kindness was greatly appreciated for taking on this very demanding work. Running the committee without that post being filled would be like trying to keep fish without water. Also welcomed on to the committee for the purpose of organising and running the craft and trade stands for 1988 was Mr Jim Larkin. The case of VAT had now been solved and we had to register by March of this year. VAT could then be set against all expenses once we were registered. Therefore we would have to be very careful with all expenditure, as invoices would be needed.

Grants to be made from this last show to date were as follows: to Uffington C. of E. School, for an extra computer – £850; Thomas Hughes Memorial Hall, to replace boiler – £1,500; to the sports and social club, to complete the car park and help with field maintenance – £2,500; Uffington Church – £2,000; Woolstone Church – £2,000; Baulking Church – £2,000; towards the village minibus, which had to be replaced – £2,500.

1988

In the meantime, Sir Adrian Swire had confirmed that we had the use of his fields again for 1988. This was good news, as the workload is never quite as much second time around. Teething problems such as those experienced in 1987 can be ironed out with a certain amount of ease because they stick in one's mind and you make notes of these to compare with other members. We knew that certain adjustments would have to be made for the layout in 1988, because we had been lucky enough to find volunteers to take on the rare breeds and poultry side of the show. The volunteers were Mr and Mrs Don North and Mrs J Cooper. With an extra sixty-by-thirty marquee to accommodate this attraction, and by pushing everything back a little closer to the outside, this would cause no problem.

We were beginning to realise that, no matter how many field plans we could produce and present to the committee during the course of the planning stage, it would always need altering for someone. We thus hung on as close to the last meeting before the show before producing the plans; in this way we had fewer headaches than if we produced them early. It seemed near impossible to explain that, with the best will in the world, at some time in the building of the showground it would invariably not fit as originally planned. After all was said and done, the main arena had to be set in the smoothest part as near to the centre as possible, and this determined more or less where the rest of the field was set. To us it made common sense to then fit the trade stands around the main arena. In any case, when the time came to set everything into the show field, we found that the fault-finders were conspicuous by their absence.

It was very unfortunate that Grove Rugby Club had very badly let us down concerning the car parking in 1987, with insufficient marshals on duty in the car parks to keep the traffic from building up on the roads. A very strong letter had been received from

Inspector Griffiths of Thames Valley Police concerning the poor way in which the car parking had been marshalled; this was duly sent to Grove Rugby Club.

It was therefore decided to seek other bodies to carry out these duties; this duty was costing the show £580, and it seemed, therefore, that we could at least expect a good job to be achieved for this sort of money. In the end Cricklade Railway Society came forward with the offer to carry out these duties for the same price, together with the promise that they would have the minimum of twelve adults on duty at all times. This was accepted by the committee without hesitation.

On Monday 29 August we had what I believed to be the most spectacular star attraction that we had ever had at a White Horse Show; this was due to the sheer persistence of Colonel Tony Bateman. It was only through his contacts that we secured one of the attractions from the Royal Tournament at Earl's Court. That attraction was to be the Household Cavalry Musical Ride. To have a star attraction of this class performing in the village of Uffington was certainly going to be a big publicity boost to the show. But, unfortunately, I have always asked since, did we in fact get the publicity right? I think not; we had had quite a lot of disagreement on the cost of advertising after the 1987 show. Frankly, I could not see why anyone could find fault with that side of the expenditure for the 1987 show; after all, we had beaten all previous records on attendance and profits at that time. The arguments just did not stand up to the facts, but one or two hawks on the committee seemed determined to go down that road to cut expenditure. However, the proof will come to light in the end.

The Household Cavalry Musical Ride was commanded by Captain T J K Faulkner and the Life Guards riding master Captain B J McKie.

The Household Cavalry is formed from two regiments – the Life Guards and the Blues and Royals (Royal Horse Guards and the 1st Dragoons). At present the Life Guards are stationed at Windsor, where they have an armoured reconnaissance role, and the Blues and Royals are equipped with Chieftain tanks. One mounted squadron from each regiment is maintained to continue the traditional 300-year-old role as the personal cavalry of the sovereign in London.

The Household Cavalry Regiment (Mounted) is stationed at Hyde Park Barracks in London and may be seen throughout the year at Horse Guards where each day they provide the Queen's Life Guard. They also provide a sovereign's escort and other escorts on occasions such as the Queen's Birthday Parade (Trooping the Colour), the State Opening of Parliament, visits of heads of state and royal weddings.

Household Cavalry Musical Ride, 1988

The Musical Ride is a development of the ride first performed by the 1st Regiment of Life Guards at the Royal Tournament in 1882. There are sixteen dutymen dressed in Mounted Review Order, eight Life Guards and eight Blues and Royals. There is also one kettle drummer, four trumpeters and two farriers. The full-dress uniform worn by the Ride is the same as that worn on all ceremonial parades. The uniforms of both regiments have remained almost unchanged since the days of the Prince Regent, later King George IV, who died in 1830. The regiments substituted helmets for cocked hats and polished steel cuirasses, which were first worn when the Prince Regent became King in 1820. The helmets worn at our 1988 show came into use in 1842 and are worn with a white plume for the Life Guards and a scarlet plume for the Blues and Royals. All trumpeters wear scarlet plumes and ride grey horses for recognition on the battlefield. The farriers carry axes which were used in the old days for despatching wounded horses. The Life Guards farriers wear a black plume and a blue tunic.

The Household Cavalrymen taking part in the ride will spend about three years with the Mounted Regiment, after which they return to their parent regiments. The Musical Ride appeared by kind permission of the Lieutenant Colonel commanding the Household Cavalry, Colonel A H Parker-Bowles, OBE.

Music for the Household Cavalry would be supplied by the St George's Band of the Royal Regiment of Fusiliers, commanded by Bandmaster WO1 C C Attrill. They appeared by kind permission of Lieutenant Colonel J C Gunnell, commanding officer of the 2nd Battalion Royal Regiment of Fusiliers.

The total cost of this attraction would be £4,900. Therefore, Tony should be congratulated for obtaining this event. If the advertising and publicity were not any different from last year, the crowds could be expected to roll up for this event.

The programme for both days over the August bank holiday was very full, in fact, as follows:

Sunday 28 August

- 12.00 Show opens
- 12.00 Dressage Display, 'We're a Couple of Equestrienne Swells'
- 12.20 Wasps Motorcycle Display Team
- 12.50 Swan Majorettes
- 13.20 K9 Commandos, a demonstration by military trained guard-dogs, mainly Alsatians
- 13.30 Cricklade Town Band, by refreshment tent

Monday 29 August

- 10.00 British Driving Society
- 12.30 Wasps Motorcycle Display Team
- 13.00 Parade of Vintage Tractors
- 13.00 Hungerford Town Band (by refreshment tent)
- 13.30 Wantage Gymnasts
- 13.45 Lawnmower Racing begins (own arena)
- 14.00 Flying Dragons Freefall Parachute Team
- 14.30 Wasps Motorcycle

13.30 Lawnmower Racing starts in its own arena
13.50 Melton Mowbray Tally-Ho Band
14.40 Dressage Display
15.00 Wasps Motorcycle Display Team
15.30 Freefall Parachute Team, The Flying Dragons from the Queens Regiment
15.30 Cricklade Town Band (by the refreshment tent)
16.00 K9 Commandos
16.35 Parade of Historic Motorcycles
17.00 Marlborough Aerobatic Display
17.30 Melton Mowbray Tally Ho Band
18.00 Show Closes

15.00 Musical Ride of the Household Cavalry with St George's Band of the Royal Regiment of Fusiliers
15.30 A Country Sporting Pageant
15.30 Hungerford Town Band (by the refreshment tent)
16.00 Swan Majorettes
16.30 Parade of Historic Cars
17.00 Marlborough Aerobatic Display
17.30 Musical Ride of the Household Cavalry with St George's Band of the Royal Regiment of Fusiliers
18.00 Show Closes

To this was added the heavy horse show, which commenced at 11.00 in its own arena, and consisted of the following. Officials: Judge – Mr August from Alton in Hampshire; Stewards – Mr P Matthews, Wilton, Salisbury, Wiltshire and Mr Ken Freeman, Goosey, Oxfordshire; Announcer and Commentator – Mr Frank Chambers, Uffington, Oxfordshire.

> Class 1 – Best Mare in hand. Three years upwards. For the Isis Construction Perpetual Challenge Trophy.
>
> Class 2 – Best Gelding in hand. Three years upwards. For the Jewson & Sons Perpetual Challenge Trophy.
>
> Class 3 – Best Suffolk/Percheron/Ardennes/any other breed other than Shire. Any age, any sex. For the White Horse

Show Perpetual Challenge Trophy.

Class 4 – Fillies/Colts. One year. For the R J Brickell Perpetual Challenge Trophy.

Class 4(A) – Fillies/Colts. Two years. For The White Horse Show Perpetual Challenge Trophy.

Class 5 – Brood Mare, in foal or with foal at foot. For the J Calder Perpetual Challenge Trophy.

Class 5(A) – Foal, produce of above. For the R J Brickell Perpetual Challenge Trophy.

Class 6 – Novice. Any age, breed or sex, never having won a first prior to the day of the show. For the Clarks Mill (Wantage) Perpetual Challenge Trophy.

Championship – 1st & 2nd of above classes. For the Fawley Stud Perpetual Challenge Trophy. Presented by Mr D Muir, North Farm (Fawley) Limited.

Class 7 – Best single decorated horse in harness. For the Corona Perpetual Challenge Trophy.

Class 8 – Best single agricultural horse in harness – working harness (Black Steel) only. For the Farmers Perpetual Challenge Trophy.

Class 8(A) – Best single agricultural horse in harness – show harness. For the Mr and Mrs K Freeman Perpetual Challenge Trophy.

Class 9 – Best single turnout – Trade Only. For the D Herring Perpetual Challenge Trophy.

Class 10 – Agricultural turnout – any horse-drawn machine/cart used for agricultural purposes. For the R J Brickell Perpetual Challenge Trophy.

Class 11 – Best pair in harness. For the P White Perpetual Challenge Trophy.

Class 12 – Best pair, unicorn or team turnout. Trade or agricultural. For the Ben Smith Memorial Rose Bowl (Perpetual).

The committee greatly appreciated the generous sponsorship of Morrells Brewery Ltd of Oxford, which helped to make the running of the heavy horse show possible at the White Horse Show each year.

As anyone can see from these few details of the 1988 show, a lot of planning and hard work was required to run such an event. But, given fine weather and some good luck, it certainly benefited the three villages financially.

It seems that some things stand out at each show; unfortunately at this one it was a very bad accident. It took place by the helicopter: a girl could not wait to get on the helicopter in the proper manner and tried to run round the back. As a result she got struck a blow on the arm by the rear rotor blade, which in turn severely lacerated her arm. If this girl had done the same as all the other passengers and waited for the helicopter staff to take her to the helicopter, the accident would never have happened. I think that she was exceptionally lucky not to have lost her arm or even her life, but it certainly marred the rest of the show.

The rare breeds, which made a welcome return to this show, certainly turned out to be a great attraction. A Gloucester Old Spot sow with nine very small piglets only a few days' old really caused great interest, particularly with the small children. In fact, to get inside the rare-breed marquee was an achievement, let alone to get anywhere near the pen with the piglets in. Another success this year was the car parking, which was undertaken by the Cricklade Railway Society. With no outstanding build-up of traffic on the roads leading to the show, the police were happy, which speaks for itself. Another successful refreshment profit was reported by Stella and Kath, who thanked Greta and the Girl Guides for all their sterling help over the entire show. Although the profit was down a little on last year it still left £500 to be donated to the Mary Lodge and £500 to the British Heart Foundation, which had to be appreciated by these charities.

The overall profit for the show was down on the previous one, but we realised that we just could not keep breaking records every year. But, with a profit of £8,000, I think everyone was well pleased. But, again, I expected that we would be getting earache from the hawks who would say we could have done better if we had kept the spending down. I will always maintain that if we cut back on advertising and publicity then sooner rather than later the crowds will drop off, and with that the profits will also go down.

The disaster fund was now to be increased to £20,000. This made sense with the rising cost of running the show. This money was not just sitting in a bank account doing nothing; it was in fact invested, with the profits from this investment being paid out in grants by the trustees, which were in the bounds of the trust. Other recent grants were as follows: Tom Brown's Museum, £600; Uffington Church, £500; Baulking Church, £500; Uffington Cubs and Scouts, £589; Uffington Jubilee Field Play Area, £1,000; Uffington Sports Club, £400; Thomas Hughes Memorial Hall, £500; Craven Sports Field, £100.

1989

Again we were set to look for yet another site for the 1989 show. With the present pattern of agriculture and crop rotation this was what we had to expect in this day and age. The site we had used for the past two years was due to be ploughed up for cereal crop from Lea, therefore move we must.

Another change that we faced for 1989 was that our chairman Barry Godsell was resigning due to work pressure, but would remain on the committee. I was pleased about his decision to remain with the committee, as he always had a great sense of humour; no matter what the situation was, Barry could always see a funny side to it.

Working with people of this nature always made the work go easier, no matter how hard it was. The post of chairman would be taken over by Mr Viv Boaler, who had been on the committee for a number of years and of course knew what the score was.

Before I go any further I think that it is time to give a run-down of the names of the committee at this time, as they do change occasionally.

Chairman, Mr V J Boaler; treasurer, Mr J P Erskine; secretary, Mrs S Philo; arena events, Mr B Mills, Mr R. Jay; publicity, Mr M C Thomas; craft and trade stands, Mr J Larkin; refreshments, Mrs S Mattingley, Mrs K Larkin; bar, Mr B White; sign writing and field, Mr D Chester; public address and electrics, Mr W Mattingley; historic vehicles, Mr and Mrs D Kelsey; driving society and army displays, Colonel A J Bateman; heavy horses, Mrs C Keen; dog show, Mr M Elliott; rare breeds, Mr and Mrs D North, Mrs J Cooper; stationary engines and vintage tractors, Mr C Philo; field services, Mr P Smythe; printing, Mr J Packford; showground, Mr B Tilling, Mr M Connors, Mr R Cummins, Mr B Godsell, Mr W Mitchell; police and security, PC Dave Platts.

As can be now well seen, a lot of people put in a lot of work to run a White Horse Show.

By early January the owner of Sower Hill Farm, Mr Jim Soden, had offered fields on the approach road to White Horse Hill. If these fields could be used for the 1989 show it would rate as one of the best possible sites ever. Who could want a better site with the backdrop to the show being White Horse Hill itself? One could now look forward to the White Horse Show at last coming home.

Vintage tractors and machinery, 1989

After some discussions with Jim about just what we could do as regards the entrances and exits from the proposed show field and car parks, I thought what a very cooperative gentleman he was. He sanctioned the installation of an extra gateway into the main car park and an extra gateway through to the main show field from the car park. As for the gateway into the main show field from the road, this was already a double-width entrance and, in my opinion, was ample to the needs of the show. As far as the car park and public entrance went, Jim was perfectly happy for this work to be undertaken by the committee. On explaining that the entrances would need hardcore of some description tipped into them nearer the time of the show, he was also happy with this situation.

On leaving Jim I thanked him for his outstanding cooperation, but said I would leave the finer points of the discussion in the hands of Barry and Tony. On departing, Jim said that if there was anything else that I thought of afterwards to by all means come and see him again. After consulting with Mr David Coxhead as to the feasibility of getting any large articulated lorry through the gateway into the main show field, he assured me that there was ample room for this. The next thing there was to do now was to get a very tight measurement of the show field; this Daniel and I carried out on one very wet Sunday afternoon. But, on doing so, we decided that we were going to be spoilt in the amount of room we had at our disposal. It was therefore left for Barry and Tony to visit Jim to negotiate the terms regarding the question of rent.

As for the field-sub, we were extremely happy with the site overall. At our January meeting the committee accepted the new site by a large majority. One of the most pleasing aspects of it was that we were to have this site for some considerable time, as Jim was not an arable farmer. In Jim's words he 'did not believe in destroying the countryside by chopping down every hedge in sight'. In fact, he was going to be the opposite and undertake a tree-planting scheme. On explaining to the committee that there would be a certain amount of expenditure on the show site to bring it up to the standards that we always tried to achieve, this seemed to acceptable. But, unfortunately, we had to sit and listen to the short-sighted idea that expenditure could be trimmed on the advertising and publicity side. We still could not seem to convince these people that if you fall down on publicity, then the public fail to hear what you have to offer in the form of entertainment and do not bother to come. This then becomes the slippery slope to failure, and that road was one which we did not want to go down.

On preparing the site for the show we found, as usual for a new site, the workload was going to be a lot extra, and it was going to be touch and go to be ready in time. Another thing that was usual was that though extra hands were promised for help, they seemed to think that turning up on the Friday evening prior to the show was soon enough. How short-sighted can you get? One extra job that was done that was not really needed was an extra printed sign that Daniel made to go next to the large manure heap; that sign read 'Adventure Playground'. Alas, some committee members did not see the funny side of this and removed it. But the next day I pulled on a pair of wellington boots and planted it right in the middle and on the top. Needless to say, it never got moved again until we cleared the show field after the event. I wonder why?

One other problem that came up was the footpath that ran up the full length of the car park. We therefore decided to wait until the Sunday morning of the show to quietly remove the sign in order to replace it afterwards. We hoped this would not be noticed, but unfortunately we got rumbled and would have to fence this confounded thing off the next time. Eventually we did overcome the workload in preparing the field, but it was the closest call of any so far.

The programme of events for 1989 was as usual very full, as can be seen from the following:

Sunday 27 August

11.30 Gun Dog Parade
12.20 Wasps Motorcycle Display Team
12.50 Funtasia
13.20 Sheep Dog Demonstration
13.40 Swan Majorettes
14.10 Demonstration Lawnmower Race
14.40 Wasps Motorcycle Display Team
15.10 Sheep Dog Demonstration
15.30 Armoured Display by the Royal Wiltshire Yeomanry
16.00 Funtasia

Monday 28 August

10.15 British Driving Society
12.10 Funtasia
12.40 Wasps Motorcycle Display Team
13.10 Parade of Vintage Tractors
13.40 Demonstration Lawnmower Race
14.10 Funtasia
14.40 Parade of Heavy Horses
15.00 Band of Her Majesty's Royal Marines, Flag Officer Plymouth
15.30 Working Dog Demonstration
16.00 Wasps Motorcycle Display Team

16.35	Parade of Historic Motorcycles	16.30	Parade of Historic Cars
17.00	Toyota Aerobatic Display	17.00	Toyota Aerobatic Display
17.30	Swan Majorettes	17.30	Band of Her Majesty's Royal Marines, Flag Officer Plymouth
18.00	Show Closes		
		18.00	Show Closes

Monday only: Heavy Horse Show in its own arena, 11.00 to 16.00.

Both days: Cricklade Town Band, 11.00 to 12.00 and 16.30 to 17.10.

A rundown on this show's attractions in brief follows, as described in the programme:

> *Swan Majorettes* – This girls' marching band from Swindon is making a return appearance after their highly successful debut at last year's show. The band were West of England champions in 1987. Their members, who range in age from eight to nineteen years, put on a really sparkling spectacle.
>
> *The Toyota Aerobatic Team* – A star attraction in past White Horse Shows has been this exciting display of formation and synchronised aerobatics. The Toyota team never fail to thrill spectators with their breathtaking display.
>
> *Rare and minority breeds* – This display of unusual breeds of farm animals, including pigs, sheep, goats, ponies, poultry etc., has always been a popular favourite at the show and as a bonus there is a demonstration of wool spinning by hand. The Rare Breeds Survival Trust also has a stand to answer questions.
>
> *Cricklade Town Band* – It is a great pleasure to welcome back this top-class band, whose fame has spread throughout the south of England. Their extensive repertoire has given great pleasure to audiences as far afield as France and Germany.
>
> *Army Displays* – The Army Careers Information Office of Reading present a static display courtesy of Lt. Col. Lord Allenby. They

are supported by Army youth-training teams of the Royal Electrical and Mechanical Engineers and the Light Infantry Division Training Team, who will erect a climbing tower.

The Band of Her Majesty's Royal Marines, Flag Officer Plymouth – Directed by Lieutenant David M J Rogerson, LRAM, ARCM, RM, the band of the Flag Officer Plymouth is based at the main new entry and training establishment of the Royal Navy, HMS Raleigh, in Torpoint, Cornwall. The band undertakes a wide variety of ceremonial work of national importance, as well as fulfilling its main role of providing music for the establishments and ships which are under the auspices of the Flag Officer Plymouth. The band perform in the knowledge that wherever they appear they are welcomed by an appreciative audience that enjoys the sound and the spectacle for which the bands of Her Majesty's Royal Marines are famous throughout the world. The band appears by kind permission of the Flag Officer Plymouth, Vice Admiral Sir John Webster, KCB.

The Royal Air Force – There is a static display by RAF Abingdon, illustrating career opportunities in RAF engineering and the work of the station. The display is by kind permission of the Station Commander Group Capt. S P Burdess. There is a raffle in aid of the RAF Benevolent Society.

Working Dog Demonstration – A varied display of dogs in action in the main arena. This includes gun dogs, sheep dogs and a police dog, by kind permission of Chief Superintendent David Lindley, Thames Valley Police. The hounds of the Old Berks hunt, who are kennelled at Faringdon, also appear, thanks to the joint masters, Mr Frank Caldwell, Viscount Astor, Miss C Allsopp and Mr Michael Green. This display is rounded off by the Grove Branch of Guide Dogs for the Blind, for whom a collection will be taken.

Morris Dancing – We are delighted to welcome again the Icknield Way dancers, who perform traditional dances on Monday.

Sheepdog Display – Ron Webb demonstrates his skills as a shepherd with his three dogs, Zak (ten), Ben (three), and Meg (six). Ron, who has shorn over 20,000 sheep this summer, trained the dogs himself. Basic training can be accomplished in as little as two months, but the finer points may take a year or more. Ron's dogs have regularly won prizes at Great Shefford and many others, including a recent victory in Sussex. In this demonstration half a dozen ewe lambs will be driven through gates and penned using whistled and verbal commands. Those unfamiliar with this ancient technique should watch out for the five main commands. 'Come by' means go clockwise; 'away to me' means go anti-clockwise; 'come on up' means bring the sheep towards me; 'walk on' means drive the sheep away and 'lie down' is self-explanatory. If you hear 'do as you're told', that's just what the dog wasn't doing.

At this year's White Horse Show you could find dozens of craft stalls catering for every possible interest. There were too many to list, but they included: pottery, painted eggs, wood turning, hand-made knitwear, models, dolls, clocks, candles, leatherware, glass blowing, painting, enamelled coins, board games, framed photos, lace, ceramic vases, home-made cakes, dried flowers, porcelain, corn dollies, horncraft, pyrography, cushions, wooden toys etc.

There were also a number of trade stands who could sell you anything from industrial clothing to a new car, or from a plant to a conservatory.

There were informative stands about blood transfusion, crime prevention, kidney donation and AA. The National Childbirth Trust at Stand 133 operated a crèche to give weary mums and dads a break. Several charities ran stalls including Save the Children Fund, Friends of ARMS, RNLI, and the British Heart Foundation. If the wind was right Ron Gunter, the 'Kite Man' who has won the National Kite Flying Championship, would give a demonstration of his expertise.

> *The British Driving Society* – Combining the elegance and style of days gone by with the skills of handling horse and vehicle. Displays of competition driving and *concours d'elegance* organised by Major and Mrs Northern, local representatives of the society. Thanks also to area chairman, Mr Richard Ellis and to Major Tony Lake. Participants compete for a cup presented by Mr S Warren.
>
> *Wasps Motorcycle Display Team* – These boys and girls aged from six to sixteen present a thrilling display of skilful motorbike

riding. Based in the Southampton and Portsmouth area, they travel widely to put on displays, which, as well as funding their own club, raise money for handicapped children.

Lawnmower Racing – This unusual sport began back in 1977 in Wisborough Green, West Sussex. The brainchild of Jim Gavin, it has developed into a popular hobby with meetings being held throughout the country. Races take place over both days of the show and include the White Horse Show Grand Prix on Monday. There will also be demonstration races in the main arena. Mowing the front lawn will never be the same after you've watched this.

The Dixie Rebels Western Show Team – Founded by Tex Cascade, this team of enthusiasts re-enact a whole programme of Western scenes. Performances take place in their own Western township throughout both days of the show. A must for Cowboys and Indians fans of all ages.

Johnny Carr's Children's Funtasia Show – Action-packed show for children that parents get involved in! An arena show with competitions, games, dancing, music and lots and lots of prizes and giveaways.

Helicopter Rides – There is even more to Uffington than the White Horse Show. Attendees are urged to take a short trip in the helicopter and look down on the White Horse itself, and see Uffington Castle as well as Wayland Smith's Cave.

On the two days of the show the helicopter was very busy indeed; on talking to the operating crew they said that the amount of photographs that had been taken of the White Horse from the helicopter must have been a record.

The clay-pigeon shooting was also another success and created a lot of interest; the only drawback was that all the straw bales were left in the adjacent field, and these had to be carried back over the brook into the car park for loading away. This extra work was left to just a few after the show, and would have to be faced before the next show.

At the wash-up meeting after this show I made my feelings very plain to all concerned about the unnecessary amount of work left to clear the site. If, due to the thoughtlessness of a few, we failed in our commitment to clear the site within the seven days, how could we expect to keep the goodwill of the landowners? The good news at this meeting was that a profit in excess of £10,000 had been made. It was therefore decided that the disaster fund should be increased to £20,000. I feel at this point that a word of congratulation should go to Jim Larkin on the amount of income that he had obtained from the trade stands this year. This part of the show had contributed £7,131 to our income. Well done, Jim!

An additional field had been acquired from Mr and Mrs Seymour next to the main car park for extra parking. When asked about the cost of this facility they said that they did not require any payment for themselves, but would appreciate a donation being made to St Mary's Church. This I thought was a great gesture towards the local church, which always needed extra funds for its upkeep. The gesture would have no doubt pleased John.

At our March meeting in preparation for the 1990 show, we had the pleasure to sanction the recommendation of the trustees for the following grants:

To Tom Brown's Museum, £3,000; to the Jubilee Field Play Area, £500; to Uffington C. of E. School, £700; to the White Horse Playgroup, £200; to the Afternoon Club, £200; to Baulking Church, £2,500; to Uffington Church, £2,200; to Woolstone Church, £2,000; to the Craven Sports Field, £2,000; to the local Red Cross, £300.

This made a grand total of £13,600 which was to be paid out by the trustees. This of course would not have been possible if it had not been for the White Horse Show. This goes to prove that the hard work, headaches, and to a certain degree the worry that we get in running the show is really worth the while. It also goes to prove that our committee works because we accept the majority decision and still stick to that commitment no matter whether we agree with the decisions or not. All members of the committee must be congratulated on that commitment. I believe that we all get a great feeling of satisfaction from the success of the White Horse Show.

St Mary's Church and Tom Brown's School (now Thomas Hughes Museum), trust beneficiaries

1990

The ordering for the 1990 show had nearly been completed by this time. For instance, five marquees were in hand for the trade stands and the booking of the spaces were going like wildfire. Jim had demanded that a deposit had to be paid for any booking to be accepted. Even this was not deterring the demand for stands; this just goes to show that the show was a success story. A larger marquee had also been booked for the rare breeds, and this must speak for itself, as this section of the show was becoming even more popular than ever.

The portable toilets had also been booked, together with two disabled ones to be positioned at two different spots in the main show field. We had been severely criticised over the poor state of toilet facilities in the past, together with the dirty state of them. I think that now is the time to put this criticism in perspective: when these toilets arrive in the show field prior to the show they are in very good condition and certainly very clean. When the contractor arrives with them they have to be signed for as clean by a member of the committee, and no member would put his name to that fact if they were not. I should not have to explain that it only needs a very few members of the public to turn them into the filthy state that some are left in. With this in mind they are quite expensive to hire – the fee for the 1990 show will be £2,128 plus VAT. How much easier our job would be if that section of the general public would treat them with respect. One thing is certain, we will not be going back to the toilet arrangements of the 1974 and 1975 shows down in Craven Field, when we had to partition an old wooden shed with tarpaulin sheets and place buckets inside. That was very primitive, but unfortunately it was all that could be afforded at that time. When the buckets required emptying the shed had to be cleared to enable myself, Bill Mitchell and Mick Connors to carry them out and tip them in a pit round the back. Furthermore, I cannot see anyone volunteering for this sort of work now or in the future.

With the confirmed attendance of the Army's Royal Artillery motorcycle display team, 'The Flying Gunners', for 1990, the main arena size would have to be increased to 110 by 80 metres. This would also have to be double-roped, with a one-metre gap between each fence. Extra rope and posts would be ordered to arrive at the show field for this purpose in the week before the show.

Morrells Brewery said that their dray and shires would be attending this year's show, which would put the icing on the cake for the heavy horse show.

With Colonel Lord Allenby offering us a free freefall parachute team for the Monday, a really full programme had emerged, as follows:

Sunday 26 August

- 12.00 Sheepdog Demonstration, by Ron Webb
- 12.30 Hampshire Skydivers Freefall Parachute Team
- 13.00 Pathfinders German Shepherd Dog Display Team
- 13.30 Isis Musical Dressage
- 14.00 The Flying Gunners, motorcycle display team of the Royal Artillery
- 14.30 GWR Drum Majorettes
- 15.00 Pathfinders German Shepherd Dog Display Team
- 15.30 Hampshire Skydivers Freefall Parachute Team
- 16.00 The Flying Gunners, motorcycle display team of the Royal Artillery

Monday 27 August

- 11.15 Swindon Youth Pipe Band
- 12.00 The Flying Gunners, motorcycle display team of the Royal Artillery
- 12.30 Parade of Vintage Tractors
- 13.00 Demonstration Lawnmower Race
- 13.15 Isis Musical Dressage
- 14.00 Royal Corps of Transport Freefall Parachute Team
- 14.30 Parade of Heavy Horses
- 14.45 Band of the Irish Guards
- 15.15 Parade of the Old Berks Hunt
- 15.30 Swindon Youth Pipe Band

16.30	Parade of Historic Motorcycles	16.00	The Flying Gunners, motorcycle display team of the Royal Artillery
17.00	Toyota Aerobatic Display Team	16.30	Parade of Historic Cars
17.30	GWR Drum Majorettes	17.10	Toyota Aerobatics Display Team
18.00	Show Closes	17.30	Band of the Irish Guards
		18.00	Show Closes

This show was on the same site as the previous year at Sower Hill, by kind permission of Mr Jim Soden. Jim was as usual cooperative and friendly, letting us on to the site on the Sunday morning prior to the show. We needed this sort of start to get all the material and equipment into the field ready to start marking out as soon as possible on the Monday morning. I still think that people do not really appreciate just what is involved in simply marking the field out, let alone erecting the arenas and preparing all the pieces that go to make the show possible. I used to be in considerable doubt about whether even members of the committee realised what a terrific workload was taken on board in the week before the show and the week after. For instance, all the posts had to be stood up ready for driving-in on the Wednesday night for when the tractor and post driver arrived, and in the end we were using about 300 posts each show. On top of this there were, on average, about 200 trade stands to peg out, and these had to be driven in by hand. The car park had to be fenced in with chestnut paling to enable pay booths to be operated to allow the public in. Also, temporary bridges had to be placed in their spots to allow the public access from field to field. Not forgetting that someone had to be on hand to make sure that everything was put in the right place when it arrived at the site.

We also had to rope the arenas and areas for the stationary engines, cars, and parking for the horse boxes, as well as an area in the main car park for the disabled. Then there was the levelling of aggregate in the gateways that required it. If we were lucky we might have a JCB for this, but it still had to be done. That is why we blessed a certain member of the Ramblers Association this particular year. She complained that on the previous occasion of our show, a public footpath notice had been removed and replaced again after the show. We were thus warned that she would be checking this year to see that it did not happen again. To counteract this situation we had to post and rope a track off the full length of the main car park. This did not come to our notice until the Thursday prior to the show. Guess what? We had to drive in eighty-two posts by hand, as the tractor had been removed the previous night. Although I must admit that these posts went in as easy as any posts I had driven by hand before, this was because I could see that woman's face in the top of every post every time I hit it with a fourteen-pound sledgehammer. I said at the time I wish I could have met her just to tell her her fortune. She would probably not have liked it; nevertheless I would have enjoyed telling her without a charge.

We used to try and keep the Friday evenings clear for setting up in the marquees. That is to say, teaming up with the committee member who was in charge of the trade stands so that we could get the trestle tables put in place ready for the mad rush that would always happen on the Saturday. The show field bore more resemblance to Piccadilly Circus than anything at this time. This is when every member of the field committee was required to split himself in numerous pieces to keep track, and make absolutely sure that everything was in the right place. Of course there was always the odd trade stand that would inevitably try to gain a little extra room and encroach on the next stand plot, and then this had to be sorted out. But, although this was certainly a very hectic time, there was always the pleasure of meeting old faces from the past years whom you at least you could reminiscence with. Then, on top of this lot, there were still the White Horse Show souvenirs to be taken care of. This was my own responsibility. These used to make about £300 profit for the show each year and were quite a good earner as well as causing a lot of interest from the general public.

At the wash-up meeting after the show there was a general feeling from all members of the committee that this had probably been the best show ever, with a profit of £14,000. But, with costs still spiralling, this year's being in the region of £31,000, very serious thought had to be given to the 1991 event, which by the kind permission of Mr Jim Soden would be on the same site. Income from the trade stands this year amounted to £6,586.25, and Jim Larkin must take great credit for this big slice of the income.

Mrs Stella Mattingly and Mrs Kath Larkin were given a very big thank you for all their hard work and help over the last seven years in raising so much money for charity. This year they raised another £1,000. They felt, though, that the time had come to hand over to someone else. This was inevitably a big blow to the committee, as we knew then that we would not be able to replace this part of the show as it had been run – that is, using it as another outlet of funds. This had been the only way that certain deserving charities such as the British Heart Foundation, the British Red Cross and St John Ambulance could benefit, as in fact they were outside the registered White Horse Show Trust. With the Red Cross and St John Ambulance always on hand at the shows it was felt in general that they should at least get some reward over and above their standard charge. As for the Heart Foundation, we must never forget the great service that Harry put into the shows at the start when we were really struggling.

The cost of stands for 1991 would have to be increased to £45 and £40 to offset some of the increase in marquee hire that was to be charged for that year. It was also proposed to increase the entrance charges to £4 per adult, whereas children and OAPs would remain the same. After receiving an invoice for £575 against the loss of twelve tables from Whitney Marquees, it was decided that a member of the committee had to be available next year to check the number of tables and chairs being left at the show field by the suppliers. Alternative quotes had to be also tried for the next year.

As there were some changes to the committee, I believe that it should be noted that the full committee now stood as follows: chairman, Mr V Boaler; treasurer, Mr J P Erskine; secretary, Mrs S Philo; military booking and organisation, Col. A Bateman; craft and trade stands, Mr J Larkin; publicity, Mr M Thomas; heavy horses, Mrs C Keen; historic vehicles, Mr and Mrs D Kelsey;

electrics and public address, Mr W Mattingley; arena events, Mr C Philo, Mr B Mills, Mr R Jay; stationary engines, Mr D Shirley; field services, Mr P Armishaw, Mr B Godsell; bar, Mr B White; rare breeds, Mr A Parsons; police, PC Dave Platts; souvenirs, Mr B Tilling; field sub-committee, Mr B Tilling, Mr J Panting, Mr D Chester, Mr R Cummins, Mr W Mitchell, Mr C Avenell.

At our first meeting for 1991, the committee were pleased to sanction the following grants put forward by the trust: Uffington Girl Guides, £300; Uffington Church, £2,000; Woolstone Church, £1,000; Jubilee Field Play Area, £500; Uffington Scouts, £500; Baulking Church, £1,000; Uffington Playgroup, £200; Uffington Mother and Toddler Group, £100; Uffington Beaver Scouts, £200; Uffington Afternoon Club, £200; Tom Brown Museum, £1,600; Uffington School, £1,000; Thomas Hughes Memorial Hall, for new furniture, £500; Thomas Hughes Memorial Hall, for extension, £5,000.

These grants were approved unanimously. The remaining £3,700 would be held for dealing with any further applications. The disaster fund was raised to £22,000.

The same number of marquees booked with Whitney had increased in cost by 10% on last year. As regards the refreshments, these had gone out to contract as follows: Quick Food Vans franchise had been agreed at £1,700 plus VAT, the tea tent to get 15% of profits.

1991

The annual headache with the toilets was solved early this year by the employment of a new contractor. There were to be fifty separate loos, together with two disabled ones, plus the firm's representative to be in attendance. All this came at a cost of £2,300 plus VAT, against last year's cost of £2,000. But this year the committee did not have to anything with the toilets; therefore, this had to be a good deal as in other years we debated this subject for countless hours. Maybe we could put this headache to rest at last; we had to wait and see with our fingers crossed. The booking for trade stands inside and out was well up at this time against other years.

At our June meeting it was reported that the advertising and publicity was all going well. Adverts had been placed in the following papers: *Swindon Evening Advertiser, Oxford Times* group, *Newbury Post, What's on in Faringdon, Wiltshire Gazette, Reading Chronicle, Faringdon Folley, Wiltshire & Gloucester Standard*. This was at the total cost of £1,100. Advertising in the programme had all been taken; it may be noted at this point that the rates for this lay unchanged since 1989. They were at this time: full-page, including VAT, £70.50; half-page, £41.13; quarter-page £23.50, all with a 25% discount for local companies.

A quote was received on the printing of programmes at £1,629 for 4,000, which compared favourably with the previous year and was accepted. As far as advertising on the radio was concerned we would stick with GWR at £800, leaving the total advertising budget just below £2,000.

An additional piece of interest was being introduced this year in the animal marquee. This was going to be spinning wool directly from sheep fleece, which I was sure would create a large amount of interest. Anthony requested that the name of this section of the show be changed from 'rare breeds' to 'farm animals'. This would enable him to expand a little more without crossing the path of the Rare Breeds Association. This was of course accepted, as there would still be rare breeds in attendance.

Committee member 'Mad Daniel' bungee jumping, 1991

There had been nine skips booked and this was appreciated by the field-sub, as in past years we had had difficulty piling everything in the available skips, although we had compressed them down with a JCB bucket. The new portable loos this year did not need any water tankers, which was very good news. Everything now seemed ready for yet another show. A new attraction appeared at this year's show, which the general public could try their hand at if they were brave enough. That was bungee jumping from the hundred-foot jib of a crane. One of our own committee members said that he would be participating. Quite frankly I would rather it be him than me. Good luck, Daniel, you mad idiot! The full programme for the 1991 show was as follows:

Sunday 25 August

12.00 Ron Webb, Sheepdog Demonstration
12.30 Hampshire Skydivers

Monday 26 August

11.30 Mid-West Rodeo Show
12.00 Fleet Air Arm Helicopter Display

Time	Event	Time	Event
13.00	Mid-West Rodeo Show		Team
13.30	Fleet Air Arm Helicopter Display Team	12.30	Parade of Vintage Tractors
14.00	Army Cadet Force, Mock Attack	13.00	Demonstration Lawnmower Racing
14.30	Ron Webb, Sheepdog Demonstration	13.30	Army Cadet Force Mock Attack
15.00	Band of the 17th/21st Lancers & Tent Pegging Team	14.00	Mid-West Rodeo Show
		14.30	Parade of Heavy Horses
		15.00	Band of the Coldstream Guards and Royal British Legion Muster
15.30	Hampshire Skydivers		
15.45	Fleet Air Arm Helicopter Display team	15.30	Parade of the Old Berks Hounds
16.00	Mid-West Rodeo Show	16.00	Fleet Air Arm Helicopter Display Team
16.30	Parade of Historic Motorcycles		
17.00	Toyota Aerobatics Display Team	16.15	AAC Freefall Parachute Team
17.30	Band of the 17th/21st Lancers	17.00	Toyota Aerobatics Team
		17.30	Band of the Coldstream Guards and Royal British Legion Muster
18.00	Show Closes	18.00	Show Closes

I will follow this programme up with a description and information about the origin of some of the arena participants in this show:

> *The 17th/21st Lancers* – A short history: the 'Death or Glory Boys' was the nickname given to the original 17th Lancers and continued in use by the 17th/21st Lancers, one of England's finest cavalry regiments. The 17th Lancers were formed by direct order of the King after the fall of Quebec in 1759, and it was the King's wish that the regimental badge should be the much-coveted death's head, with the motto 'Or Glory'. The most notable of the regiment's many actions was the gallant Charge of the Light

Brigade down the 'Valley of Death' at Balaklava.

The 21st Lancers were raised by the Marquis of Granby in 1760 and their most famous action took place in the Sudan at the Battle of Omdurman. They were amalgamated with the 17th Lancers in 1922 to become the regiment as it is known today. Since the Second World War, the 17th/21st Lancers have played an active part in the Royal Armoured Corps as far afield as Palestine, Hong Kong, Borneo and Cyprus. They have also served as part of the 1st British Corps of the British Army of the Rhine in West Germany.

The regimental band of the Death or Glory Boys has its roots in the early eighteenth century – the days when troops were inspired to deeds of great personal valour by the rousing music played by their band. The band returned from the Gulf on 21 March 1991 and rejoined the regiment after a period of well-earned leave in April. The regiment has been posted to Tidworth after a tour in Munster, Germany, lasting ten years. The band is under the capable hands of the bandmaster, WO1 (BM) K J Harrod BBCM, who joined the army in 1973. He became a musician in the Queen's Lancashire Regiment as a euphonium player in 1974, and in 1985 went to the Royal Military School of Music, Kneller Hall, for a three-year bandmaster's course. On passing the course he joined the 17th/21st Lancers in May 1988 and has since spent the last three years with them. The band and Display Team 17th/21st Lancers appeared by kind permission of Lieutenant Colonel R D S Gordon, Commanding 17th/21st Lancers.

The Band of the Coldstream Guards – The regiment was formed in 1650 by George Monck, a general in Oliver Cromwell's 'New Model Army'. In 1661, after a long march from their home in Coldstream on the banks of the Tweed, they were instrumental in quelling the riots in London prior to the restoration of the monarchy. In appreciation of this gallant act they were asked to lay down their arms and to immediately take them up again in the name of the King, and in doing so became Household Troops. From the earliest days, the regiment had drummers, and a 'Band of Musik' from 1742. This was, in fact, eight civilian musicians who were hired monthly by officers of the regiment to provide music for Changing of the Guard at St James's Palace.

In 1785 the officers asked the Duke of York, colonel of the regiment, for a regular attested band. Twelve musicians were sent over from Germany and the instrumentation consisted of two oboes, four clarinets, two bassoons, two horns, one trumpet and one serpent. In 1815, the year of the regiment's distinction at Waterloo, the total strength of the band was increased to twenty-two by the addition of flutes, keyed bugles and trombones. As was usual in the British Army at the time, the Coldstream Guards' early bandmasters were of German extraction.

In 1825 the first truly British bandmaster, Charles Godfrey, took over. It was under his baton that the foundation of today's musical and military expertise began. By the end of the nineteenth century, the band had grown to thirty-five in number. Its importance, both within the Army and the British way of life, had also grown. As a matter of interest, it was Queen Victoria who decreed that all members of the Household Division Bands would be known by the title of 'Musician' and not as 'Bandsman', as they were known in the rest of the Army.

The band now consists of fifty musicians, and within its ranks are many fine soloists who greatly enhance the vast and varied repertoire, which is as diverse as the music of Andrew Lloyd Webber, Handel, Shostakovich and the Beatles. The versatility of the band provides the spectacle of a first-class marching band, a concert band, fanfare team, an orchestra, a brass quintet and a dance band.

Whatever the occasion, the band's presentation and style has endeared them to audiences around the world. Like their regimental motto, *Nulli Secundus*, the Coldstream Guards Band are second to none. The band of the Coldstream Guards appears by the kind permission of Colonel Sir Brian Barttelot, BT, OBE, DL, Regimental Lieutenant Colonel, Coldstream Guards.

The band is conducted by Captain D J Marshall, ARCM, LTCL, BBCM, psm, Director of Music, Coldstream Guards.

Army Cadet Force – These local lads, aged twelve to fifteen, are based at Shrivenham. They will carry out various manoeuvres and stage a section attack with regular soldiers as the 'enemy'.

The Royal Air Force – There will be a static display by RAF Abingdon, illustrating career opportunities in RAF engineering and the work of the station. RAF Abingdon attends the show by kind permission of Group Captain P W Henderson, MBE, RAF, Station Commander, Royal Air Force, Abingdon.

Royal British Legion – Formed from the three existing ex-services organisations in June 1921, the British Legion became 'Royal' after completing fifty years' invaluable support to our ex-servicemen and their families. 1991 is the seventieth anniversary of the founding of the Royal British Legion. To commemorate the occasion, the personnel of the Berkshire and Vale of White Horse Royal British Legion were at this show parading their standards in a display of countermarching and drill to music from the band of the Coldstream Guards. There are fifty-one branches of ex-service personnel in the county, and thirty-five women's section branches, and they were joined by invited members from Oxfordshire and Surrey. The Royal British Legion muster are under the command of their ceremonial officer, Mr Albert Dunham (ex-Royal Marines). They appear by kind permission of the president and officers of the Royal British Legion of the Royal County of Berkshire and Vale of White Horse.

The AAC Freefall Parachute Team – Formed in 1985 by the current team leader. During its first season, the team became outright army champions, and last year one team member was in the winning team at the British Parachuting Championships. He took part in the World Parachuting Championships in Spain, where the British team came fourth. Other team members include an ex-British National Parachuting Champion and a member of the Royal Marines Canopy-Stacking World Record Team. The team also include two of the country's leading freefall photographers. One is a video expert and the other has had many of his photographs published in the national press and other publications. Both were the official photographers at the fifty-way British record freefall formation, completed at the International Air Show 1988 at Middle Wallop. Over 100,000 spectators saw a joint services team smash the existing record of thirty-two. Six of the parachutists involved were AAC team members. During 1990, the team carried out displays in the UK, USA, Malaysia, Germany and in Switzerland. Members of the royal family and other VIPs have watched the team display. The AAC is the air arm of the army. As such, it is probably one of its more glamorous elements. Approximately 50% of the 1991 team are helicopter pilots and the others are either ground-crew or technicians. Parachuting can be a hazardous activity. Although the Army Air Corps Freefall Parachute Team members are highly capable, there is always the possibility of unforeseen accident. Spectators watch at their own risk.

The Sharks Helicopter Display Team – 705 Squadron of the Fleet Air Arm, based at the Royal Naval Air Station, Culdrose, has been responsible for basic helicopter flying training of the navy's pilots since 1959. Its instructors are some of the most experienced helicopter pilots in Britain. In the last six years, the squadron has gained first place, and the majority of other prizes, at the British Helicopter Championships. In 1989 the Culdrose instructors were also well represented in the British team, which took third place in the World Helicopter Championships in Paris. The Sharks display team celebrated its fifteenth anniversary last year. We are delighted to welcome their solo display pilot, who is flying a Gazelle HT2 Helicopter. This appearance is by kind permission of Captain T Taylor, Royal Navy, Captain HMS *Seahawk*, Royal Naval Air Station, Culdrose.

Mid-West Rodeo – This is an exciting new event for a White Horse Show, full of fun, action and laughter. It includes a colourful mounted flag parade, cowboy-riding demonstration and surprises from Joey the Clown. Then volunteers from the public are invited to try their hand at bareback riding. Overalls and safety helmet are supplied and you could be the winner of a cash prize plus the rodeo trophy. So, if you are sixteen years of age or over, why not have a go?

Mid-West Rodeo is licensed and registered under the Performing Animals Act, 1925. They want to assure spectators that there is no cruelty in their show, which has been seen by the RSPCA, who had no complaints.

The Hampshire Skydivers – the Hampshire Skydivers Freefall Display Team, who attend this year's event, are one of the most experienced civilian display teams in the country. In past seasons the team have been invited to perform at many popular events, such as the Jersey Battle of Flowers, the FA Cup semi-final at White Hart Lane and the final match of the Britannic Assurance County Cricket Championships, when they delivered a giant winner's cheque by 'Air Mail' to Worcester Cricket Club. Spectators at this year's White Horse Show are invited to watch and meet the team members who will be pleased to answer any questions about the exciting sport of skydiving. The team extend sincere thanks to the organisers for the invitation to attend, and wish them luck and success with this year's event.

The Hounds of the Old Berks Hunt – the hounds, which are kennelled at Faringdon, appear by kind permission of the joint masters.

The Cricklade Band – the White Horse Show Committee were extremely pleased to have with us again this first-class band, who are well known throughout the south of England. They have also toured the continent of Europe and their extensive repertoire has given great pleasure to the many thousands of people who have been lucky enough to have listened to them. They play by the refreshment marquee at the following times: 12.00 to 13.00 and 16.00 to 17.00. We strongly recommend the audience to sit down and listen to them.

Johnny Chuckles – Johnny has been delighting children at our shows for fifteen years now and has always performed his own unique brand of entertainment, and not only to the children at times, I may add. His Punch and Judy show never fails to attract crowds of fascinated spectators, who are equally spellbound by his mysterious tricks and brilliant sleight of hand.

Team Toyota Aerobatics – Nigel Lamb, leader of Team Toyota, has won the British National Aerobatics Championships for the last five years in a row. At the White Horse Show this year he is joined by team-mates Steve Johnson and Steve Privett in a breathtaking three-plane display of close-formation, synchronised, solo and opposition flying. Steve Johnson is new to the team, having recently completed three years as a pilot with the renowned Red Arrows. Another new acquisition for the team is Nigel's Extra 300 plane, a new generation display machine, which can deliver even better performance than the Extra 230 it has replaced. Team Toyota has been a thrilling and highly popular event at our show in recent years. We are very pleased to have them performing again in our 1991 programme.

Farm Animals – This display includes most of the animals found on smallholdings today and in the past. Some are rare breeds, which enthusiasts are working hard to preserve in this country, others are more established. There are several breeds of sheep and goats; there are pigs, a cow and a wide variety of poultry, including a selection of eggs. Victor, an ex-beach donkey, can also be seen. Almost all the animals are raised for a purpose, whether for milk, wool, meat, eggs or for breeding stock. There are displays (and proud owners) to explain the different qualities of the breeds to the visitors. It is displays such as this one that keep reminding us that we are still running a country show. After all, this is what Uffington used to be all about.

As a bonus there is a demonstration of wool spinning throughout the day. The Rare Breeds Survival Trust has a stand to answer questions.

Star attraction of the animal marquee, 1990

Clay Pigeon Shooting – Dunmore Shooting puts on a forty-bird sporting trophy shoot. There are five categories: Open, Novice, Ladies, Side by Side and Colts. Sportsmen of all ability levels, including complete beginners, are welcome. There is no obligation to compete – people can just have a go.

Historic Vehicles at the White Horse Show – from the very start, the White Horse Show has hosted a display of historic cars, motorcycles, commercial vehicles and military vehicles. From very small beginnings with just a handful of cars on show, we are now treated to around 200 beautifully prepared and lovingly displayed vehicles, each one at least twenty years old and many much, much older.

What makes the White Horse Show so special for the owners of these treasures from our motoring past and why do the public find them so attractive? After twenty years of talking to exhibitors and public alike, I think we know some of the answers. One of the first things that can be noticed is the sheer variety of the vehicles on display. At virtually every show we can see cars and bikes from the earliest days of motoring and motorcycling, to the sort of vehicles we might have owned ourselves not so long ago.

The very early cars, those built before the end of 1904, are defined as 'veterans', those built between 1905 and 1914 are called 'Edwardians', and those built before the end of 1930 are called 'vintage'. There is something very English about these definitions; there is no special reason in the development of the car to pick 1904 as the first cut-off point; King Edward died long before the end of the 'Edwardian' period and this classification totally ignores the fact that cars continued to be produced outside Europe during the Great War.

On the other hand, 1930 did mark a great change in the way cars were made and this, combined with the Depression, meant that for most car makers the cars of the thirties were that little bit more cheaply made. They were often less well engineered and altogether different from the cars which went before. This does not mean that they were bad cars, far from it, but the great days were gone and most of the companies which survived the Depression simply concentrated on making cars to an attractive price, rather than to a high-design standard.

The very best cars of the thirties are called post-vintage thoroughbreds and these include some of the very finest cars ever made at any time in the motor car's history. There are always many examples of these lovely cars, the Bentleys, the Rolls-Royces and the like at the show; but never forget that the Austin and Morris Tens and Twelves are far more typical of the period.

There is no generally accepted classification for cars of the post-war period. Some call them 'historic', others call them 'classics'; wisely the show organisers avoid these problems and welcome cars over twenty-one years old. For many of the visiting public, these are the cars they know best and many have fond memories of the cars 'just like that' which they or their families owned not so long ago. Historic commercial vehicles have a delightfully simple rule: they must be twenty-five years old or older to be eligible for their events.

Why do the car owners choose this show rather than any one of the dozens of others around the country on this, or any other summer weekend? For some it is their local show; others may have travelled many miles to be here. They all enjoy a show where every vehicle is respected for what it is – a special part of our motoring heritage – and the humble Ford Popular can be as much admired as a mighty Bentley, a Jaguar sports, or a veteran from the dawn of motoring. For each and every one of them it is a chance to share their pride and joy with you for a few hours. Every one of the vehicles on display has a fascinating history and their proud owners will be only too pleased to tell you all about it; so why not go and talk to them? You will be glad you did.

As a result of a very successful show last year, the trustees of the White Horse Show were able to make grants to various local organisations to the tune of £15,000. Together with income that local organisations made at the 1990 show it proved to be a very successful time for all concerned.

With a programme like this, together with the high class of arena events, our committee could not get complacent; to maintain our profit margin we could not let the class of arena events slip below that which the public had come to expect to see at a White Horse Show. In my mind there was only one way that we as a committee could achieve the continuance of the show for years to come, and that was to maintain the very high standard of the show, together with the value in cost that the public paid as the entrance fee. With the ever-increasing rises in interest rates it was the people with families that were hardest hit. With the White Horse Show being built on family entertainment since its beginning in 1972, if the families found that we had got too expensive for Mother and Father with two or three children to attend, then we would be on the slippery slope to failure.

I sincerely hoped that we would not go down this road; but, listening to the hawks, we could have been heading for a problem. One thing that we had not done since our inauguration in 1972 was to try and set a profit margin prior to every show. The one main philosophy that we had had over those years had been to put a good show on that was real value for money and that the public would patronise. At present we had £22,000 in the disaster fund, which was there for the purpose of a guarantee to see the continuation of the White Horse Show.

The wash-up meeting for the 1991 show was filled with the same earaches as before. Problems were still very apparent, and yet we had still just made £10,000 profit. To me and others this was becoming unbelievable. The gate takings had gone up over what they were at the 1990 show, but also the same applied to the cost of putting the show on. A lot of us on the committee felt that, yes, our profit margin had gone down from the previous year, but we had still made a sizable profit. This was 'swings and roundabouts' and was something that we had to accept. To think that we could go on year after year increasing our profits each time would be living in cloud cuckoo land.

Two sad resignations from the committee also came in at this meeting, the first being Roger Cummins and his wife Greta. Both had served the committee very well over a number of years, not forgetting that Roger also had the enormous task of taking over as chairman of the committee after the tragic loss of Harry. As they were leaving the district Roger would also be leaving the trustees at the same time. The committee were quick to say how pleased we had been to have had their services over the time they had been with us, and to wish them all possible luck in the future.

The second resignation was our treasurer, Mr Peter Erskine, who would be only too pleased to stay on as treasurer of the trust. This was of course accepted by the committee with great reluctance. Peter had over his time been a great source of guidance to us through the change from the Thomas Hughes Trust to the White Horse Show Trust, and also in the era when we moved into the VAT bracket. He will be sadly missed by everyone on the committee.

I think at this stage it would also be appropriate to list some of the organisations that the White Horse Show relies on each year to ensure the smooth running of the show, together with the safety side.

They are as follows: the St John Ambulance Brigade; 1861 (Wantage) Squadron Air Training Corps; Swindon and Cricklade Railway Society Ltd, for the organisation of the car parking and supplying car park attendants; the chief constable of Thames Valley Police and his officers for their support; Freeman's Transport of Uffington, for the supply and loan of trailers.

The committee are also most grateful to Lieutenant Colonel Lord Allenby and the staff of the Reading and Oxford Army careers offices for arranging the army displays. They are also indebted to the numerous firms that are generous in their sponsorship of various parts of the show.

The one good thing to come from this meeting was that we had already got permission from Mr Jim Soden for the 1992 show to be held in his fields again. So we had to wait and see what would transpire in the next episode of the White Horse Shows.

1992

The first meeting relating to the 1992 show arrived with the committee giving their blessing to the recommendation from the trustees for grants as follows: the Uffington Playgroup, £200; the Afternoon Club, £300; the Jubilee Field Play Area, £1,000; Thomas Hughes Memorial Hall, for kitchen refit, £2,500; Tom Brown School Museum, for redecoration and steps to be sloped for the disabled, £1,000; Baulking Church, £3,000; Uffington Church, £2,000; Woolstone Church, £3,500. This left £5,000 still in the hands of the trustees and waiting for grant applications.

It was agreed also that these grants should be published in the local *Courier* to keep the three villages aware who the grants were being given to.

It was also confirmed by Tony that the combined bands of Royal Scots Dragoon Guards with pipers would perform with the 17th/21st Lancers on both days, with two performances, for £4,900. Hopefully this would be under the VAT limit. This would be the last time they would be performing together as they were to be disbanded.

Other good news that came to this meeting was that I myself had been nominated to fill the vacancy on the White Horse Show trustees left by the resignation of Roger. This was something that I did not need time to consider, as I thought it to be a great honour. Therefore I accepted this post without hesitation. It still gave me the freedom to work and speak out in defence of the White Horse Show and all that it stood for. By being a trustee and a member of the show committee I would see both sides of the differences that very occasionally arose between the thinking of both committees. These were not serious differences in a sense, but, nevertheless, they did arise from time to time. This is why any grants awarded always came before the show committee to get the final blessing, or to be questioned. After all was said and done, why should the show committee not have a chance to at least comment on these awards? If it was not for all the hard work put in by these people there would be no such awards to make.

At the April meeting we had been lucky in the fact that a new treasurer had come forward. That brave person was Mr Graeme Clark. Graeme was given a hearty welcome to the committee by all present. The committee unanimously agreed to the changes in the banking system that would enable him to carry out these duties.

Even at this early time, in excess of £2,000 had been taken on the trade stand side; the show was still generating interest amongst the businesses that contributed so much to our income. The cost to date for the arena programme was £11,900, and this of course did not cover the side show and stationary entertainment still needed; so far, so good.

There had also been four more applications for grants before the trustees. The trustees were thus recommending the following to the show committee for approval: to Uffington C. of E. School towards extension over the boiler house, £1,500; to Uffington C. of E. School for an alarm system, £600; to the Sports and Social Club for tennis court maintenance work, £1,000; towards a new day centre being set up in the village hall for the sick and elderly, £500.

Needless to say these grants were given the blessing from the show committee.

During the lead-up to this show I myself had to get very forceful about the number of straw bales that we needed in the field for use during the show. In the end I had to make it quite plain that any bales that were offloaded in excess of 300 would, as far as I was concerned, remain on the site until the culprit responsible for their presence removed them. Needless to say, the total number of bales in the show field was kept down as low as 250. I therefore think that the message had at long last got through. It was about time, because the week after every show it was the same two members left to pitch the remaining bales in the field up on to a trailer to be taken away.

The number of vehicles booked in this year was also well up on other years; at the August meeting a total of 251 had already booked, and on the day you could bank on quite a few more turning up. The booking on stationary engines was also well up on the previous years. This meant that I had to order another 120 rally plaques over the phone, then make time before the show to go to Catras Leather at Whitchurch near Aylesbury to fetch the same. This I did not mind in the least, as it was possible to go to those people at nearly any time; to see the other products being made there was a bonus. In any case the plaques were a necessary reward to the participants in the show for bringing their motorcycles, cars, military vehicles and stationary engines to our show for the enjoyment of the public.

A run-down on some of the entertainment that went to make up the arena events at this show is as follows:

Sunday 30 August 1992

- 11.30 Heart of England Falconry
- 12.00 Rockwood Dog Display Team
- 12.30 EL Caballo De Espana
- 13.00 Magnificent Seven Motorcycle Display Team
- 13.30 Red Devils Freefall Display Team
- 14.00 The combined Military Band, Pipes & Drums of the Royal Scots Dragoon Guards and the Band of the 17th/21st Lancers
- 14.30 Heart of England Falconry
- 15.00 Rockwood Dog Display Team
- 15.30 EL Caballo De Espana
- 16.00 Magnificent Seven Motorcycle Display Team

Monday 31 August 1992

- 10.45 Hampshire Skydivers
- 11.00 Heart of England Falconry
- 11.30 Magnificent Seven Motorcycle Display Team
- 12.00 Rodeo Dave and the Rodayos
- 12.30 Historic Tractors Parade
- 13.00 Red Devils Freefall Display Team
- 13.30 Parade of the Old Berks Hunt
- 13.45 Heart of England Falconry
- 14.15 The combined Military Band, Pipes & Drums of the Royal Scots Dragoon Guards and the Band of the 17th/21st Lancers
- 14.45 Hampshire Skydivers
- 15.00 Rodeo Dave and the

16.30	Historic Motorcycles Parade		Rodayos
17.00	Toyota Aerobatics Team	15.30	Magnificent Seven Motorcycle Display Team
17.30	The combined Military Band, Pipes & Drums of the Royal Scots Dragoon Guards and the Band of the 17th/21st Lancers	16.00	Parade of Heavy Horses
		16.30	Parade of Historic Cars
		17.00	Toyota Aerobatics Team
		17.30	The combined Military Band, Pipes & Drums of the Royal Scots Dragoon Guards and the Band of the 17th/21st Lancers
18.00	Show Closes	18.00	Show Closes

The Cricklade Band will play at various times during the day by the refreshment marquee.

The Heavy Horse Show will be in its own arena from 11.00 to 16.00.

The Cricklade Band will play at various times during the day by the refreshment marquee.

A description with some of the history relating to the performances of our arena entertainers follows, to the best of my ability. This information was obtained from them through other members of the White Horse Show Committee. I sincerely hope that it will be of interest to most people.

Team Toyota – Team Toyota's display is 'designed to delight'. More than a display of formation aerobatics, it is an exciting aerial dance of approximately thirty-two non-stop manoeuvres. All in all an exuberant demonstration of top-quality flying: solo, synchronised, opposition and close formation.

Team Toyota's pilots have well above average flying ability, including great precision and natural flair. British Aerobatic Champion Nigel Lamb leads the team and is one of the UK's most experienced formation aerobatic display pilots. He has been flying displays worldwide since 1981 and is the overall British

Aerobatic Champion, a title he has held for six consecutive years. He also currently holds the British Freestyle title.

Steve Johnson leads the duo section. He joined Team Toyota from the RAF where he flew 2,500 hours on the Harrier and Hawk. He was European display pilot for the Harrier before being selected to fly with the famous Red Arrows and led their synchro pair in 1990, his last year with the RAF.

Lee Proudfoot is the team's newest member. He has amassed over 2,500 flying hours on a diverse range of aircraft. His rich flying background includes flying Twin Otters with the British Antarctic Survey in the frozen south doing survey and photographic work. He flies in the number-three position and is thoroughly enjoying the challenge of his first season with the team.

Just as the pilots must be very carefully selected, so too must the aircraft. The rugged 200 hp Toyota Pitts Special biplanes are designed specifically for aerobatics and are just as happy flying upside down as the right way up. Nigel leads the team in the Lexus Extra 300, a new-generation display and competition machine with its carbon-fibre wing and 300 hp engine.

The Bands of the Royal Scots Dragoon Guards – The Royal Scots Dragoon Guards is Scotland's senior cavalry regiment. The regiment was formed in June 1971 from an amalgamation of two famous regiments, the Royal Scots Greys (2nd Dragoons) and the 3rd Carabiniers (who had themselves been constituted from the union of the 3rd Dragoon Guards and the Carabiniers in 1922).

The regiment can trace its history back to 1678, when Charles II ordered that an independent troop of dragoons be formed in Edinburgh. Since then, the battle honours of these three famous regiments have reflected the campaigns of the British Army. Amongst these are the wars of the Austrian and Spanish succession, the Napoleonic and Crimean wars, the Indian mutiny, the Afghanistan Campaign, the Boer War and the two World Wars. The regimental standard displays over fifty of the regiment's battle honours, in which the officers and soldiers of this gallant regiment fought with honour and distinction.

Since the formation of the Royal Scots Dragoon Guards, the regiment has served in many countries, including Germany, Cyprus, Hong Kong, Canada, and Belize. The regiment has recently returned from BAOR, where, equipped with Challenger tanks, they formed part of the 1st Armoured Division during the

Gulf War. Today the regiment is equipped with Chieftain tanks and at present regimental headquarters and 2 Squadron are at Catterick with a squadron at Tidworth, Hampshire, in England. The regiment will return to Germany in 1995.

Apart from the military side, the regiment also has a very healthy musical tradition. There are two bands, the Pipes and Drums and the Regimental Band. When these high-calibre musicians are not playing, they take on a very different main role: the Pipes and Drums revert to tank crewmen and the bandsmen provide medical assistance to the regiment. The two bands are renowned throughout the world for their high quality of military music and have performed in countries such as Australia, Canada, America, Italy (including a papal audience) and most of Europe.

In 1971 the bands produced a long-playing record which included 'Amazing Grace'. Nearly a year after the album was released it was played on English radio, which resulted in so much pressure that the record company issued a single. Within weeks it was in the British charts, where it remained at number one for six weeks, the first time an Army band had hit the charts.

Just after this record of 'Amazing Grace' had been in the hit parade, the White Horse Show had the pleasure of the presence of the Pipes and Drums of the Royal Scots Guards. On the day they played 'Amazing Grace' in the arena I have never seen so many spectators around an arena before, or since, as far as that goes. The applause they received as they left the arena on that day was tremendous, with no one sitting down anywhere. This was thoroughly deserved.

Individually, the Pipes and Drums has been awarded the status of Grade One by the Royal Scottish Pipe Band Association, the only British Army pipe band to achieve this. The Regimental Band holds the grading of 'Outstanding' from the Royal Military School of Music. The Band is conducted by Bandmaster WO1 R Falshaw, LRAM, ARCM. The Regimental Band of the Royal Scots Dragoon Guards appears by kind permission of the commanding officer, Lieutenant Colonel N D A Seymour.

Magnificent Seven Motorcycle Display Team – This team was formed in 1979. The Magnificent Seven have performed all round the UK and Europe. The team hold various world and British records including a record for twenty-two men on a motorcycle, the world record trolley-jump and the world record for twenty-five walls of burning fire. Their programme of events includes formation riding, backwards and ladder rides, wheelies and unbelievable car jumps, spectacular fire stunts and balancing acts.

Laser Clay Pigeon Shooting – Shoot to thrill! Insight Lasersport are putting on laser clay-pigeon shooting for show visitors this year. Players use a modified shotgun to fire an infra-red beam at clays launched from a conventional clay launcher. The sounds of the shotgun being fired and the clay breaking are realistically reproduced, and electronic indicators show instantly whether the player has hit or missed. Up to five people can participate at a time, using authentic but de-activated twelve-bore guns. Lasersport is totally safe, can be enjoyed by people of all ages and does absolutely no harm to the environment. It provides a wonderful opportunity for everyone from the complete beginner to the expert to enjoy the thrill and excitement of clay-pigeon shooting. So why not have a go?

Rockwood Dog Display – The team consists of seven handlers and eight dogs and is based in Caerphilly, South Wales. Their aim is to promote the enjoyment that can be obtained from a trained pet dog. There are various breeds demonstrating progressive stages of obedience such as loop jumping, egg retrieval, a working gun dog, a spectacular fire retrieval and a dog walking a tightrope. The display also shows the skills of an operational security dog and includes dogs competing against each other. The Rockwood Dog Display Team have shown their skills on national television and have played many roles for the commercial and film industry. They are sponsored by Omega pet foods. With action and excitement throughout, this is a display not to be missed.

Heart Of England Falconry – Steve Wright presents a varied selection of hawks, falcons and owls. Their spectacular aerobatics are accompanied by an entertaining and informative commentary. Audience participation is welcomed and, when the birds are not flying, you can photograph them and put your questions to Steve.

Rodeo Dave and the Rodayos – This is a sensational Western trick riding display with thrills and spills in the style of the Wild West. The fast-moving show consists of three riders and two horses giving a display of trick shooting, stunts and trick riding, as well as Western dressage. If you're a cowboy fan, enjoy Westerns or just appreciate horsemanship, don't miss this exciting display.

The Red Devils, The Parachute Regiment Freefall Team – The Red Devils, under Captain T C Carroll, team commander, are a world-class freefall parachute team who regularly represent the Parachute Regiment, the Army and Great Britain. All team members are serving soldiers, selected for their exceptional parachuting skills, and most are in the elite Parachute Regiment, some having served with the regiment in the Falklands.

Each year the Red Devils appear at over 200 public events in the UK and abroad. Some highlights from 1991 were the NatWest Cricket Final at Lords, Gulf Appeal Day in front of Prince Charles and the Duchess of York, and TV appearances on *The Generation Game* and *You Bet!* They also represented the UK at the world championships in Czechoslovakia.

If you feel inspired to try a jump for yourself and live within fifty miles of Aldershot, you might like to consider the Red Devils' 'One Jump' introductory training course for civilian volunteers at the Parachute Regiment depot. The Red Devils are sponsored by the *Sun* newspaper. The Red Devils, the Parachute Regiment Freefall Team appear by kind permission of Colonel D C Parker, regimental colonel of the Parachute Regiment.

Lawnmower Racing – This unusual sport epitomising eccentric English pastimes began some eighteen years ago in Wisborough Green, West Sussex. The brainchild of Jim Gavin, it has developed into a popular hobby, with meetings held throughout the country. Around a dozen races will take place over each day of the show and will include the White Horse Show Grand Prix on Monday. Most races last about five minutes, but the Grand Prix is three times as long. Once a year there is a twelve-hour race. There are two main classes of lawnmower participating at this year's show:

Group 3: Ride-on tractor types, capable of up to 55 mph.

Group 2: Conventional lawnmowers with rollers and grass boxes, able to reach 40 mph.

Nowadays the Group 1 Machines – the 'run behinds' – are not seen too often in public!

All machines must have conventional lawnmower engines, but the gearing system can be changed. The drivers are all amateurs who compete throughout the season for a championship title. The society boasts a membership of around 200, and between thirty and forty machines are expected at our show. A special welcome to the competitor from Huddersfield.

El Caballo de Espana – For hundreds of years the sight of man working in harmony with horses has thrilled all, and never more so than in Spain. This is a rare opportunity to see a group of horses perform the movements of the 'High School' – the pirouette, the half-pass, the *piaffe*, and the *levade*. See the impressive Spanish Walk, seldom performed in this country, and the colourful, traditional riding costumes of Spain, usually reserved for the fiestas. This is a unique and enthralling display which demonstrates the Spanish style of training and riding, giving an insight into Spanish culture and horsemanship.

Amusements and Sideshows – These include roundabouts, bouncy castle, coconut shy, swings, twister, helicopter rides, pony rides, go-karts, archery and dodgems.

Craft and Trade Stalls – At this year's White Horse Show you will find dozens of craft stalls catering for every possible interest. There are too many to list, but they include: sugar craft, puppets, pyrography, hand-painted porcelain, wood-turned items, English wines, painting on shells, pottery, apple dollies, decorated eggs, hand-made knitwear, wrought ironwork, leatherware, glass engraving, paintings, calligraphy, brass and copper jewellery, ceramic vases, home-made cakes, dried flowers, corn dollies, terracotta pots, wooden toys etc. Further details are available from the committee bus. Don't miss the stall selling very attractive White Horse souvenirs. You'll find T-shirts, tablemats, horse brasses, bookmarks, pint and half-pint tankards, porcelain thimbles, pens and lots more at amazingly cheap prices.

Charity and Information Stalls – There are informative stands about crime prevention, the Fire Service, kidney donation, the Royal British Legion and Samaritans, to name but a few. Several other charities will be running stalls, including Save the Children Fund, RNLI, Prospect Foundation, Guide Dogs for the Blind, RSPCA, Wantage Deaf & Hard of Hearing, Churchill Kidney Unit, Friends of Stowford House, Macmillan Nurses and Worldwide Fund for Nature.

It would be wrong not to include something about one of the main parts of the show on the Monday, the heavy horse show. I did, a few shows back, list all of the classes in the show and the contributors of the trophies; these are so far unaltered and remain the same. The judge for this year's show was Mr A J Wass, the stewards being Mr Dibben from Salisbury, Wiltshire, and Mr Ken Freeman from Goosey, Oxfordshire. The commentator was Mr Peter Davies. We were indebted to the generosity of Morrells Brewery of Oxford for their sponsorship of the heavy horse section of our show.

Judging of Shire horses, 1992

It would also be wrong not to include something about the lovely friendly giants that make a show like this possible – yes, the horses themselves.

An average heavy horse weighs around a ton and is capable of pulling enormous weights. At one time almost all of Britain's land was worked by horses – ploughing, drilling seed, raking and turning and carting the hay. In the mid-1940s the tractor began to appear on farms and, by the mid 1950s, it was obvious that the days of these lovely animals were numbered, as far as the mainstay of farming was concerned. Oil was then cheap and machines were comparatively inexpensive. Now the engines are more expensive to run and we are anxious that oil supplies will come to an end. With other countries, such as those of OPEC, being able to virtually blackmail us on its price, horses are becoming more popular. A broodmare will have a foal every year or every other year, and in three years the foal itself is ready for a long working life.

The white marking down the front of the face is commonly known as a 'blaze', and the hair round the lower leg is known as 'feather'. The unit of measurement for horses is the 'hand', which is equal to four inches. A horse is measured to the top of its shoulders; this is also known as the 'withers'.

Britain has four main breeds of heavy horse: the Shire, the Clydesdale, the Suffolk Punch and the Percheron. A brief description of these lovely animals follows.

The Shire – Body colour is black, brown, bay or grey. Black horses with four white socks (legs) are very popular with display teams as they are easily matched. Stallions must be at least 16.2 hands high (1.68 metres).

The Clydesdale – Clydesdales are so called after the old name for Lanarkshire, and the Clydesdale is, therefore, the heavy horse of Scotland. The Clydesdale stands much the same height as the Shire but tends to have more white on the legs and belly.

The Suffolk Punch – Every pure-bred Suffolk alive today may be traced back to a single ancestor – a stallion called Crisp's Horse who was foaled in 1768. All are the same colour, chesnut (Suffolk breeders omit the central 't') of which there are actually seven shades. The Suffolk is sometimes known as 'Punch', from the use of the word to mean short and thickset, as they are generally lower slung than the Shire.

The Percheron – The Percheron is black or grey; the grey may go almost white with age. Percherons are usually docile and their sound legs are free from feather, which is an advantage to farmers. Stallions should weigh up to a ton and stand 16.3 hands (1.70 metres) with mares weighing 16–18 cwt and standing 16.1 hands (1.65 metres).

Other breeds of heavy horses, not often seen in this country include the Belgian, the Ardennes, Jutland, Rhenish, Dutch Draught and Zeeland.

At the 1976 White Horse Show, we had the pleasure of welcoming a British record breaker to the heavy horse section at that time. This was the tallest Shire horse on record, being 18.8 hands. It belonged to the Calder brothers from Kidderminster in Worcestershire. This Shire's name was Prince and he was four years old when on show at Uffington. Though having been in the country all my life, I have never seen such a massive horse before or since.

The weather leading up towards the show had been very stormy and changeable and, needless to say, we were all hoping for a change for the better. I am sorry to say our hopes were not fulfilled. On the Sunday prior to the show, when Jim, Daniel and myself tried to get the posts, pegs etc into the show field ready to start building, we got extremely wet. Nevertheless, on the Monday we were in the field in good time to start our task. At least it had stopped raining, but it was extremely wet underfoot. With a good gale blowing and as the side of the hill was chalk it would soon dry out somewhat.

But, unfortunately, during that day the storms insisted on starting again in the afternoon and becoming more frequent still in the evening. But, not to be deterred, we kept pressing on with the marking out of the arenas, marquees, and the boundaries for the other things in the field. This we had to do, as we had always tried to get the post driving finished before we called it a day on the Wednesday evening. Sometimes in the past even in good conditions we were very late finishing on the Wednesday evening. Some people at times thought we were mad, but, after all, this was one of the qualifications for being a committee member. But this year proved to be an exception in every way; we were not just absolutely mad but completely certifiable. The staff of Whitney Marquees just gave us all the screaming abdabs with their complete non-cooperation. They appeared in the field during the Tuesday afternoon; the erecting staff had obviously come straight from the unemployment queue with no experience whatsoever of erecting marquees. After offloading the marquees all over the field, nearly all in the wrong places, they came over to inform us that the wind was too rough to erect any today, but they would return to start on Wednesday morning. Needless to say, they did not take too kindly to me informing them that, in my opinion, that was a load of rubbish. I said that as a committee we would require these marquees erected in good time for the exhibitors to start setting up on the Friday evening. Also, when told that the Pewsey Marquee Company had erected the marquees in the Craven Field back in 1974 with a gale blowing, they refused to believe that also.

After they had gone I remarked to Jim and Daniel that we could well have problems before the week was out. As far as building the show field was concerned, we had absolutely no spare time on our hands. If to get through our usual workload before the Saturday night we had to rely on this bunch of cowboys, then we were in trouble. They duly arrived back in the field on the Wednesday around mid-morning, looking like they had had no sleep whatsoever. After a further three-quarters of an hour they at least started to look interested in performing their duties. By lunchtime they had in fact got as far as having one roof of a marquee up. After this they went on to start on another marquee, without putting the skirt of the first one in position. This made it completely plain to us that they did not know what they were doing as, if the wind increased any further, this first one would be like a huge balloon and would certainly come to grief.

Daniel decided to walk over to them to explain the trouble that could well come their way. Needless to say, the warning that Daniel gave them fell on deaf ears. About an hour afterwards we could see that the tent pegs were working loose in the ground. This was entirely due to the extra wind being caught in the roof and snatching the guy ropes. This would have been a great deal less problematic if the skirt had been fitted straight after the roof had been raised. The next thing we saw was the whole lot down on the ground. On going over to this marquee we could see that one of the main upright poles had snapped. Before anybody could do anything to stop it, it happened to the other one. With this the owner of Whitney Marquees arrived in the field, came over to us, and stated that it was far too windy to erect marquees. With this I explained that we had warned the men to fit the skirt straight away to keep the wind-pull down to a minimum. He admitted that he could not get experienced staff to carry out the job. But, nonetheless, he would have to stop the work until the wind dropped. I became extremely angry and let him know in no uncertain terms that, if this resulted in the failure of the White Horse Show, then he should be held entirely to blame. If he, in taking a contract on, could not fulfil its terms, then he alone should be made liable for any loss the show incurred due to his shortcoming. But this was something that the committee would have to discuss.

As it was we were post driving on the Wednesday evening without any canvas up anywhere, and that was the first time that we had had no marquees up so close to a show before that I could recall. One thing was certain, a statement would have to be got from Whitney Marquees as to their position on erecting the marquees. As it was, it was obvious that without extra help forthcoming we were going to be stretched to the limit in getting the field ready. Until the marquees were up we were unable to put any exhibitors' tables in position, let alone mark their pitches out with their names on.

On Thursday we were working on the car park, which had to be fenced all the way across with chestnut paling. The posts were already driven in, admittedly, but it was still a three-man job to erect the paling and keep it tight at the same time. Also, gaps had to be left at intervals wide enough to allow the passage of a car for pay booths, with a flap left loose to enable them to be closed when not in use. A footbridge had to be put in place to allow pedestrians to get from the reserve car park to the pay booths. This entailed the removal of three barbed-wire fences that had to be rolled up and placed handily, ready for replacing after the show. Whilst we were doing this work we were being continually hindered by the so-called marquee erectors. This continued until we had to manage these tasks with just two, to allow Daniel to stop these pitiful idiots making every excuse imaginable not to put up the marquees at all. As time wore on it looked all the more likely that if this show were put on it would lose money. But somehow we had to try and run the show to recoup some of the outlay that had already been spent, or that we had committed to spend to stage this show. Why did we have to be blessed with this outfit on our twenty-first show?

As time moved on into the Friday, tempers were becoming more frayed than ever. In the end we were trying to assist the Whitney mob with erecting some of the marquees. But the substandard steel tent-pegs were bent so badly it was near impossible to get them into the ground and stay firm. In 1974 when Pewsey Marquees had the same windy and wet conditions, we were hammering in three long steel tent-pegs in a triangle about a foot apart; that would have worked this time, had we had the equipment to hand.

In the end we had to relent and erect some marquees in the car park on the sheltered side of the hedge. Even then we were going back up the main show field to the marquees that had been erected to drive in full-size fence posts at an angle. This was to substitute the useless bent steel pegs already in, which were not holding in the ground due to their very poor condition. If this was not bad enough already, on examination of one of the marquees that had been erected in the car park, we found that the men had used one of the main top cross-poles that had been badly cracked when it collapsed earlier in the week. When this was pointed out to the person in charge of Whitney Marquees he decided that this could be put right and that he would do so. But, as it was getting late on the Friday evening, it would have to wait until the Saturday morning.

On the Saturday morning they were in the process of binding the pole with rope after getting it down when they were caught red-handed by our health and safety advisor, Mr Jim Butler. When questioned by Jim as to what they intended to do with it, they informed him that they were going to put it back in the roof, as it would be safe enough. Jim told them in no uncertain terms that they would not be doing this; he then introduced himself to them and explained his duty to the White Horse Show Committee. With this they went all the way back to Whitney and returned with a replacement. With the continuous heavy showers still coming down at regular intervals we had to keep shutting one gate and opening another to try and spread the traffic flow. This was the only way we could hope to keep the gateways passable; but even then they were getting quite bad. On top of this we were ordering more hardcore to be tipped in the car park gateways to try and keep them clear for use on the Sunday morning. We eventually completed the roping of the arenas etc. fairly late in the evening. As a result we were putting the tables into the marquees with the assistance of car headlights, but, nonetheless, we completed what we had set out to do. But we also knew that we would still have some severe problems to face on Sunday morning. Maybe with our local parson attending to hold a short service in the main arena on Sunday morning the weather would be kinder; we would have to wait and see.

On the Sunday morning the weather was bright and breezy but at least it was dry, although the forecast was for heavy and frequent showers. As we had agreed, we three musketeers were up in the field early. The first job was to burst some bales of straw open and scatter this as much as possible in the main pedestrian walkways. Just before 7 a.m. the exhibitors started to arrive. The majority of these knew what they were doing when driving in these wet conditions, and drove in a sensible way. That is, they knew not to rev the engine as if they were about to take off in an aeroplane, but just to keep the engine running smoothly, and not on any condition stop. But, needless to say, there were the few that *would* stop and ask for directions right in the gateway instead of continuing until they were well inside and then finding out from the members of the committee. We were fortunate to have some very keen vintage tractor owners, who I must say were quite enjoying the experience of towing these people to their allotted places. Again we were indebted to Mr Jim Matthews for his kindness in loaning us his spare tractor for towing duty. Daniel thoroughly enjoyed this and was always on hand to deal with the big and heavy towing work. Also, we were just as thankful for the usual helpfulness of Mr Charley Walters of Baulking Grange Farm who was also on hand to help out. Charley had just turned up on the morning with another load of bales. These we decided to leave under-load by the committee bus so that we could use them when and where required.

But somehow we did manage to get the show under way; don't ask me or anybody else how, because we would not be able to tell you. The biggest problem in the end was the aggro from the trade-stand people, who would not accept that we had had problems all week from the marquee company. I believe that some of these people thought that not only should we have been able to control those inexperienced dole-queue marquee erectors, but that we could have controlled the weather even better. But fair play to the majority that I had to deal with, who were courteous, sympathetic and were prepared to give the show a chance to prove itself a success. After setting the stall up for the sale of souvenirs we decided that it was at last time to sit down to down a cup of tea. But, to be perfectly honest, after all the aggro and abuse that we had received it made you wish that it was at least a full barrel of beer.

With the sun shining, at 10.45 prompt the local vicar, Reverend John Gawn-Cayne, led his flock to the main arena for the short service that he had arranged. But, with storm clouds gathering, we wondered if he would be able to manage to complete this task in the dry. Unfortunately this was not to be; just as this service was coming to an end the rain came down by the bucketful – the only thing missing were the buckets. Dare one say it – well I am going to anyway – the heavens just opened; it was then, when he eventually ran into the marquee, that I realised that – yes! – John had a great sense of humour. I also can say that this fact, together with other comments concerning his blessing of the show, was remarked on at quite a number of show meetings afterwards.

The Sunday was marred by frequent showers, but the arena events carried on despite the weather. Of course the attendance was well down, but the people who did attend seemed to enjoy themselves and were appreciative of the class of show that was put on. Although the very small minority did complain, this was not much above the usual complaints that we were always going to get anyway. The main complaint was that there was nowhere dry to sit down. We were all at a loss to know how we were going to provide this with the weather that we had had leading up to and during the show.

On the Sunday evening, after the show was over for the day, we had the additional severe problem of getting the trade-stand holders out of the field. Yet again we appreciated the kind help of Mr Jim Matthews, Mr Charlie Walters and the vintage tractor owners for their help in towing the people out who got bogged down in the gateways. After we had got everybody out and on their way home we had to attend a committee meeting in the committee bus. When it started I made it quite plain that I had had about enough for one week, so I was not prepared to sit and listen to any idle chatter; after all, we were tired and had another week of good slog to pack the equipment away when the Monday part of the show was over. But in all honesty the meeting was quite brief and straight to the point. We made what arrangements we could in preparation for the Monday morning, including having Daniel with Jim's tractor and myself on standby by the gateway into the main show field at 6.30, so as to assist the heavy horse boxes to the heavy horse arena. This had to be done as one of these boxes was a very large articulated box and always had a trailer on tow, with its wagons etc on board.

We had a certain amount of luck with the weather at long last. It had been a dry night with quite a lot of wind, and this was what was wanted, but the gateways were still very wet. At least they had got no worse than they were the night before. The big test arrived at the gate bang on time – the large heavy-horse box. On discussing the situation with the crew it was decided to uncouple the trailer out on the road and tow the box in first. This proved to be a very wise move; whilst towing the box just inside the gateway, the body of the box was actually dragging on the mud. But all the same we got the heavy-horse box to the park all right. It only remained to go back and collect the trailer, which caused no problems whatsoever.

Thankfully the field was drying quite fast by the time the majority of the stallholders arrived; the day in front of us looked to be set for better weather. But some of the general public still needed to put their brains in gear before complaining about how difficult it was to get around the ground. One such lady went out of the field complaining something terrible, but on looking down and seeing that she had no shoes on I noticed that she was carrying a pair of sandals with stiletto heels. This, coupled with the foul language that she was using, I thought said everything that needed saying at that particular time. I must say also that some of the stall holders were very upbeat about it all, saying, all in all, that they were not doing too badly at all. Admittedly there were others who were ranting and raving, 'We want our money back,' as there will always be. We told them that they would have to write to the show committee after the show, when every application would be looked at on its merits.

It seemed that, due entirely to the adverse weather in the week and over the two days of the show, the attendances were going to be well down on previous years. Needless to say, the preachers of doom were giving us all a headache before the show was over. This of course gave us the incentive we had to have to start the big tow-out job on the Monday evening. But things did not turn out to be as bad as at first thought: during the Monday afternoon a fair amount of sunshine and a fairly stiff wind had dried the field no end. Therefore, with a little care and a lot of thought, people were getting out of the field fairly well, which was a credit to them. This helped us no end as we could concentrate on towing the heavy vehicles out, and we were all thankful to be having an easier time than we had anticipated. Nonetheless we were thankful when it was time to go home and have a well-earned rest.

The week after the show, I am pleased to say, was a lot less stressful than the previous week, although there were one or two heated arguments with the marquee gang concerning their attitude before the show. However, Jim and myself got our act together and we were clear of the field by the following Friday evening. Considering the conditions we had experienced before the show we were very pleased with this performance. One worrying thing was the muddy conditions on the road on the Tuesday morning, but the council were true to their word and had a sweeper at the site by mid-morning. The job this sweeper did was a credit to the operator; we had a good clean road by midday. This certainly made my work a lot easier getting all the equipment back to the store without skidding on the road. For our overall performance regarding the show we would have to wait until the wash-up meeting, and this I did not look forward to. I could hear the hawks already and wondered what sort of arguments would be coming.

This meeting took place a lot later than was the normal custom, but eventually was held on 19 October. This was mainly due to the fact that for the first time we had actually lost money; this did not surprise me in the least. The final figure was a loss of £3,400. To only lose this amount was a relief to some of us, but to others it was a crime of great magnitude. After all was said and done, this was the whole idea and thinking for the disaster fund: to clear any debts from this show and still have funds to start the wheels rolling ready for the next one. Personally I did not see a problem over this. Yes it was a great disappointment to lose money with all the very hard work that had gone into organising and running a show of this size, but it was not the end of the world – we had ample funds left to guarantee a show in 1993.

At this meeting we had to deal with the complaints of the trade stand holders. These had to be given plenty of thought as, if we were running another show in 1993, trade stands would give us a good income. It was thus decided that certain stand holders would be given a generous discount next time. This was left in the hands of Jim Larkin, who had already indicated that he was willing to again organise that part of the show for 1993. It was at this stage of the meeting that it became certain that we would still be running a White Horse Show next year. The really sour thing at this meeting related to a claim from a person for compensation for a car accident. Apparently this car skidded on the road two days after the show and ended up in a ditch. The claimant was not named at the meeting, which I thought was rather odd. But the amount of times that I personally used this road after the show meant I thought that we could ignore this claim anyway. In my opinion any person who had come to grief after the council had cleaned the road was not driving within the speeds required on this country road. As I had already stated, the council had done a great service in returning the road to its normal condition. I did, some time after this incident, learn the name of this claimant, but as the show committee received no more letters on this incident I shall therefore remain silent on the matter.

A claim for grass seed for reseeding the bare patches of the show field was not even questioned, as we all knew that this would have to be done when the ruts were levelled and harrowed over. During the show I had had quite a long talk with Jim over the damage that we were doing to the field and found him adamant that this was not going to cause too much of a problem – nothing that patches of reseeding would not cure. I was also surprised by his insistence that the show would be welcomed back in the same field for 1993.

It was decided that we should go ahead and invite tenders for the marquee hire, and that Whitney Marquees should also be invited to tender. This was met with my complete disapproval, considering their performance this year. But it was thought that we could leave ourselves open to charges of unfair tendering if they were not invited. But whoever did get the contract for 1993 would have to provide their own site attendants over the two days of the show. This decision was made and accepted by all, as we could all discuss this subject in full when the tenders were received early in the New Year.

Thank-you letters were sent to the following, as without their support no show would be possible: Dibbles, Mr J Matthews, the Lonsdale Estate, Mr Charlie Walters and Mr and Mrs Seymore.

With a long and, at times, frustrating meeting over, the first meeting for the 1993 show would be on 9 January 1993 at the Sports and Social Club. I believe that all of the committee were looking forward to a well-earned rest until the New Year.

1993

At the first meeting of the 1993 show, the treasurer confirmed that the loss from the 1992 show was £3,452. Nevertheless, this had to be put behind us now to face the task ahead, which was the 1993 show. It was decided that the cost of trade stands would have to be increased to: inside Sunday, £25; Monday, £30; both days, £45. Outside Sunday, £20; Monday, £25; both days, £40. It was also agreed that admission should stand as last year; that is, adults £4, children and OAPs £1.

Several quotes for the marquee hire had been received, but Paul was asked to negotiate with the three most suitable suppliers and endeavour to make a decision before the end of March. To avoid the fiasco of last year a specified erection time of Thursday evening would be demanded. This the field-sub had requested, as we certainly were not prepared to be treated this year as we were last year. Even after the disastrous weather of last year we were receiving competition for the broadcasting from the showground; this was between GWR and BBC Wiltshire Radio.

At our March meeting Mr Neil Eades was welcomed to the committee; he would be working with Mike Thomas on the publicity side of the show. Mike had been seeking help for some time, as this side of the show also encompassed sponsorship; a fair amount of time needed to be spent on this subject. This also had the effect of cutting costs on our own expenditure. Paul also informed us that the marquee contract had been let to Clycan. These people had of course undertaken to have all erecting of marquees completed by the Thursday evening prior to the show. They would also erect them in the order that we required them. This was great news for the field team, and meant we would not experience the trouble that we had had the previous year. Jim Larkin confirmed also that the Cricklade Railway Society were prepared to carry out the car-parking duties again, and this was accepted.

It was also at this meeting that I was able to confirm that I had been made redundant by British Rail after forty-three years' service, for which I was very thankful. This year I would not be tied to the two weeks as in the past, but would have more time to spare.

The following awards recommended by the trustees were also approved: Uffington Day Care Centre, £200; Jubilee Play Area, £500; White Horse Playgroup, £200; Old Folks Afternoon Club, £300; Baulking Church, £1,000. This was made possible because there had been a little money left over from the previous year, together with the interest that the treasurer of the trust, Mr Peter Erskine, had gained from the disaster fund.

It had already been noticed that tree planting had taken place in the show field where the lawnmowers' arena had been last year, so this would involve a new layout plan for this year. To achieve this we needed to be informed what space each arena would need, together with the amount of room needed for trade stands, in plenty of time. This information had to be in our hands at least a week before the show, to enable us to build the show field in the week leading up to the actual show.

My worst fears were realised at the April meeting; the way in which it was done still fills me with anger to this day. At our first meeting back in January it had been decided to leave the admission for the 1993 show at the same level as it had been for the 1992 show. With publicity already published and distributed to this effect our new member Mr N Eades proposed that the admission be raised for adults to £5. To my utter amazement the chairman allowed the proposal to stand. To cap it all he took a vote on this proposal and, of course, the hawks won the vote by the margin of seven for and five against. Yes, with only twelve members present the motion was deemed to have been carried. Therefore the missing fourteen committee members who could not attend this meeting were being ignored. I thought that this took the biscuit, and promptly said so. Increasing this admission was going to hit just the people that the White Horse Show had always tried to represent – it was entertainment for the family. With the interest rate still sky-high this idiotic way of going forward was sure to put us in reverse.

It was deemed to be an impossible task to get these people to understand that the working class were still having a rough time with very high interest rates. It was always my argument that we should try to keep the high standard that we had always set, even if it was lowering the profit margin to do so. As long as we could break even but keep the show going, the economy would eventually take a turn for the better, and then we should be in a position to forge ahead again. But the hawks, with their computers trying to predict what the human being would do, will never replace the human brain. Working-class people would always look after their families first and foremost. When the attendance levels dropped, which they were bound to do, what would these people do then? Probably cut down on the arena events and drive even more people away. The entire thought behind this philosophy was idiotic in the extreme. The dissatisfaction and anger amongst some of the committee was only to be expected. But we were not going to walk away at this time; we had to hang in together to try and keep the White Horse Show on the road, as John Little would have wished. I eventually talked Jim and Daniel out of packing it all in as they threatened to do and kept them in the fold for at least one more show. Two other members of the committee said that if we were prepared to keep going then they would do the same.

At our June meeting the field-sub were asked for a layout plan for the show. This was answered very quickly: the main arena and heavy horse arena would be in the same place as last year, as would the marquees. Vintage and veteran cars and the stationary engines would be in virtually the same place as last year. But, as far as anything else went, we could not oblige; we were at a complete loss as to how much space would be required by the events that we had not, as yet, been told of. With this very blunt answer we were very soon furnished with the information that we were waiting for. Therefore, we would present a revised plan for the next meeting, bearing in mind that a final layout would be an impossibility if Jim Larkin was able to take stand bookings up until the last minute. Let's face the facts – this was what was required if we were going to make use of every piece of the field. Jim should be allowed to continue as before. That is why we had always been adamant that we mark out the trade stands with Jim in attendance on the Friday afternoon prior to the show; by working in this way Jim could keep us posted right up to the last minute. We would then leave about six or so spaces between marquees or odd places. Jim knew just where these were; therefore, if anybody turned up on the day Jim was left in the position of being able to take their money. If we had to save expenses it made sense to me that we should also be in a position to take money. This method of marking the field out had worked well over the last twenty-one years and made the work of building the show field straightforward, so I saw no reason why it should not work now.

At the August meeting we did inform the committee that the lawnmower arena would be in the top of the car park, as we could not provide enough room in the main show field to meet their requirements. However, I had been in touch with Jim Gavin, and he was happy with that site. Also, we had programmed the clay-pigeon shoot to be over the stream in Mr and Mrs Seymour's field. This left just enough room for the Buscot Archers to be in the main show field. This was done because two members of the Buscot Archers were disabled, leaving us the simple task of placing one of the two disabled toilets close by.

The good news as far as the field-sub was concerned was that the marquee firm would be in the field on the Tuesday, which as far as we were concerned was exactly right. The marquee places would be marked ready and the marquees could be offloaded spot-on. I wondered if we were going to get any language problems with their staff as they were foreigners coming all the way down from Scotland. Yes, this is a fact – the marquee hire firm that had tendered for this contract came all the way from Edinburgh and was competitive enough to win the contract.

The programme would be near to forty pages this year, with the advertisements bringing in some £2,200 of income. Writing about the programme brings us on to the schedule which we had lined up for the 1993 show, and another fine programme of events it promised to be as well. With the show commencing earlier than ever before, we were indebted to our show arena events coordinator and show commentator, Colonel Tony

Bateman. On his shoulders fell the responsibility of collating all of the arena events and working out the time allowed for performing in the arena. Then, to add to his headaches, he had to stay in the control caravan to commentate for all the events. But the committee had no fears in this direction as Tony had performed this task with accuracy and precision for a number of years now, and this showed in the smooth way that the arena events complemented the show.

Sunday 29 August

10.20	Heart of England Falconry
10.50	Wasps Motorcycle Display Team
11.20	Pathfinders Dog Display Team
11.45	Mid-Wales Axe Racing Team
12.15	Greater Manchester Police Field Gun Competition
13.00	City of Coventry Corps of Drums
13.25	Wasps Motorcycle Display Team
13.55	Pathfinders Dog Display Team
14.15	Heart of England Falconry
14.45	Mid-Wales Axe Racing Team
15.15	Greater Manchester Police Team Field Gun Competition
15.55	City of Coventry Corps of Drums

Monday 30 August

10.30	Heart of England Falconry
11.00	Wasps Motorcycle Display Team
11.30	Pathfinders Dog Display
12.00	Greater Manchester Police Field Gun Competition.
12.40	Historic Tractor Parade
1.05	Band of the Scots Guards
1.35	Heart of England Falconry
2.05	Wasps Motorcycle Display
2.35	Greater Manchester Police Field Gun Competition
3.15	Pathfinders Dog Display Team
3.35	Devil's Horsemen Jousting
4.15	Red Devils Freefall Parachute Display Team
4.40	Band of the Scots Guards

16.15 Red Devils Freefall
Parachute Display Team
16.40 Historic Motorcycles Parade
17.00 Toyota Aerobatics
18.00 Show Closes

The Cricklade Band to play at various times during the day by the refreshment marquee.

Lawnmower Racing in its own arena throughout the day from 11.00 to 17.30.

5.10 Parade of Historic Cars
5.30 Toyota Aerobatics
6.00 Show Closes

The Cricklade Band to play at various times during the day by the refreshment marquee.

Lawnmower Racing in its own arena throughout the day from 11.00 to 17.30.

The Heavy Horse Show in its own arena from 11.00 to 16.30.

The committee thanked Mr J Soden for the use of Sower Hill Farm fields as this year's showground and car parking. We also extended our thanks to Mr and Mrs Seymour of Britchcombe Farm for the use of fields for car parking and clay-pigeon shooting.

Thanks also to: St John Ambulance Brigade for their valuable help in ensuring a safe and enjoyable show; 1861 (Wantage) Squadron Air Training Corps for selling programmes and clearing up after the show; Swindon and Cricklade Railway Society Ltd for providing the staff and organising the car parking; Uffington Sports Club for manning the bar; Mattingley and Sharps for the public address system; the chief constable of Thames Valley Police and his officers for their support; Freeman's of Uffington for the loan of trailers; Mike Durham and SW Transport Ltd, for the loan of the trailer used by the Cricklade Band.

We cannot leave this list of thanks without conveying our sincere thanks to the volunteers who man the pay booths over the two days of the show. Remember that these heroes take all the flak thrown at them from some of the general public and then return each year to do the same task again. It is these people who we rely on; without them there would not be a show.

Following is some information about some of the attractions at this year's show, not previously covered:

The Greater Manchester Police Youth Field Gun Competition – This exciting new event at our show is based on the competition that has been held every year by three Royal Navy crews at the Royal Tournament for over seventy years. A field gun and limber, weighing over a ton, are manhandled over an obstacle course in the shortest possible time by teams of youths who have undergone a rigorous, twice-weekly training programme in fitness, self-discipline and teamwork. Started by an officer with the Greater Manchester Police in 1982, the project has benefited more than 500 young men, including many from underprivileged inner-city backgrounds. Between them they have raised many thousands of pounds for charity.

The standard is so high that 'B' Division has become affiliated to the Portsmouth Field Gun Crew and 'K' Division to the Fleet Air Arm. They have appeared on television and at the estate of Lord Lichfield, and both crews have competed at Portsmouth in what has been called 'The Toughest Team Sport in the World'.

Pathfinders Dog Display – The Pathfinders, established in 1968, are probably unique in being the only civilian display team using just German shepherd dogs. They have performed all over Great Britain at shows, carnivals, military tattoos and many other events, including numerous TV appearances. A high standard of training is achieved by a combination of firmness and kindness, resulting in a display that both dogs and handlers really enjoy. The varied programme includes obedience, agility, criminal work and a spectacular fire tower, as well as comedy and audience participation. The Pathfinders Dog Display Team, under the direction of Bruce Grantham, are sponsored by Edward Baker Ltd, producers of Bakers Complete high-quality dog food.

Mid-Wales Axe Racing Team – The team first formed themselves into a club in 1975, but some of the members started log chopping as early as 1966. Current membership is fifteen, of which five or six members normally participate in each demonstration. The team have been all over the world, including America, Ireland, Australia and Belgium, and are competing in the World Championships in Melbourne. Amongst their number are past British champions in various individual events, and the team have also been British Team Champions. They have appeared on TV, including Marti Caine's *Your Best Shot*, and this year they have already competed in the Royal Welsh and New

Forest shows as part of the British Championship.

In this daring display with razor-sharp axes, you will see tree felling, tree climbing, an amazing 'chainsaw vs. axe' race and small articles cut from a two-foot-long log with a chainsaw. The Mid-Wales Axe Racing Team really are something very different and we are delighted to have them at our show.

Devil's Horsemen Jousting – For the first time in Uffington, Gerard Naprous and his Devil's Horsemen will entertain and astound you with their skill and daring. You will see heroes such as the darling Harry Hotspur doing battle at the tilt with the villainous Black Knight. Lances, swords and battleaxes will flash as in the days of yore, and all for the favour of a fair maiden.

The steward of the court will preside over competitions such as the 'quintain' and also 'deadly combat'. The knights in full medieval dress, attended by their squires, present a magnificent display full of colour and pageantry.

Icknield Way Morris Men – The Icknield Way Morris Men are the local morris side, based in the Vale of White Horse in Oxfordshire. The side is named after the Icknield School in Wantage, where it was formed in the mid-1950s. The Icknield Way is also the ancient name of the Ridgeway passing White Horse Hill. The side dances in blue waistcoats, each bearing a west-facing golden wyvern, the standard of the kings of Wessex in olden times. Wantage is the birthplace of Alfred, the most famous of these ancient kings.

The side performs dances from a number of dancing traditions, which originate mostly from the local area. The dances come from the Oxfordshire villages of Adderbury, Bampton, Ducklington, Fieldtown (Leafield) and Stanton Harcourt, as well as from Bledington (Gloucestershire) and Lichfield (Staffordshire). Both stick and handkerchief dances are performed in the time-honoured manner to bring good luck, fertility and to ensure a good harvest. The side dances to the melodian, piano accordion, fiddle and pipe and tabor, in various combinations, using the traditional tunes associated with the dances.

As in previous years, we will be dancing on August bank holiday Monday at the White Horse Show and at various times during the day we can be found dancing at different points around the showground. We do hope you will appreciate our dances and help us to make the day an enjoyable one for all.

The Band of the Scots Guards – Director of Music: Lieutenant Colonel D E Price psm – The Scots Guards were formed by King Charles I in 1642 for service in Ireland. The earliest trace of any music in the Scots Guards seems to be of drum, fifes and bagpipes twenty years later. By the late eighteenth century there was a band comprising two each of oboes, clarinets, French horns and bassoons. Players were drawn from the London theatres and were exempt from military law. In the following century, flutes, trumpets, trombones and serpents were added, together with three coloured men called 'time beaters' who were attired in exotic uniforms and played tambourines and Turkish bells.

The band of today numbers fifty players, all of whom are among the finest instrumentalists in the services. Stationed in London, it shares with other guards bands the duties of daily guard mounting at Buckingham Palace. It is also present at various state occasions throughout the United Kingdom, two of the most notable being the ceremony of Trooping the Colour on Horse Guards Parade and the Remembrance Parade at the Cenotaph in Whitehall. A fair proportion of the musicians are 'double-handed' or capable of playing both a string and wind instrument, as the band is often called upon to produce an orchestra to play at investitures and state banquets in Buckingham Palace.

The musicians wear the traditional uniform of Her Majesty's Household Troop and can be distinguished from the other footguards regiments by the buttons on the scarlet tunics that are arranged in groups of three, signifying that the Scots Guards are the Third Regiment of Foot Guards. On the collar is emblazoned the Order of the Thistle. The famous black 'bearskin' headgear, worn on parade, was copied as a battle trophy from Napoleon's Imperial Guard.

In recent years the band's travels have taken it to the USA, Canada, Kenya, Germany, Italy, France, Spain, Malta, Hong Kong, Cyprus and Australia. During the Gulf War the band was deployed in its secondary role as medical assistants in support of British and Allied forces in Saudi Arabia.

Lieutenant Colonel D E Price, psm began his musical career in the army in 1960 as a junior bandsman. In 1973 he took up his first bandmaster post with the 1st Battalion, the 22nd (Cheshire) Regiment. Since then he has had a number of distinguished appointments, becoming director of music to Her Majesty's Scots Guards in December 1987 and senior director of music of the Music Household Division in February 1993.

The band of the Scots Guards appears by kind permission of Brigadier A G Ross, OBE, Regimental Lieutenant Colonel, Scots Guards.

GWR Roadshow – An exciting first at this year's show will be the GWR Gold Roadshow who, on Sunday, will provide four action-packed hours of fun from 11.30 to 15.30 including loads of free giveaways and some great music. Presenter Gary Vincent is appearing at 13.15 and he will be doing some interviews from the show live on GWR. Whatever you do, don't miss this.

Wasps Motorcycle Display Team – These boys and girls aged from six to sixteen present a thrilling display of skilful motorbike riding. Their show includes precision and trick riding as well as a touch of comedy. Based in the Southampton and Portsmouth area, they travel widely to put on displays which, in addition to funding their own club, raise money for handicapped children.

Army Stands – If you're interested in a military career or would just like to find out more about the Army, why not have a chat to the soldiers who will be at this year's show? For the youngsters there's even a mini-assault course to give them a flavour of Army life and use up some of that excess energy.

City of Coventry Corps of Drums – The City of Coventry Corps of Drums, under their commanding officer Mr J T Rose, JP, travel extensively in the UK and Europe, performing their musical arena displays at many major venues. Their travels abroad range from appearances at almost every holiday town along the Belgian coast, to appearances at many towns and cities through Holland, Germany, France, Switzerland, Liechtenstein, Austria, Denmark, Luxembourg, Norway (where they took prizes at the Hamar International Music Festival) and, last but not least, the grand Macy's Parade through Manhattan, New York. In 1984 they were the National Marching Band Champions.

The boys' ages range from ten years up to the late teens. They perform a programme of music and drill movements which they have committed to memory during an intensive winter of training. Their uniforms are formal and are based on the style of HM Royal Marines. We are sure you will not fail to enjoy this entertaining performance by a very energetic, enthusiastic and proficient group of young people.

Before I go any further I believe that now is the time to give an update on the committee, in case I have missed recording any new members and the responsibility that they oversee for the show. Therefore, the full committee was as follows: chairman, Mr Viv Boaler; treasurer, Mr Graham Clark; secretary, Mrs Sue Philo; arena events, Mr Barry Godsell and Mr Barry Mills; publicity, Mr Mike Thomas and Mr Neil Eades; craft and trade stands, Mr Jim Larkin; bar, Mr Brian White; sign writing and sign posting, Mr Daniel Chester and Mr Roger Jay; electrics and communications, Mr Bill Mattingley; White Horse souvenirs, Mr Brian Tilling; historic vehicles, Mr Derek Kelsey and Mrs Ann Kelsey; army displays and army events, Colonel Tony Bateman; heavy horses, Mrs Christine Keen; farm animals and rare breeds, Mr Anthony Parsons; stationary engines and vintage tractors, Mr Charles Philo; field services, Mr Paul Armishaw; printing, Mr Jeremy Packford; showground, Mr Brian Tilling, Mr Jim Panting, Mr Daniel Chester, Mr Bill Mitchell, Mr Clive Avenell; police, PC Dave Platts.

I believe that our local bobby Dave Platts was one of the unsung heroes of the White Horse Show over his time in the village of Uffington. He was always ready to commit himself to the aims of the show and of course was always on hand over the show days to stop any trouble, even before it started. If we look over the period that the show has been running we can all be proud of having a virtually trouble-free time. Thanks for everything, Dave! When you consider that the main qualification for being on the White Horse Show Committee was that you had to be completely mad, I am left to ask where you would find another place where there were twenty-six mad people living in such close proximity at the same time.

One of the events of the show that you could always see causing a large amount of interest was the heavy horse section. The person that we have to thank for this innovation was Mr Peter White and his wife Angela, whose brainchild this was. Thanks to Peter and his wife, the strength of this part of the show has gradually built up over the years. With the White Horse Show now being a qualifying show for the heavy horse Section of the Royal Bath & West Show, I feel I therefore must include at this stage some extracts from the standard of points for Shires issued by the Shire Horse Society.

> Standard of Points for Shires – A scale of points for the breed has been carefully drawn up, and this has been amended when necessary to meet modern requirements. For instance, years ago, a great characteristic of the Shire was the wealth of hair, or feathers, on the legs. Today the demand is for a cleaner-legged horse, with straight, fine, silky hair.
>
> The standard of points laid down by the council is as follows. Stallions:
>
> Colour – Black, brown, bay or grey. No good stallion should be splashed with large white patches over the body. He must not be roan or chestnut.
>
> Height – From 16.2 hands high. Standard 17 hands and upwards. Average about 17.2 hands.
>
> Head – Long and lean, neither too large nor too small, with long neck in proportion to the body. Large jaw bone should be avoided.
>
> Eyes – Large, well set and docile in expression. Wall eyes not acceptable.
>
> Nose – Slightly Roman nostrils, thin and wide; lips together.
>
> Ears – Long, lean, sharp and sensitive.
>
> Throat – Clean-cut and lean.
>
> Shoulder – Deep and oblique, wide enough to support the collar.
>
> Neck – Long, slightly arched, well set on to give the horse a commanding appearance.
>
> Girth – The girth varies from 6 ft to 8 ft in stallions of between 16.2 and 18 hands.
>
> Back – Short, strong and muscular. Should not be dipped or roached.
>
> Loins – Standing well up, denoting good constitution (must not be flat).
>
> Fore-end – Wide across the chest, with legs well under the body and well enveloped in muscle, or action is impeded.
>
> Hind-quarters – Long and sweeping, wide and full of muscle, well let down towards the thighs.
>
> Ribs – Round, deep and well sprung, not flat.
>
> Forelegs – Should be as straight as possible down to pastern.
>
> Hindlegs – Hocks should be not too far back and in line with the hindquarters, with ample width broadside and narrow in

front. 'Puffy' and 'sickle' hocks should be avoided. The leg sinews should be clean-cut and hard like fine cords to touch, and clear of short cannon bone.

Bone Measurement – Of flat bone 11 in. is ample, although occasionally 12.5 in. is recorded. Flat bone is heavier and stronger than spongy bone. Hocks must be broad, deep and flat, and set at the correct angle for leverage.

Feet – Deep, solid and wide, with thick open walls. Coronets should be hard and sinewy with substance.

Hair – Not too much; fine, straight and silky.

A good Shire stallion should stand from 16.2 hands upwards, and weigh from 18 cwt to 22 cwt when mature, without being overdone in condition. He should possess a masculine head and a good crest, with sloping, not upright, shoulders running well into the back. Shoulders should be short and well coupled with the loins. The tail should be well set up and not what is known as 'gooserumped'. Both head and tail should be carried erect. The ribs should be well sprung, not flat sided, with good middle – which generally denotes good constitution. A stallion should have good feet and joints; the feet should be wide and big around the top of the coronets, with sufficient length in the pasterns. When in motion, he should go with force using both knees and hocks; the latter should be kept close together, he should go straight and true before and behind.

A good Shire stallion should have a strong character.

Modification or Variation of Stallion Standard of Points for Geldings:

Colour – As for mares.

Height – 16.2 hands and upwards.

Girth – From 6 ft to 7 ft 6 in.

Bone measurement – 10 to 11 in. under knee, slightly more under hock and broadside on; of flat hard quality.

A gelding should be upstanding, thick, well balanced, very active and a gay mover; he should be full of courage, and should look like he can and be able to do a full day's work. Geldings weigh from 17 to 22 cwt.

So, next time anyone thinks that the judge wearing his black bowler hat is taking a long time looking at and feeling a horse, they can now appreciate and know that he has a terrific number of points to take into consideration – and all before he can witness the horse in movement. I hope this will be of some use to the people who enjoy watching these wonderful animals at the show.

Another side of the show that has come a long way since the very first show in 1972 is, of course, the historic and vintage vehicles. This has been due to the keen organisation of Derek and Ann Kelsey, who have built the attendance figures up over the last eleven years or so.

As for the stationary engines, the White Horse Show has had support since the beginning from a dedicated group of enthusiasts who spend their free time in the winter months renovating the farm machinery and power units they come across, sometimes in ditches and often in pieces. Many originate from the early part of this century and have been brought back to their original working condition after many hours of hard and tedious work.

At the end of the day the 1993 show was back in profit, although the profit margin was only around £2,500, a loan from the disaster fund of £1,500 to clear away the 1992 disaster having been repaid. I found it disappointing to have to sit and listen again to the idiotic ideas of the hawk side. They were preaching, yet again, that we would have to cut costs and increase charges. If we went down this road we would have major problems on our hands; the general public will not pay extra to see an inferior programme of events. With the interest rates still high, working-class people were still in the grips of recession, with families still the hardest hit out of the population. To yet again increase prices would mean these would be the first people to find the show too expensive to attend. To try and predetermine the profits of a show was therefore the road to ruin. It was my own thinking that the only thing we could do as a committee was to carry on creating a show that was in the price range that these families could afford. Having done this, we had to sit back and hope that a profit was returned, but attempt to at least break even. A computer would not give us the answer to what a human being was intending to do. I also thought that, as a committee, we had a duty to ensure the continuance of the White Horse Show for the benefit of the future population of the three villages.

The one thing that must be remembered about the White Horse Show Committee was that, from time to time, we have had to sit through some very bitter arguments about policies and the way forward. But the one thing remaining supreme was that all the decisions were made by the majority of members present at the meeting. Once this was achieved it was accepted as a fact by the minority, at times with great reluctance, in order to get on with the running of show. It was with this spirit that the committee had kept going and were still working as a team to organise and run the shows. This was, of course, much to the annoyance of the knockers and preachers of doom, who said that it would never last when we first started the shows in 1972. Now, twenty-three years later, we were still up and running and achieving what we set out to do in the first place – that was, to supply a source of income and finance to the benefit of the three villages. After all the arguments we had had there was only one thing to do and that was to get on with the job of the 1994 show.

1994

The site was the same as in the previous years, at Sower Hill, by kind permission of Mr Jim Soden of Sower Hill Farm, and the car-parking field by kind permission of Mrs Marcella Seymour, of Britchcombe Farm. The site would not give us too many headaches until some of the committee wanted the plan altered at the last minute.

The main arena events booked to appear at the 1994 show again contained a good and varied programme to cater for a large cross section of the general public. The programme was:

Sunday 28 August

- 11.00 Heart of England Falconry
- 11.30 Solent Eagles Motorcycle Display Team
- 12.00 Pathfinders Dog Display Team
- 12.30 Cricklade Band Lunchtime Concert
- 13.00 Greater Manchester Police Field Gun Competition
- 13.20 Dingle Fingle's Clowntime Crimewatch
- 13.45 Romford Drum and Trumpet Corps
- 14.15 Heart of England Falconry
- 14.45 Greater Manchester Police Field Gun

Monday 29 August

- 10.30 Heart of England Falconry
- 11.00 Solent Eagles Motorcycle Display Team
- 11.30 Pathfinders Dog Display Team
- 12.00 Greater Manchester Police Field Gun Competition
- 12.20 Cricklade Band Lunchtime Concert
- 12.45 Dingle Fingle's Clowntime Crimewatch
- 13.10 Parade of Historic Tractors
- 13.40 City of Coventry Corps of Drums
- 14.10 Heart of England Falconry

	Competition	14.40	Pathfinders Dog Display Team
15.10	Parade of Historic Motorcycles	15.10	Greater Manchester Police Field Gun Competition
15.50	Pathfinders, Dog Display Team	15.30	Parade of the Old Berks Hunt
16.20	Dingle Fingle's Clowntime Crimewatch	15.50	Parade of Historic Cars
16.50	Solent Eagles Motorcycle Display Team	16.30	Dingle Fingle's Clowntime Crimewatch
17.20	Romford Drum and Trumpet Corps	17.00	Solent Eagles Motorcycle Display Team
17.40	Show Closes	17.30	City of Coventry Corps of Drums
		18.00	Show Closes

The Cricklade Band will also be playing at various other times during the day.

The Cricklade Band will also be playing at various other times during the day.

At 11.00 in Arena 2 the Heavy Horse Show will be taking place, until approximately 16.00. Handouts on the programme can be obtained from that arena.

Over both days lawnmower racing will be taking place in its own arena.

The committee were again most grateful to Lieutenant Colonel W F Clarke, OBE, and the staff of the Reading and Oxford Army Careers Offices for arranging the army displays. The display of logistic vehicles was by kind permission of the commanding officer, 4 General Support Regiment, the Royal Logistic Corps, Lieutenant Colonel J R Wallace.

The committee also thanked all those companies who had generously supported the show through programme advertising and sponsorship of events.

The committee extended thanks also to Ken Freeman, Charlie Walters, Jim Matthews, and Lonsdale Estates for their assistance and co-operation in putting on the show.

Some interesting facts on our attractions are as follows:

The British Lawnmower Racing Association – The association (motto, '*per herbam ad astra*') boasts a membership of around 200. Between thirty and forty machines are expected at our show. A dozen races will take place over each day of the show and will include the White Horse Grand Prix on Monday. Most races last about five minutes, but the Grand Prix is three times as long.

Solent Eagles – These boys and girls aged from six to sixteen present a thrilling display of skilful motorbike riding. Their show includes precision and trick riding as well as a touch of comedy. Based in the Southampton and Portsmouth area, they travel widely to put on displays which, in addition to funding their own club, raise money for handicapped children.

Johnny Chuckles – We are very pleased that once again Johnny will be entertaining children at the show, as he has for many years. As well as being able to see a traditional Punch and Judy show, they can wonder at his magical tricks which he will be performing regularly throughout both days.

Helicopter Rides – A regular feature of White Horse Shows has been the opportunity to take a helicopter flight, affording a superb aerial view of the showground, the Ridgeway, Uffington village and, of course, the famous White Horse itself. This year's helicopter is provided by Diamond Aviation (Helicopters) Ltd.

Dingle Fingle's Clowntime Crimewatch – A new attraction at this year's show – especially, but by no means exclusively, for our younger visitors – will be Dingle Fingle, undercover policeman, out to catch Slippery Sid, the notorious car thief – with your help! Featuring a replica 1920s Aston Martin and other props, including a mobile water cannon, Dingle Fingle's act will delight you with its innovative, entertaining and participative brand of clowning.

Romford Drum and Trumpet Corps – Our marching band on Sunday this year will be making their White Horse Show debut. Comprising some forty youngsters, this prestigious band has a glittering track record of appearances. They have performed before HM the Queen, HRH the Princess Royal, HRH Princess Margaret and the Prince of Wales. They have also taken part in the Lord Mayor of London's procession on more than twenty occasions. Their busy schedule has included international music festivals and contests in France, Germany, Belgium and Holland, where they have had the honour of representing the youth of Great Britain. We are delighted that the White Horse Show will now be added to their list.

Farm Animals – In this marquee you will find many animals found on smallholdings today and in the past. Some are rare breeds which enthusiasts are working hard to preserve in this country; others are more established. There are sheep, goats and pigs; also a Red Poll cow. The South Oxfordshire Poultry Club are showing a wide variety of poultry as well as laying on an egg competition. The Didcot and District Rabbit Club have an exhibit with lots of breeds of rabbit together with information for rabbit keepers. Almost all the animals are raised for a purpose, whether for milk, wool, meat, eggs or for breeding stock.

There are wool-spinning demonstrations throughout the days of the show. The Friends of Cogges Museum have a stand and demonstration of various country crafts. Feedstuff is kindly provided by White Horse Animal Feeds of Childrey. Lonsdale Estates of Kingston Lisle are supporting the display through the loan of hurdles.

Morris Dancing – Morris Dancing is probably the oldest surviving folk custom in England today. It is thought to have pre-Christian pagan origins, but these connections have faded over the centuries. 'Morris' is probably a corruption of 'Moorish' or 'Morisco', meaning strange or outlandish. Nevertheless, morris dancing seems to have been widespread and at one time perhaps every village may have had its own group, dancing in the particular style of the village.

The custom was extensively practised in the Middle Ages, the dancers being associated with the bringing of luck, fertility and healing. The dances were ritualistic and still retain a ceremonial nature today. By the end of the nineteenth century, however, few traditional styles remained and morris dancing was unknown outside the communities where it was still practised. These were mainly in the Cotswold villages of Oxfordshire and Gloucestershire, and the Welsh-English border country.

The survival of this colourful tradition today is largely thanks to a chance meeting in 1899 between Cecil Sharp and William Kimber, the musician of the Headington Quarry morris side. Sharp began to collect the dances of the Cotswolds, and his collection still forms the backbone of the repertoire of today's revival sides. Many of the tunes are themselves quite old and may be traced back to the popular songs of the seventeenth and eighteenth centuries.

Morris Men dance to maintain this long tradition and preserve a valuable heritage, but not least because they enjoy it. The dance is traditionally one of good luck and the audience is invited to participate by encircling the dancers, so that when a hat is passed round they may share in the good luck the morris brings by making a small contribution.

The Icknield Way Morris Men are the local morris side, based in the Vale of White Horse in Oxfordshire. The side is named after the Icknield School in Wantage where dancing was formed in the mid-1950s. The Icknield Way is also the ancient name of the Ridgeway passing White Horse Hill. The side dances in blue waistcoats, each bearing a west-facing golden wyvern, the standard of the kings of Wessex in olden times.

Great West of England Heavy Horse Championships – The champion and the harness-class winner from the White Horse Show will qualify for the championships, where they will compete for the titles of 'In-hand Champion' and 'Harness Champion' respectively. These West of England titles are open to all four main breeds of heavy horse of two years and over. If a qualifier from the White Horse Show has previously qualified, the next eligible horse will go forward. The two White Horse qualifiers, who will receive special rosettes, will join the twenty-two qualifiers from the eleven other qualifying shows in competing for the titles. Winners will be declared 'Champion of Champions' in each class.

The winner of the In-hand Championship will receive a sash and trophy together with £100 in prize money. They will also hold the Sheila Adlam Trophy for one year. Prize money is given to the other qualifiers up to tenth place. A prize of a bottle of whiskey and £10 is awarded for the best plaited full tail and £10 is awarded for the best-dressed groom.

The winner of the Harness Competition receives a sash, a limited-edition horse brass from the National Horse Brass Society and a martingale together with £150 in prize money. They will also hold the Bristol and West Trophy for one year. All other qualifiers in the harness final will receive £30 prize money. The Kingham Cup is awarded for the best plaited full tail.

The White Horse Show is one of only twelve shows in the West of England in which competitors can qualify for the Great West of England Heavy Horse Championships. The championship finals will take place at Countryside Cavalcade at the Royal Bath & West Showground on Sunday 4 September.

This has explained to us, the White Horse Show Committee, why our heavy horse section had been becoming more and more popular over the last couple of years. Congratulations must go to the organiser of this section of the show, Mrs Christine Keen.

Historic Cars – The committee are most grateful to Laporte Absorbents (Baulking) Ltd for their kind sponsorship of the exhibition and parade of historic cars. Judges for this year's historic cars are Clive Avenell, Jack Clark and Tim Hills.

Military and Commercial Vehicles – Lt. Col. Richard Unwin will judge this year's exhibition of military and commercial vehicles.

Vintage Tractors – The judges are T Sawtell, Dorchester-on-Thames and M Neal, Bicester. The commentator for all events is Mr D Sarney. Details of entries are available from the organisers' caravan.

Historic Vehicles and Historic Motorcycles – The judges for this year's parade and exhibition of historic motorcycles will be Derek and Iris Guy.

The White Horse Show Committee would like to thank all those who have kindly agreed to act as judges at the 1994 show. The display of historic motorcycles at this year's show is as good as can be seen in many motor museums and is, in fact, better than most! Some of the machines date back to the turn of the century and when one looks at their immaculate condition, it is not hard to imagine the many hours of skilled work and loving care that has been bestowed upon them by their proud owners.

The competition is divided into two classes – those machines produced prior to the 1939–1945 war and those produced after that war. Prizes will be awarded for the first, second and third places, plus an award for a highly commended entrant.

A large number of the motorcycles you see today were produced in the heyday of the British motorcycle industry and even their names will evoke nostalgic memories: BSA, Triumph, Norton, Panther, Rudge, AJS and Ariel, to name but a few. It is interesting to see that machines that were produced as economy transport are now attracting the restorers' skills. The humble BSA Bantam is a good example, but for a real daydream is there anything one can compare with a Manx Norton? Run on Castrol R of course!

The restoration of any form of machine can evoke much lively discussion. How far should the restorer take this project? Returning a machine to the manufacturers' original specification is the aim of many enthusiasts, while others endeavour to improve upon the finish and presentation.

The committee owe a great thanks to both Derek and Ann Kelsey for the hard work they have put in to continue and expand this section of our show.

Charity and Information Stalls – There are informative stands about crime prevention, the fire service, kidney donations, the Royal British Legion and the Samaritans, to name but a few. Several other charities will be running stalls including Save the Children Fund, RNLI, Prospect Foundation, Guide Dogs for the Blind, RSPCA, Foundation for Nephrology, Friends of Stowford House, Churchill Kidney Unit, Swindon and Wootton Bassett Cats Protection League, the Worldwide Fund for Nature, West Oxon Animal Rescue and the RAF Association. The RSPCA would like to remind all dog owners that 'Dogs die in hot cars'. Water for dogs is available at their stand.

Craft and Trade Stands – At this year's White Horse Show you will find dozens of craft stalls catering for every possible interest. There are too many to list, but they include: sugarcraft, pyrography, hand-painted porcelain, wood-turned items, English wines, pottery, hand-made knitwear, wrought iron, needlecraft, leatherware, glass engraving, paintings, brass and copper jewellery, ceramic vases, home-made cakes, dried flowers, wooden toys, Mexican jewellery and clothes, lace, doughcraft, caricatures, greeting cards, shells, walking sticks, hats, canal-boat art, thatching etc. Further details are available from the committee bus.

In Marquee Six this year you will find stands specially devoted to models and other hobbies.

Don't miss the stall selling some very attractive White Horse gifts and souvenirs. You'll find T-shirts, table mats, horse brasses, bookmarks, half-pint tankards, pens and lots more, at amazingly cheap prices. We also have a number of trade stands who can sell you conservatories, plants, new cars, clothes and lots more.

Thunderboxes and Baths – This you will find among the trade stands. Mr Wells of Shepton Mallet has been exhibiting at shows for over twenty years. He tries to put together a different collection of exhibits every year.

This year he is concentrating on old toilets. For the last twenty-five years he has been in possession of a 'Two Holer', which originated in Pollyfont, Cornwall. It is made up with a timber and paper enclosure to show what it was like in olden days. The Rev. Henry Moule invented the 'earth closet' and this was patented by him in 1860. The one in Mr Wells's possession is circa 1900. The bucket beneath it is rated at twenty charges. Mr Wells has a number of adverts and articles from old newspapers on this facility.

He is bringing a sponge bath which is about 3 ft 6 in. diameter and 6 in. deep. This is circa 1900–1910 and comes with literature on its use for bathing in eau de cologne or whisky. He also has a small wooden bath that was used in his family for bathing children and doing washing.

The weather for the two days of the show was excellent and with the crowds pouring in it looked as though all the effort that had been put in to get the show back into the decent profit margin again would come good. After the show was over on the Monday we had had a really good turnout. We were pretty sure we had made a good profit with this one. It always gave me, and I am sure others on the committee, a great feeling of satisfaction. Here we were with yet another success on our hands despite all the heated arguments that we had as a committee as to the best way forward. There is little doubt that we would again be doing the same thing, as soon as the results of this one were put to rest.

Again I must reiterate that when the public turns a show like this into a success story, it is not only the show overall that benefits. All the local organisations that take the trouble to work and run their stalls at the show also gain financially for their efforts. This of course gave the White Horse Show Trust quite good guidance when it came down to awarding grants from the main fund. It was also rewarding to the show committee to see the local organisations that were prepared to try and help themselves.

The wash-up meeting for this show was duly held and some very interesting figures were produced. The profit for this show was in fact very pleasing, turning in a surplus of £7,513. With a turnover of £43,823, the profit margin was yet again insufficient to satisfy the hawks. Yet again we were going to hear how we must cut down on the expenditure – just where I did not know. At this show we got an income from the gate money of £29,505, with the recession still being felt in no uncertain terms by working people. If those savings were forced through and the standard of the shows fell, then we would be back to 1972 and Queer Street.

A brief rundown on the income side is as follows: income from all stands, £7,819; from the catering contract, £1,800; souvenir sales, £798; programme advertising, £1,175; programme sales, £885; sponsorship, £790. I am a firm believer that if we cut down on the quality of our shows then all of these incomes could, and would, fall dramatically.

To look at the expenditure side is also interesting: cost of all events, £10,829; public address and electrics, £1,954; hire of toilets, £2,450; marquee hire, £6,401; cost of police, £1,809; cost of car parking, £1,200; publicity and advertising of show, £3,151; insurance, £1,000.

If we look at the marquee hire and trade stand income on just the figures, a false impression immediately appears. First of all, the marquee used by the farm animals had to be paid for, but how could we balance this with the volume of people going through to see the animals inside? Before I go any further, anyone that saw the crowds of children and adults milling around the pig pen over both days to see a litter of very small pigs would verify how unbelievable this was. To try and put an income side to this was just impossible; to cut this marquee out as a loss would be suicidal. Congratulations must go to Anthony Parsons and his wife for putting on such a great show and creating this amount of interest in true country life.

On the hire of toilets: surely we did not have to have another never-ending debate yet again on this subject. Whatever the cost was on this facility I couldn't see us finding volunteers to dig holes and empty buckets again. On top of this, we couldn't get Sid to build transparent ones; he had gone away and, yes, the field-sub still missed him very much. With my own health not being too good after a heart attack in January of this year, I was hoping to be able to carry on fighting in the corner of the working people – they were who this show relied on for the profit margin. However, now I was on the waiting list for bypass surgery, and we would just have to be patient with the idea, as I doubted whether I would be in a position to attend all the meetings.

My thanks must go out to the wonderful help I received from the whole committee in the preparation of field for the 1994 show. My own shortfall on my normal workload made extra work for Jim Panting, Daniel Chester, Roger Jay and Paul Armishaw. They also made it quite clear to me that they would be watching me very closely to make sure that I did not overstep the mark in 1995. Of course I was very grateful for their support; it would enable me to keep an active interest in the show.

1995

I was able to attend all the meetings up to and including the December 1994 meeting and take part in all the debates regarding the cost and expenditure for the 1995 show. But on 14 December 1994, I was called into hospital for heart surgery. Therefore, I was unable to attend meetings for at least two months. But, on the bright side, I was told by the medical profession that after this time I should be fit to resume normal duties. After this I would be looking forward to doing just that.

The first meeting that I was able to attend was in March 1995. The committee had changed a little in my absence. For the benefit of myself, the full committee now was as follows: chairman, Mr Viv Boaler; secretary, Mrs T Monk; treasurer, Mr Graham Clark; arena events, Mr Barry Mills; publicity, Mr Mike Thomas; sponsorship, Mr Cuan Ryan; craft and trade stands, Mr M White; electrics and communications, Mr Bill Mattingley; historic vehicles, Ann and Derek Kelsey; Army displays, Col. Tony Bateman; heavy horses, Mrs Christine Keen; farm animals and rare breeds, Mr Anthony Parsons; stationary engines and vintage tractors, Mr Paul Armishaw; field services and sign writing, Mr Roger Jay; printing, Mr J Packford; souvenirs, Mr Brian Tilling; showground sub-committee, Mr Brian Tilling, Mr Daniel Chester, Mr Jim Panting, Mr Nigel Tilling, Mr Clive Avenell, Mr Bill Mitchell; police, PC Dave Platts.

By this time a very good selection of arena events had been booked and the 1995 show looked like another fine attraction. Our thanks must go again to Mr Jim Soden, on whose land the show would again take place. Going back to the same site year after year made the work of the field-sub just that bit easier. Our thanks must also go to Mrs Marcella Seymour for the use of her land for car-parking facilities. Thanks also to Mr Ken Freeman for his kindness in the work of mechanical post driving; to Mr Charlie Walters and Mr Jim Matthews for the delivery and supply of straw bales and to the Lonsdale Estates for the loan of hurdles. Without the help of these kind people the show could not take place.

A full and interesting programme had been booked to appear over both days, as follows:

Sunday 27 August

- 12.00 Double Decker Bus Demonstration
- 12.30 Seamarks Sheepdog Handling Display
- 13.00 Hawk Experience
- 13.30 The Coventry Corps of Drums
- 14.00 Seamarks Sheepdog Handling Display
- 14.30 Dream Team Freefall Parachute Display
- 15.00 Historic Motorcycle Parade
- 16.00 Hawk Experience
- 16.30 The Coventry Corps of Drums
- 17.00 Firebird Aerobatics
- 18.00 Show Closes

The Cricklade Band will be playing at various times during the day by the refreshment marquee.

Monday 28 August

- 11.30 Double Decker Bus Demonstration
- 12.00 Lawnmower Extravaganza
- 12.15 Hawk Experience
- 12.45 Seamarks Sheepdog Handling Display
- 13.10 The Mayflower Corps
- 13.40 The White Horse Vale VJ Day Pageant
- 14.15 Seamarks Sheepdog Handling Display
- 14.45 Dream Team Freefall Parachute Display
- 15.00 Hawk Experience
- 15.30 Historic Vehicle Parade
- 16.30 The Mayflower Corps
- 17.00 Firebird Aerobatics
- 18.00 Show Closes

The Heavy Horse Show will be taking part in its own arena from 11.00 to 16.00.

The Cricklade Band will be playing at various times during the day by the refreshment marquee.

Some interesting facts about our attractions:

VJ Day Pageant – At this year's show will be the VJ Day Pageant. The pageant is to commemorate World War II, from 1939 to 1945, and the final end of fighting – VJ Day. The war resulted in the defeat of evil, brutal and totalitarian regimes, but at the cost of millions of human lives and enormous misery and suffering.

Vale of White Horse Pageant with the Royal Scots Dragoon Pipe Band to commemorate the 50th anniversary of the end of World War II, 1995

The story of the conflict will be traced from its start on 3 September 1939 until the climax of VJ Day. It will be told in sound, by commentary and recordings of famous speeches and music, and by action, and will be staged in the main show arena. The pageant will depict the end of peace; preparations for war; the conquest of western Europe by the German forces; the evacuation of Dunkirk and the Battle of Britain; the effects on life at home; the worldwide battles of 1941 to 1944 on land, sea and in the air; D-Day; the end of fighting in Europe and then in the Far East and VJ Day.

The pageant will include an aerobatic display by an original World War II Spitfire, provided by The Fighter Collection, Duxford

Airfield. The committee wish to acknowledge and thank all who have helped to make this pageant possible. Particularly those taking part, notably: Members of the Berkshire, Oxfordshire and Buckinghamshire branches of the Royal British Legion; The Burma Star Association, Swindon branch; SSAFA, Faringdon and Wantage branches; Abingdon Sea Cadets; Mr Brian Gibbon of Start Audio & Video; Mr Ken Selway for providing his horse and wagon; the owners of the historic vehicles taking part; all members of the cast.

The committee are also thankful to Col. Peter Rosser for organising this VJ Day commemorative pageant.

The pageant will be accompanied by the Royal Scots Dragoon Guards Pipe Band, who appear by kind permission of Lt. Col. R A B Ramsden, commanding the Royal Scots Dragoon Guards.

Firebird Aerobatics present the Rover Group Aerobatics Team – A highlight of this year's show will be an aerobatic display by the Rover Group Aerobatics Team. Sponsored by Rover Group, the team pilots are the very experienced duo of Brian Lecomber and Alan Wade. A former British Freestyle Aerobatic Champion, Brian Lecomber has flown more than 2,000 displays in the past sixteen years – almost certainly a world record for any single pilot. Alan Wade has been a professional display pilot with Brian's company, Firebird Aerobatics, for the past six years, flying the air show circuit in Britain and Europe.

After an intensive work-up period the team have created a spectacular display which is notably different to any other team.

'Most teams start with good formation pilots and develop the more esoteric aerobatics later,' says Lecomber. 'We are doing it the other way round, with two unlimited solo men to begin with. This means we have all the wild manoeuvres – *lomcevaks*, knife-edge flicks – which are not normally used by teams.'

The brand new Extra 300s used by the team are the latest state-of-the-art specialist aerobatic machines: 300 hp providing acceleration of nought-to-sixty in five seconds on take-off, carbon-fibre wing stressed to over 20 G, and a roll-rate of 370 degrees per second. They even have passenger seats.

Hawk Experience – Hawk Experience is one of the country's leading falconry display teams. It provides an opportunity to see breathtaking birds from around the world. Its many film and TV appearances have included *The Really Wild Show*, *Emmerdale*, *Yorkshire Glory* and numerous regional programmes. At the White

Horse Show you will see dramatic free-flying displays of hawks, falcons and owls, as well as the magnificent splendour of a roaring eagle. All the birds are flown to perfection with an informative commentary and audience participation. In between displays you will be able to see the birds close up and the falconer will be available all day to answer your questions.

Seamark's Sheepdog Handling Display – Norman Seamark is chairman of the international sheepdog society. He is a member of the judges' panel and has judged interstate trials in the USA and extensively on the continent. Two years ago Norman organised and judged the first ever Italian sheepdog trial. He was on the panel of judges at the first BBC 2 series of *One Man and His Dog*.

Norman trained Paul Heine to work a sheepdog and then compete at the prestigious Woburn Trial for the BBC's series *In at the Deep End*.

Norman demonstrates the skills of the dogs working the sheep at home on the farm. Each phase of the display is part of the everyday work needed to shepherd the 2,000 sheep kept on the farm. Children are invited to take part in the display, to act as obstacles. Please, parents, if your child is invited let them take part, as they will come to no harm. It will also let them know what country life is all about.

The Mayflower Corps – The Mayflower Corps from Billericay was formed in 1973 as an all-girls' drum and trumpet band. They soon became recognised as one of the leading youth bands in the country. In 1985 the band opened up its membership to boys in order to maintain its high standards. The band has a fully valved brass section and a comprehensive percussion section. These, together with the colour guard, offer a unique style of musical presentation with precision formation marching. The corps changes its music and display every year to give an entertaining and colourful performance. The corps is a member of both the British Youth Band Association and the British Drum Corps Federation. It has appeared on television on several occasions including Channel 4's *Bands of Gold*. The corps has twice been invited to take part in the Lord Mayor's Show in London and has on two consecutive years opened the City of London Festival. They are also well known at fêtes, carnivals and similar functions throughout the country, and have frequently travelled abroad to give displays in Holland and other European countries.

The Dream Team Parachute Display Company – The Dream Team are one of the most professional civilian display teams in the country. Based in Northamptonshire, the team train at RAF Weston-on-the-Green, utilising the superb facilities of the Royal Air Force Sports Parachute Association. The Dream Team offer a very colourful display package, utilising flags and streamers, which are trailed by each member of the team after their parachutes are opened.

The standard team format is a four-man display from a Cessna aircraft at 4,000 feet. They have only ten seconds in which to link together while travelling in freefall at 120 mph.

The Dream Team was started by Geoff Wood who is an ex-RAF parachute jumping instructor. Hand-picked from ex-services personnel, the team now includes some military 'guest' parachutists whose skills and expertise are called upon from time to time to complement the team line-up.

RAF Weston-on-the-Green is a full-time Military Drop Zone (DZ) which operates a weekend club for civilian and guest members. The centre offers instruction in all aspects of parachuting, from novices to professional skydivers, and is the home of two current British National Championship Teams who will be representing Britain at the World Championships in September. Parachute courses are available to anyone over the age of sixteen and instruction ranges from full weekend courses using either square or round parachutes, to tandem parachute jumps and accelerated freefall.

Throughout the season the PDC Dream Team will perform over twenty displays at air shows, village fêtes, football stadiums, rock concerts and many more. Last year, team members performed in front of the Prince of Wales as part of the Prince's Trust, and were privileged to be introduced personally before the display. During the 1993–94 season, PDC directors Geoff Wood and Simon Ward jumped into most of the European Grand Prix Races dressed as 'Sonic' and 'Tails', as part of the SEGA sponsorship of Williams Renault and Damon Hill. Some avid football fans will probably have seen PDC skydivers perform as 'The Labatt's Skydiving Mounties' when they landed in the Nottingham Forest football ground in front of 26,000 spectators, watched by an estimated 2 million viewers on Sky TV.

Skydiving and display parachuting are not as dangerous as some people would like to believe. In the hands of experts, a parachute display is one of the most graceful, exciting and thrilling spectacles you will ever see.

Watership Brass – We are very pleased to welcome Watership Brass, who are performing for the first time at the White Horse Show. They will be playing a selection of band music at various times on Sunday.

The Model Exhibition in Marquee Two – In Marquee Two can be found a varied display of brilliant hand-made models by the exhibitors. A list of exhibitors and their models are as follows:

Joe Scutts and his wife Sadie – Joe and his wife Sadie from Swindon have been exhibiting at our show for twenty years now and have always created an immense amount of interest in their fairground and gypsy caravan models and many others. Joe and his family have won many awards up and down the country. Joe's daughter Kay has a lovely collection of canal boats. Joe has exhibited at the International Model Show at Halton for many years. It is always a pleasure to see Joe attending our show, where there will always be a welcome for him and his family.

Richard Eeles – Richard Eeles ('Riding all the time!') from Bampton has displayed his models at the International Model Show. He is in the process of building an Orbiter, a replica of the one travelling with Wilson's funfair from the Birmingham area. With Richard will be the 'Grand Old Man of Modelling', Ted Miles from Witney, with his miniature organs, traction engines and caravans. Ted has been on the modelling circuit for many years. He is one of the organisers of the traditional church service on Noyce's Gallopers at the famous Witney Feast. He is a believer in traditional fairgrounds.

David James – David from Swindon has one of the best model funfairs in the country today. David has been exhibiting his funfair rides, all built from cereal packets and scrap materials, since the age of twelve. He has travelled to the International Model Exhibition many times. People cannot believe that the whole layout is made from scrap. This exhibit takes David two hours to set up.

Mrs Maureen Cook – Maureen from Swindon, with her collection of hand-knitted cottages and church, has only been exhibiting on the modelling circuit for the last three years. This exhibit has been the talking point wherever it is shown. It has won first prize at the Hobbies Exhibition in Bedfordshire, first prize at the West of England Show at St Agnes in Cornwall, and last year it won first prize at the Essex Country Show. A few weeks ago it won first prize for best non-working exhibit at Banbury Traction Engine Rally.

Ian Gerrard – Ian hails from Oxford and will be displaying his model for the first time. This is a collection of buildings representing a foundry-smithy and wagon works, known as 'The Foundry'. The original is now extinct, with new houses on the site.

Philip Webb – Philip comes from Swindon and is well known for his working model fairground rides. They have been displayed at the International Model Exhibition. They won first prize at the Hobbies Exhibition in Bedfordshire and also at Eversley Model Show.

Unfortunately lack of space and information prevents us giving more details here on the other exhibitors taking part. They include Brian Arlott – road transport; Ron Collins – Southdown buses; Mr and Mrs Philip Bratley – period room sets; Ray Pitts – Wantage engine; Ray Goldsmith – Mamod steam models; Mr and Mrs Hamilton – railway and lifeboat.

With the marquee measuring 20 ft by 60 ft and packed to capacity, there are plenty of exhibits inside to interest a large cross section of the general public; it is well worth a visit.

John O'Groats to Land's End Run – We are delighted to welcome a team from the Territorial Army and Royal Yeomanry who are running from John O'Groats to Land's End on behalf of Marie Curie Cancer Care. Please support them generously as they do their lap of the show field.

Double-Decker Bus Driving – Have you outgrown your Mini and want to try something bigger? As a child did you have a secret ambition to be a bus driver? Or are you just curious about what it is like to drive a bus? Well now is your chance. At this year's White Horse Show for a moderate fee you can try your hand at driving a real double-decker bus under the supervision of a fully qualified professional instructor. And, whether or not you are going to have a go yourself, be sure to watch him demonstrate in the main arena how these huge vehicles can be manoeuvred with pinpoint accuracy.

Finally, a message from the police – We hope that you have an enjoyable time here at the White Horse Show, but please do not become a victim of crime. Twice in the past opportunist thieves have struck, with our visitors being the unfortunate losers. A lady's purse was stolen when she momentarily put it down to admire articles on a stall, and a stall holder had goods stolen when her attention was distracted. The message is simple – do not make it easy for the thieves. Wallets and purses that can be seen in back pockets and on top of handbags give thieves an easy opportunity.

Visit the Thames Valley Police stand here at the show. Officers there will be pleased to answer any questions you may have on crime prevention. Here's hoping for a safe, crime-free White Horse Show.

I was pleasantly surprised at the amount of work that I was able to undertake after my recent health problems. I even had to prove to myself that I was probably fitter now than I had been for the past two years. To do so I had to wait until the coast was clear. When it was, I had to try some post driving with my fourteen-pound sledgehammer. To my amazement I found that I could use this tool without getting breathless like I did before. So there was hope that I would be able to carry on assisting with the White Horse Show.

However, with good weather over the two days of this, the 1995 show, the profit margin did drop to £5,000. With the gate receipts practically identical to the 1994 show, one only had to look at the cost of the VJ Pageant, which stood at £2,500. With the rest of the income and expenditure nearly identical to that of the 1994 show, it was plain to see why the profit had fallen by £2,500. To me, and thankfully the majority of our committee, this was money well spent. Perhaps this would bring home to a great deal of people the gratitude that we owe to the unfortunate people that did not return after this terrible conflict. The fallen had paid the extreme price, to give us a better world to live in. That should never, ever be forgotten. I for one will never forget this terrible chapter in our history and intend that these memories will be passed down through my family.

As for the pageant, this was a great spectacle, bringing home some of the very hard times that this chapter in our life had given us. The committee were certainly grateful to all those that took part.

With the 1995 show over and behind us, more exciting things

were looming. The 1995 show was our twenty-fourth, so next year we would be celebrating our Silver Jubilee – yes, twenty-five years of White Horse shows. This was some achievement and certainly something to celebrate; where were all the preachers of doom and knockers who said it would not last? For some unknown reason they seemed to have lost their voices; I wonder why?

Of course there have been annual summer fairs and celebrations going on in and around Uffington and the famous White Horse for centuries, but the present Uffington White Horse Show had been going for 'only' twenty-four years.

Considering that this was a venture organised by the late John Little, with help from a dedicated group of village volunteers in their spare time, this was nothing short of a great achievement. I am sure that John, Harry and Hugh ('The Three Wise Men') would have been pleased with the result, especially after our great struggle in the first two or three years to get the whole thing up and running. Now we were about to enter 1996 with the task of making that show something special. We had talked about quite a few things, informally, over the last few weeks. Now was the time to start putting some of these things to the forefront and making them a reality.

1996

The first task was to compile a list of the committee members since the inaugural show in 1972 and try to trace their whereabouts now. As there were only two of the original 1972 committee still on the present one, and just me with a complete set of minutes from 1972 to the present day, I had that task to perform. This would give me something to occupy my mind during the long dark evenings in the winter. The only other member of the original task force was, of course, Bill Mitchell. It seemed impossible that Bill and myself would be entering our thirty-sixth year since we first started in April 1960 to raise money for a new village hall. This was the twenty-fifth year since the shows were started by John Little in 1972. How time flies.

However, after many nights meticulously going through all the minutes, I had finally compiled a list together with each member's organising responsibilities and time spent on the committee. I just hoped that I had not missed anyone out. The list was as follows:

- Mrs Joan Little – assistant secretary, 1972; secretary, 1973 to 1978; printing 1979 to 1987. Also widow of the late John Little.
- John Little – founder of the White Horse Shows, 1972; chairman, 1972 to 1978; president, 1979 to 1986.
- Mrs Ivy Curzon – secretary, 1972.
- Mr Derek Witts – trade and model stands, 1972 to 1977.
- Mrs Peg Connors – founding members of the Village Hall Building Fund Committee in 1960. In 1972 this Committee was enlarged to form the Thomas Hughes Memorial Trust and White Horse Show. Peg retired in 1982.
- Mr Mick Connors – like his wife, Peg, Mick was a founding

member; general fund-raising, 1960 to 1972; showground services, 1972 to 1988.

Mrs Evelyn Adams – another founding member of the Village Hall Building Fund Committee in 1960; general fund-raising, 1960 to 1982.

Mr Hugh Shorten – Hugh had the unthankful task of being treasurer of the Thomas Hughes Memorial Trust, 1972 to 1982; the White Horse Show treasurer, 1972 to 1978.

Mrs Marion Wallis – secretary to the Thomas Hughes Memorial Trust, 1972 to 1982; assistant to treasurer at White Horse shows, 1972 to 1978.

Mr Ron Liddiard – involved with the gymkhanas, 1972 to 1977; umpire at period cricket match, 1972; welly-wanging, 1974.

Mr and Mrs John Mace – show field, 1974 to 1981.

Mr Peter Erskine – show treasurer, 1979 to 1991; White Horse Trust treasurer, 1982 to present time.

Mr Roger Cummins – trade stands, 1976 to 1983; vice chairman, 1979 to 1983; chairman, 1983 to 1985; field services, 1985 to 1990.

Mrs Greta Cummins – trade stands, 1983 to 1988; show secretary, 1987.

Mr Barry Godsell – field services, 1980 to 1983; vice chairman, 1983 to 1985; chairman, 1985 to 1988; arena events, 1989 to 1994.

Mr and Mrs Peter White – founding members of the heavy horse show; heavy horse show, 1976 to 1981; arranged Dick Chipperfield's Racing Camels, 1978.

Brigadier Harry Hopkinson – founding members of the show, 1972; buy-a-brick campaign, 1972 to 1975; organisation, 1975 to 1979; chairman, 1979 to 1983.

Mrs Ann Hopkinson – widow of the late Brigadier Harry Hopkinson; organised and ran dog show, 1979 to 1986.

Mrs Trish Follows – show secretary, 1980 to 1986.

Mrs Lynda Chester – show secretary, 1979.

- Mr David Dowst – publicity and arena events, 1979 to 1984.
- Mr Sid Warren – organiser of gymkhana, 1981 to 1986; showground, 1981 to 1987.
- Mr John Clarke – stationary engines, 1981 to 1985.
- Mrs Josie Drew – refreshments, 1977 to 1983.
- Mrs Stella Mattingley – refreshments, 1984 to 1989.
- Mrs Kath Larkin – refreshments, 1984 to 1989.
- Mr Jim Larkin – trade stands, 1988 to 1994.
- Mr Alton Bailey – field services, 1976 to 1984.
- Mr Paul Smythe – field services, 1984 to 1989.
- Mr Charles Philo – stationary engines, 1984 to 1990; assistant to arena events, 1991 to 1993.
- Mrs Sue Philo – show secretary, 1988 to 1994.
- Mr and Mrs Don North – rare and minority breeds, 1988 to 1990.
- Mrs J Cooper – rare and minority breeds, 1988 to 1990.
- Mr Roger Jay – field services, 1990 to 1995; road signs, 1994 to 1995.
- Mr Martin Elliot – dog show, 1987 to 1989.
- Dr Alan Rosevear – showground services, 1978 to 1981.
- Mr Dave Shirley – stationary engines, 1989 to 1991.
- John and Betsy Mathews – rare and minority breeds, 1984 to 1988.
- Mr Neal Eades – publicity and sponsorship, 1993.
- Mr David Whitfield – Sports & Social Club representative, 1981 to 1983.
- Mr Reg Keen – car parking, 1979.
- Mr Dave Mularkey – car parking, 1976 to 1978.
- Mr J Packford – sign writing, 1974 to 1976.
- Mr Dick Fawcett – publicity, 1976 to 1978; stationary engines, 1976 to 1980.
- Miss Ann Chambers – gymkhana, 1974 to 1980.

Mr Frank Chambers – gymkhana, 1974 to 1980; commentator on heavy horse show, 1976 to 1992.

Mr Jim Ormerod – show secretary, 1979 to 1980.

Mr Jack Jeeves – field services, 1972 to 1976.

Mr R Turner – field services, 1979.

Mr and Mrs B Mills – heavy horses, 1982 to 1983.

As can be seen from this list, it had taken a great deal of time and patience to keep this show on the road to be able to celebrate twenty-five years of what can only be described as a successful money-raising event for the three villages. We were of course extremely grateful to all fifty of these past members. During their dedicated time on this committee you could guarantee that for each one of these past members, they were outnumbered at least six to one by our critics. But these critics made our life more enjoyable when we could prove them wrong, as we had done so many times in the past. To follow this list of past committee members up to the 1996 show, the twenty-fifth in our long run, I will also list the 1996 committee and when they joined the completely mad outfit, to get us where we were:

Mr Viv Boaler – chairman; joined 1976; historic vehicles, 1976 to 1982; publicity, 1982 to 1990; chairman, 1990 to 1996.

Mrs Tina Monk – secretary; joined 1995; secretary, 1995 and 1996.

Mr W Clark – treasurer; joined 1991; treasurer, 1991 to 1996.

Mr Cuan Ryan – publicity; joined 1994; publicity, 1994 to 1996.

Mr M White – craft and trade stalls; joined 1995; craft and trade stalls, 1995 to 1996.

Mr W Mattingley – electrics and communications; joined 1983; electrics and communications, 1983 to 1996.

Colonel Tony Bateman – Army displays; joined 1981; gymkhana, 1981 to 1986; Army displays, 1984 to 1996.

Mr and Mrs Derek Kelsey – historic vehicles; joined 1982; historic vehicles, 1982 to 1996.

- Mr Barry Mills – arena events; rejoined 1992; arena events, 1992 to 1996.
- Mrs Christine Keen – heavy horse show; joined 1982; heavy horse show, 1982 to 1996.
- Mr Anthony Parsons – farm animals and minority breeds; joined 1990; farm animals and minority breeds, 1990 to 1996.
- Mr Paul Armishaw – stationary engines and vintage tractors; joined 1990; stationary engines and vintage tractors, 1990 to 1996.
- Mr Roger Jay – field services and sign writing; joined 1990; field services and sign writing, 1990 to 1996.
- Mr Brian Tilling – souvenirs and showground layout; joined 1960; souvenirs, 1973 to 1996; showground layout, 1972 to 1996.
- PC David Platts – police, security and traffic; joined 1988; police, security and traffic, 1988 to 1996.
- Mr Mike Thomas – advertising and publicity; joined 1989; advertising and publicity, 1989 to 1996.
- Mr Daniel Chester – showground layout; joined 1983; showground layout, 1983 to 1996.
- Mr Bill Mitchell – chairman, Village Hall Building Fund Committee and showground; joined 1972; chairman, Village Hall Building Fund Committee, 1960 to 1972; showground, 1972 to 1996.
- Mr Clive Avenell – showground; joined 1980; showground, 1980 to 1996.
- Mr Jim Panting – showground; joined 1983; showground, 1983 to 1996.
- Mr Nigel Tilling – showground; joined 1995; showground, 1995 to 1996.

It may seem to the layman that this was a very large committee to run a country show, but that could not have been further from the truth. I know from the time that I have spent carrying out my duties for this show that it took every one of these people a considerable amount of time and patience throughout the whole year to achieve a successful show. As well as all these dedicated people it still involved a great deal many more to make the show become a reality. The committee owed a debt of gratitude to the following over the years who had made it all possible:

Land owners that we were indebted to over the years 1972 to 1996 – Mr R Spence, Mr G Parrot, Mr J Mildenhall, the Lonsdale Estates, Mr B Cale, Mr J Matthews, Mr C Nash, Mr R Bracey, Mr J Read, Sir Adrian Swires, Mr J Soden, Mr A Seymour, Mrs A Seymour, Mr R Liddiard, Mr T Underwood and the Uffington Sports and Social Club.

Furthermore, we were also indebted to the following people, who had helped unsparingly with their time and patience over the years in supplying and assisting in the field services. Again, without their help there would have been no shows. Thanks to – Mr Charlie Walters, Mr A McIntosh, Mr Ken Freeman, Roy Avenell and sons, Mr Tony Coxhead, Mr David Coxhead, Mr Mick Coxhead, Mr C Matthews, the Lonsdale Estates, Mr Sid Warren.

When one looks at these lists they may, to some people, seem long and unnecessary. But, on the other hand, let's not forget that every person on these lists must have had the support of their partners in life. I know that I had the support of my wife, Myra, throughout my time with the show. Likewise, all the other people involved had the support of their partners; again, if that had not been the case, then the show would not have gone on. As far as the 1996 show was concerned, all the people involved over the years were going to be invited to a special celebration evening on the Sunday of the show. All past committee members were to be given a copy of the 1972 show programme as a souvenir of this, the Silver Jubilee.

Another of my tasks was to obtain some special souvenirs to sell at this show. I had already been able to get a catalogue of various small goods with this in mind. On discussing this at one of our meetings it was decided to purchase a commemorative eight-inch collectors' plate as the main souvenir for this occasion.

The firm whose catalogue we had chosen the plate from were

in Derby. This was no problem, from my point of view. I decided, after speaking to the sales department, that I would visit their premises to discuss in more detail the requirements we had. After all was said and done, my past employment with British Rail entitled me to some free passes each year. So for this purpose it was not going to cost me anything to get there.

On arriving at the firm's premises I spent all of two hours in their sales room before we actually got the outline of the White Horse to a satisfactory and acceptable shape. With all of the critics only too ready to jump on the bandwagon, if it was not to the correct shape and angle, near enough was just not good enough. The plates we were to have would be a set of 200 on a limited-edition basis, with each plate numbered 1 to 200. Three or four days afterwards, I was called back to Derby to see the first prototype plate. On arrival back at the firm's premises, lo and behold, the White Horse was perfect in every way but the years printed on the plate were 1971 to 1996. Pointing this out to the young lady in the sales room was the problem; she insisted that, if the 1996 show was our twenty-fifth, then we must have started in 1971. Pointing out her error in plain English was extremely difficult. I insisted that we actually started the shows in 1972 and that the 1996 show would be the twenty-fifth and be the Silver Jubilee – to no avail. If I had not been involved with the start in 1972, she may have convinced me that she was right and I was wrong. In the end I had to write the years down in order from 1972 to 1996 on a piece of paper, and then get her to count them. This finally convinced her that I was not joking and that 1972 to 1996 was in fact the correct solution. I made our position perfectly clear, and said that when they had made the necessary alterations I would be prepared to travel yet again to Derby to check on the correctness of the product. Needless to say, we parted in the best of spirits after a really good laugh over the whole thing.

Whilst there I did in fact place a firm order for 250 souvenir Uffington White Horse thimbles, which I could pick up on my next visit to Derby. These were also useful as we did supply other retail outlets; in this way we were able to keep the price down to a reasonable level and still make a reasonable profit for our troubles.

On my next visit to Derby everything turned out perfect, the thimbles were ready for collection and the commemorative plate turned out to be perfect this time. I was thus able to place a firm order for the 200 plates as planned. Instead of having them loose, for an extra 70p each we could have them boxed. I therefore thought that if we were going to have them numbered we might just as well do the job properly and have them boxed. Therefore for £5.35 each we had a good souvenir that hopefully we could make a reasonable profit on. We had now to find a way of having 200 authenticity certificates produced and numbered to go with the respective plates. Much to my relief, Derek and Ann Kelsey turned up trumps; they offered to get these printed, but the chairman would have to sign each one individually.

At our March meeting we decided unanimously on the grants recommended by the White Horse Show Trust, which were as follows: Sports and Social Club, £1,000; Uffington, Woolstone and Baulking minibus, £4,200; White Horse Preschool, £300; Uffington C. of E. Primary School, £500; Museum, £250; Afternoon Club, £300; Saunders Trust, £75.

As can be seen, these grants exceeded the profit of the 1995 Show by just over £2,000. This was made possible by a small surplus held over by the trust together with the profit of investment from the disaster fund. This profit on investment of the disaster fund was entirely due to the shrewdness of the trust treasurer, Mr Peter Erskine.

By this time we were well under way with the organisation of the 1996 show, as well as piecing together the Sunday evening's entertainment for celebrating our Silver Jubilee. There had been a lot of suggestions as to the best way of going about setting this up and on which day it should be held. Some of the committee wanted to do the celebrating on the Monday evening, but I personally was against this suggestion, on the grounds of our workload in clearing the field after the show was over. Soon the rest of the field-sub fell in with my feelings on this matter, as it was normal practice to start recovering the rope from around the field and car-parking areas as soon as possible on the Monday evening. We always tried to get the rope rolled up and put in the store van. This was for two reasons: one, the rope was then hung up in the dry; two, this was for security reasons. Once in particular, after the very wet Monday of the 1986 show when this chore did not get completed, a considerable amount of rope went walkies. Of course, still trying to keep expenditure under control, rope was becoming an expensive asset to have to replace. On top of this we did try also to start removing posts and placing them in heaps ready for removal from the site on the Tuesday morning. After all, the manpower on the ground after a show was always very thin – usually myself and one or two others. As we always tried to be clear of the field on the Saturday after the show, we could ill afford to lose the additional manpower that was available on the Monday evening.

At the end of the discussions on this subject the majority decision was that the celebrations would take place on the Sunday evening. With this I was very relieved as the sooner we could get clear of the field, the sooner my life could return to normal. Although I must say, even after the hard work of preparing and clearing away a show, it still gave me a feeling of satisfaction – somehow you felt that you had achieved the goal that you had set out to achieve. I am equally sure that everyone on the committee had that feeling of satisfaction and achievement after it was all over.

Tony had of course been volunteered to be the commentator for the evening's celebrations. But, true to form, Tony had been busy and had done his homework ready for the evening of the Sunday. There follows some of Tony's notes for that evening. After calling the crowd to order, he would commence cheerily:

> Good evening everyone!
>
> Tonight we are celebrating the Silver Jubilee of our White Horse Show, an annual event which has done so much for our three villages of Uffington, Woolstone and Baulking.
>
> In some ways, this show is the successor to the village feasts of bygone years. Perhaps its nearest forerunner was the annual scouring of the White Horse, last held on 17 and 18 September 1857. However, something similar occurred in association with bank holidays when they were instituted; indeed there is a photograph of such a gathering in 1899.
>
> In 1780 the event attracted 30,000 people; one wonders where

they all came from and how they got there and how long they stayed. In such times gone by, bear baiting, cockfighting and prize fighting were all features of life in the Vale, and may well have occurred at the scouring. Now we are more restrained, with vintage vehicles, air displays, parachute jumping, morris men and bands.

In 1857 events included: a jingling match (whatever that was), foot races, hurdle races, carthorse race in thill harness (for a new set of harnesses), wrestling and back-swording for handsome prizes.

Legend has it that one year Tim Gibbons, an Uffington man, turned highwayman, rode up, entered the back-swording competition, won the prize, and then galloped off to avoid arrest. There was even a 'Prize for the best grin through a horse collar'; like my tractor prizes I feel this must have been based upon pure prejudice.

However, to turn to more modern times, the event which probably led indirectly to our show was when the servicemen returned from the 1914–18 war. A collection had been raised for their benefit and very nobly they decided to dedicate this money to the purchase of a Nissen hut. This served the village as a hall until the floor rotted in 1960 and it was condemned.

So, in May 1960, a Parish Council committee was formed and tasked to raise money to build a new hall. It is very appropriate that its chairman Bill Mitchell, and members Brian Tilling and Mick Connors, who have all worked so selflessly for the show ever since, should be here tonight. Over the next eleven years they raised £3,000, some of which was used to sponsor the first real White Horse Show. This, under the inspired chairmanship of the late John Little, was called the Tom Brown's Festival, and held in 1972 on the 150th anniversary of the author Thomas Hughes' birth. The souvenir programme of that first show contains much information of importance, notably the lists of all those on whose land the show has been held since, and those who have served the show on the committee and provided practical support. The festival was huge fun and a great success. It made a profit which inspired the creation of the Thomas Hughes Memorial Trust, under whose auspices the show went from strength to strength. Gradually profits mounted from £608.41 in 1973 then to £1010 in 1974, when the late Brigadier Harry Hopkinson joined the committee. By 1976 sufficient funds had been raised to build the Thomas Hughes Memorial Hall and by 1982 to finance it. So then the Thomas Hughes Memorial Trust was wound up and its funds transferred to the existing White Horse Show Trust for the wider benefit of the community.

Over the next few years the scope of the show expanded. Peter Erskine became treasurer in 1997, and still serves as treasurer of the White Horse Show Trust. Profits continued to grow from £4,302 in 1976, to £10,886 in 1980 and in 1983 the record of £11,200.

The White Horse Show Trust remains the show's sponsor and it is under its auspices that the show is run to raise money for local good causes. These have included all three churches, the C. of E. primary school, the purchase and operation of three successive community buses, the latest replacement of which was made last year. Money has been given to support the Scouts, Guides, Brownies, cricket, football, badminton and tennis clubs, the children's play area, the Afternoon Club and the day centre. From time to time special collections have been made, notably after the Hungerford Massacre, and of course the show has provided the venue at which other charities have raised money. Last year's Royal Yeomanry Marie Curie Cancer Care sponsored run is a good example.

In total some £129,000 has been distributed over the past twenty-five years. And that is simply an arithmetic total, which makes no allowance for inflation in terms of purchasing power. For example, the £3,300 donated in 1978 would be worth £13,000 at today's values. By the same token costs have risen astronomically from £676 in 1973 to something around £44,000 this year. This fact partially reflects legislation and partly the demand for greater sophistication. Our record year for attendance was in 1987 when 18,400 tickets were sold.

Latterly there has been more competition and perhaps an element of 'event fatigue' which has depressed attendance. Nevertheless, our audiences come from far and wide, including our twin village in France.

Throughout these years the show has developed its own unique character, providing a family day out to a formula that has evolved over the years. For many years a gymkhana was a feature, initially at Ron Liddiard's Church Farm at Baulking and run by Mr F Chambers and his daughter Ann, and latterly by Mr Sid Warren and his family, with strong support from all and sundry. Some things are constant: the Old Berks hounds have been at every show since the inception; the heavy horses have been a feature since 1976; the lawnmower racing, vintage vehicles, tractors, motorcycles and stationary engines and since 1983 the rare breeds. We have seen some splendid and very varied spectacles – the flying displays, the military bands, the country sports pageant, some splendid adult and junior motorcycle displays, including the Royal Artillery's Flying Gunners, the parachutists, the Household Cavalry Musical Ride in 1987, the Manchester Field Gun Display, and last year's VJ Day Pageant.

None of this could have been achieved without the support of the landowners and the hard work of the committee and helpers. Perhaps the most important thing of all is the fact that by working together as a community the show has given us all an example of what we can achieve, and in this respect has served us well.

I like to think that the spirits of those distant folk who carved our White Horse into the hill above 3,000 years ago look down on us now and approve. The past has been remarkable – the future is for us and our successors to build on. We will be most unwise if we discard the achievements of the past, and we must certainly adapt for the future.

Ladies and gentlemen, I give you a toast – the White Horse Show and all who have made it.

The final programme of celebrations for the Sunday evening, 25 August 1996, was to be as follows:

6.30 p.m. A short run down on the origin of the White Horse Show, its aims and past achievements, by Colonel Tony Bateman. Followed by a fanfare. Tony's address and welcome to all past committee members.

Medley of local tunes, to finish with 'Congratulations'.

Races and tug of war, run and organised by Chris Holly and Dibbs Coxhead.

Band to play intermittently.

Vote of thanks to Chris and Dibbs.

8.15 p.m. Band to play various tunes, finishing with 'Auld Lang Syne'.

9 p.m. Firework display to finalise the evening's celebrations.

Bar to be open throughout the evening.

Some refreshments will be available during the evening, as a pig roast will be taking place during the celebrations.

All the public from the villages of Uffington, Woolstone and Baulking will be invited to attend free of charge. Also all the stallholders and exhibitors will be invited to stay on for these celebrations.

As these celebrations are going to alter some of the rules that usually stand for trade stands and exhibitors over this show, the acceptance of booking acknowledgements will carry special terms for this show as a one-off. They are:

To campers – The camping ground opens noon Friday and closes noon Tuesday. The showground itself opens to exhibitors from 8 a.m. on Sunday, and opens to the public from 10 a.m. to 6 p.m. on Sunday and from 10 a.m. to 6 p.m. on Monday. Cars will be allowed on the showground before and after the show but must be cleared to the car park during the show. No vehicles should be parked next to a marquee or elsewhere on the showground, except in a prepaid outdoor stall. Other vehicles may be towed away in the interests of safety. Access to the car park will be by the extreme left-hand corner away from the road.

To marquee stall holders – Each indoor stall will be provided with two tables a minimum of 5 ft long by 2 ft wide. You should provide your own chairs. If you have your own tables and stands, please respect the allocated space of your neighbours. Each outdoor site will be marked by four corner posts and will measure four metres wide by seven metres deep. No tables will be provided. The large majority of our stallholders achieve a very high quality display and we discourage jumble sale stalls.

Our arrangements with the caterers preclude trade and craft stands from competing with them. If you think this might be the case, please call at the committee bus to clarify the point and prevent any difficulties on the day. The caterers will be offering a food and drink service to the stallholders before and during the show.

To mark our Silver Jubilee, we are inviting local villagers to a celebration evening on Sunday 25 August. After the show has closed there will be a break before this celebration starts at 6.30 p.m. There will be a silver band, pig roast, bar and other activities. The evening will culminate in a firework display. Stallholders and exhibitors are very welcome to keep their stalls open during this period or just join in the fun. The marquees, however, will have to be closed at or before dusk.

Although we have a police presence during the show and celebration evening, there is no formal security for the stalls either indoors or outdoors. Therefore, you should take your own precautions for safeguarding your stock. We cannot be held responsible for any damage or loss occurring on the showground. Please be aware, if you are not intending to remain on Sunday evening, that there will be many more people than usual on the site.

Silver Jubilee souvenir stall, 1996

For those who have not been before, the site will be signposted in the Uffington area. We are looking forward to this year's show and we hope you will be successful and enjoy the occasion. This year we have some exciting aerobatic and historic aviation displays. We hope this letter answers all your queries. If not, please call at the committee bus when arriving at the show.

By mid-July Derek and Ann Kelsey had sent out personal invitations to all past committee members. They were as follows:

Dear *****,

1996 is a special year in Uffington as the White Horse Show celebrates its Silver Jubilee. Enclosed is a special-edition programme, as a souvenir, which is a revamp of the original 1972 issue – to stir memories of days gone by.

We have been involved in the show for the past sixteen years and it is our pleasure to extend a warm invitation to you. The show gates will open at 10 a.m. on Sunday 25 and Monday 26 August and we have many special attractions, including two flying displays.

On Sunday evening from 6.30 p.m. we are holding a celebration to include a silver band, children's activities, tug of war and concluding with a fireworks display. The bar will be open and a pig roast and other foods will be available.

We do hope that you will be able to join the committee sometime over the weekend to celebrate this occasion.

If you do intend to come please complete the slip below and return it, to enable us to send you complimentary tickets.

Regards,

Ann and Derek Kelsey

As the replies started to come back from the invitations, things looked quite promising. I for one was looking forward to meeting some of our past committee members. I thought that it would be interesting to hear some of the comments that would be passed on as to our position of today. It would certainly be possible to pick up some tips – perhaps on some things that had slipped by the wayside since we first started, or some new ideas that we could pursue for future shows. After all, we were always looking for new things on the entertainment front.

One ex-member who had promised to come was no other than Sid Warren; I was really looking forward to meeting Sid again. We had all had great laughs and a lot of fun with Sid, not forgetting the terrific amount of work that he had put into the running of the show. He was always ready to drop what he was doing and help anybody who required his assistance. I know only too well that some of the things he had helped me with at times were remarkable. I knew that when I met Sid again my chores would be finished for quite a while. I also knew that Mrs Joan Little would be attending, and therefore I hoped that the show would go well as we on the committee would like to think that we had not forgotten the legacy that John had left to the villages. Also, we wanted to keep the show on the road for the foreseeable future as a continuing benefit to the three villages, which is what I believe John would have liked. When one looked to the benefits and the gains that the three villages had received over the last twenty-five years, I was sure that they could not let this show fail. We all owed it to John to keep the show on the road.

Mr Paul Armishaw had been in long negotiations with the funfair owner, Mr Hebron, concerning the donation that he usually contributed to the show profits. On this occasion Mr Hebron would not be making a donation to the show, but would be footing the bill for the cost of the firework display that would take place as part of the jubilee celebrations. Paul must be congratulated for this feat, as this was a considerable saving on the cost of our celebrations. Also, sincere thanks must go to Mr Hebron for his extreme generosity on this display.

Originally we had booked the Firebird Aerobatics Display Team for this show, but Mr Cuan Ryan had been in touch with the Aircraft Museum at Duxford and had got a great offer on a flying display by World War I aircraft. With additional sponsorship it was also decided that together with the 'Blue Max' World War I Team we could also have a World War II Spitfire as well. It was therefore decided that if we could cancel the Firebird Aerobatics Display Team without too much of a penalty then we should do so, as we would not get a better chance of getting the alternative star attraction. This of course did not please the hawk section of the committee, but after a long discussion on this item a proposal was put to the committee, seconded and overwhelmingly approved. Cuan was therefore requested by the committee to proceed along these lines and report back when appropriate. On reporting back, Cuan informed us that he had been very successful and had been able to cancel the Firebird Aerobatics Display Team without any penalty whatsoever. He had therefore booked the 'Blue Max' World War I Team together with the World War II Spitfire to appear for one turn each on both days of the show.

The 'Blue Max' World War I Team would comprise one French, one German and one English aircraft from the First World War. Add to this the awesome roar of a Spitfire again over White Horse Hill and I believe that the right decision had been made. I knew for one thing that I would be outside in the show field to watch and listen to the roar of that Spitfire's engine.

In the end a full supporting programme of events was booked; as always the only thing we could hope for was good weather and the crowds to turn up. The final programme was as follows:

Sunday 25 August

- 12.00 Thamesdown Double Decker Bus Recovery Demonstration
- 12.30 Solent Motorcycle Display Team
- 13.00 Dream Team Freefall Parachute Display Team
- 13.30 Pathfinder Dog Demonstration Display
- 14.00 City of Coventry Corps of Drums
- 14.30 'Blue Max' World War I Aircraft Flying Display
- 15.00 Historic Motorcycle Display
- 15.45 Pathfinder Dog Demonstration Display
- 16.15 World War II Spitfire Flying Display
- 16.45 Solent Motorcycle Display Team
- 17.15 City of Coventry Corps of Drums
- 18.00 Show Closes

Lawnmower racing will take place in its own arena over both days of the show.

Monday 26 August

- 11.15 Thamesdown Double Decker Bus Recovery Demonstration
- 12.00 Dream Team Freefall Parachute Display Team
- 12.30 Solent Motorcycle Display Team
- 13.00 Romford Drum and Trumpet Corps
- 13.30 Historic Tractor Parade
- 14.00 'Blue Max' World War I Aircraft Flying Display
- 14.30 Historic Motor Vehicle Parade
- 15.30 Royal British Legion Pageant
- 16.00 World War II Spitfire Flying Display
- 16.30 Solent Motorcycle Display Team
- 17.00 Romford Drum and Trumpet Corps
- 18.00 Show Closes

From 11.00 to approximately 16.30 the heavy horse show will be taking place in its own arena.

The weather on the Sunday was very kind to us – dry and sunny but with a blustery wind at times. During the afternoon some of the invited old committee members started to arrive and it was certainly nice to get out into the showground and have a good chatter. It was a great pleasure to meet up with Sid Warren again and our reminiscing of the past brought back some very fond memories of past shows. In fact, if some people were near us at times when we fell about laughing they must have wondered if we had taken leave of our senses. But I am sure meeting Sid again after all this time was the highlight of this show. The Sunday evening entertainment went off very well, with a considerable gathering of local villagers really enjoying themselves into the bargain. The evening sport and fun celebrations were organised by Christine Holly and David Coxhead. These went really well and were enjoyed by both the participants and spectators alike. However, I do not think anyone really knew who won the inter-village tug of war, as spectators seemed to pile in and help the team that was losing at the time. But what mattered was that all and sundry were enjoying themselves. The evening came to an end quite a lot later than was planned with a spectacular firework display donated by Mr Hebron. To this end we must sincerely thank Mr Hebron for his extreme generosity for the fitting end to our Silver Jubilee celebrations. But end they had to, as on Monday morning it was back to business as usual.

Being a committee member right from the start, through thick and thin, the good times and the bad, I believe has had its just rewards. Yes, we have had the knockers and the preachers of doom over the years, but on the Monday when complete strangers came up to committee members and congratulated us on our achievements over that period of time, it made every one of us proud to be a part of that achievement.

The Monday part of the show was perhaps an anti-climax after the Sunday. It still went well, though perhaps the attendance was down a little on the usual Monday attendance. However, we were not complaining too much about that. After the show closed on the Monday evening we were able to get cracking on rope winding and post pulling ready for the big clean up on the following days. After the last four or five shows we always aimed to be cleared up and have the materials stowed away by the Friday evening.

At the wash-up meeting there were quite a few points that would have to be raised. One of the main ones was keeping the standard of the show up, to keep it being a draw for as big a cross section of the general public as possible. While walking around this show it was the one thing that I seemed to be hearing in conversation with stall holders and the general public alike – that they thought that perhaps the standard was beginning to drop a little on past years. The two things that I heard most were that the demonstrating of local rural crafts and the military bands were still missing.

Like it or not I had to agree with this assessment by the general public. In the past when a military band was in the arena I made a point of going on top of the commentary stand. Not only was it my favourite music, but the precision and movement of the military was something only they could perform to such accuracy. When watching them perform from this vantage point and looking to the crowd of spectators gathered around the arena, it was only then that you realised the popularity of this arena event. It was quite normal to see the public ten or twelve deep all the way round the arena. If the military bands had this pulling power over the public then they were certainly good value for the money spent on them. Also, this being a country show then, yes, we ought to be having more demonstrations of local rural crafts, thatching, pottery making, glass-blowing, smithcraft, and a cooper just to name a few. These would create more interest in a fair proportion of the general public.

At the wash-up meeting of this show there was the usual pessimistic preaching of the hawks. Their view was that we were still going to have to cut our expenditure on the shows, as we were spending far too much for such a small return. On the other side of the debate there were the rest of the committee, still with the opposite view that we had become too complacent and let the standard of the show drop. This in turn had seen the support from the general public drop as well, resulting in fewer people attending the shows. This of course would eventually see even smaller profits than in the past.

It was my own personal opinion that this was one bitter-tasting pill we were going to have to swallow to keep this show on the road. After all, the politicians were calling this period a 'mini slump', which to me was an understatement. Working people were finding the cost of living on the rise and were beginning to cut back on the amount they could spend on entertainment.

Therefore, they were not prepared to accept further increases in entrance fees as well as a drop in standards. After a long discussion on the subject it was agreed to go away and come back to the next meeting with some ideas on how we could achieve the main aim of keeping the show going. Again it was my own opinion that we had to accept that we were in a recession and that the money was not about to enable us to keep large profits coming in. But, if we kept the show going on a value-for-money basis, we would be in a position, when the recession was over, to still have a show that would continue to be of great benefit to the local community.

Somehow we had to reach a compromise at the next meeting and hopefully be able to get on with planning the show for 1997.

When the next meeting finally came upon us we did have one thing in favour of a continuation of the show. This was that we had come out of the 1996 show with a profit of £4,000. A lot of us thought this was very good, as we had incurred extra expenses because of the jubilee celebrations. But we still needed to be vigilant about the fact that we couldn't be too loose on the side of the expenditures – we all had a responsibility to keep this in check. However, on the alternative side, we could not afford the standard of the show to fall out of favour with our paymasters, the general public. It was thus decided at this meeting that the show had to carry on, but a decision had to be made on the way forward. After a long meeting it was agreed on a majority decision that a budget would have to be worked out and strictly adhered to for the 1997 show. To enable this to be worked out, each section of the show would be requested to work within their respected allocation of expenditure. If by any chance they were in difficulties on this front they would have to report back to the full committee for any extra expenditure. Again, this was agreed by a small majority as the way forward.

It was while Jim, Daniel and I were working on the 1996 show that I had indicated to these long-time show colleagues that this could well be my last large commitment to the building of the show field. I was finding without a shadow of doubt that my health was not improving as fast as at first I had hoped. This in itself caused quite a stir amongst the field-sub and I was very surprised that the same thoughts were going through the minds of Jim and Daniel. Jim was adamant that it was time for a younger person to take his place, as he was now eighty years old; Daniel was equally determined that he was looking for pastures new and would not be available for the 1997 show. When we had cleared the show field after the 1996 event, I had a long talk with my wife Myra as to what further commitment we could give to the show in the future. After a lot of thought we decided that, with Myra's health also failing, the limit that I would be able to commit myself to would be to run the souvenir stall for the 1997 show only. But, if my experience in building the show fields over the last twenty-five years was of any use, then I would be only too glad to give any advice or go to the field for that purpose.

I believe that the wash-up meeting after the Silver Jubilee show was the only meeting that I wished that I could have avoided; but I knew that attend I must. After sitting through this meeting and listening to the debate on the financial side, it made my decision to resign just that little easier. After all, I would still be retaining my position on the White Horse Show Trust, so in some small way I would still be involved. But when the chairman asked for 'any other business', still the most difficult thing that I ever had to say to that committee was that I was resigning. When Jim and Daniel also resigned, to say that you could hear a pin drop would be an understatement. But all three of us promised that, if there was anything that we could advise them on as regards to setting up the field next year, we would be only too pleased to give it. After this we were thanked by one and all for the service that we had given to the show over the years. Another resignation that also followed was that of Colonel Bateman. Tony had also given very loyal service to the show over a number of years, dealing with the Army and arranging their displays, which was going to be missed. The meeting then came to a very sombre end.

1997

At the first meeting for the 1997 show the present chairman Viv Boaler decided that he was stepping down from that office and asked for nominations for the post. He also stated that he was prepared to remain on the committee for the foreseeable future. Only one nomination was offered and that was Derek Kelsey. True to form the rest of the committee gave him their whole-hearted support. I believed that if there was one person on the committee at that time that could take on the hawks and bring the White Horse Show back to its former glory then they had now appointed him as their chairman. I was also equally convinced that Derek would achieve this task. This task would not, in my opinion, be an easy thing to achieve. After all, the quality of the show had been slipping over the past two or three years, which I had always argued against. I have said before, and I will repeat it yet again: you can't expect the general public to keep paying the same price for an inferior show. If you do, sooner or later this will backfire on you, and over the last two or three shows we had had all the signs that it was doing just that. But now with Derek at the helm, I was sure that he would stamp his authority on the show and in time pull it back from the doldrums. This would not be achievable at the drop of a hat; it would take considerable changes over a period of at least three to four years. But I for one sincerely wished him the best of luck in his chairmanship and the return of an original White Horse Show of old. I was sure that with the support that he received from his wife Ann, he would achieve that aim.

Other committee changes for the 1997 show were as follows: secretary, Ann Kelsey; treasurer, Ray Avenell; heavy horses, Katie Avenell; Cuan Ryan joined Mike Thomas on publicity. The largest load of all fell on the shoulders of Paul Armishaw: poor Paul became responsible for stationary engines, tractors and arena events, as well as being field director. But I was sure Paul would cope with a little help from the rest of the committee, as he had been helping with nearly everything possible over the previous few years. Other events would be under the guidance of Nigel Tilling, whilst Tina Monk would be assisting Malcolm White on the trade stand side.

The 1997 show would again be held in the fields of Sower Hill Farm by kind permission of Mr Jim Soden. The committee also extended their thanks to Mrs Marcella Seymour for her kind permission for the use of fields belonging to Britchcombe Farm. Thanks were also extended to Mr Ken Freeman, Mr Charlie Walters, Mr Jim Matthews and the Lonsdale Estate for their assistance and co-operation in putting on the show, and all those many individuals from the area who put in so much time and hard work to make the show possible.

The programme of events over the two days was as follows:

Sunday 24 August

- 10.00 Thamesdown Bus Company Demonstration
- 10.30 St John Ambulance Presentation
- 10.45 Island Farm Donkey Display
- 11.00 The International Falconer
- 11.30 Tricky Tykes Terrier Racing
- 12.00 City of Coventry Corps of Drums
- 12.30 The International Falconer
- 13.00 Western Bareback Barrel Racing
- 13.30 Hercules the Strongman
- 14.00 Tricky Tykes Terrier Racing

Monday August 25

- 10.00 Island Farm Donkey Display
- 10.30 St John Ambulance Presentation
- 10.45 The International Falconer
- 11.00 Tricky Tykes Terrier Racing
- 11.30 City of Coventry Corps of Drums
- 12.00 Western Bareback Barrel Racing
- 12.30 The International Falconer
- 13.00 Tricky Tykes Terrier Racing
- 13.30 Parade of the Old Berks Hounds
- 14.00 Parade of Vintage Tractors

14.30	The Flyer Yak	14.30	The Flyer Yak
15.00	Western Bareback Barrel Racing	15.00	Historic Motor Vehicle Parade
15.45	Parade of Historic Motorcycles	15.45	Western Bareback Barrel Racing
16.30	City of Coventry Corps of Drums	16.30	City of Coventry Corps of Drums
17.30	Show Closes	17.30	Show Closes

Heavy Horse Show. Monday 25 August, 11.00 to 16.30.

The show takes place with twelve different classes in Arena 2.

Judge, Arthur Rule. Ring Steward, Bob Brickell. Collecting Steward, Ken Freeman. Commentator, Peter Davies.

The White Horse Show Committee are grateful to Thames Water Utilities, who are generously sponsoring the 1997 Heavy Horse Show.

This heavy horse show is also a qualifying event for the Royal Bath & West Show.

This will be the twenty-sixth Uffington White Horse Show, the very first having been in 1972. The event was originally staged under the chairmanship of John Little with the sole aim of raising money to replace the Uffington village hall, which had hitherto been an ageing Nissen hut dating from the First World War.

The current village hall known as the Thomas Hughes Memorial Hall was opened in 1975, but it was 1982 before the show had raised sufficient funds to finance the building and guarantee its running costs. Having achieved its original goals it was then decided that the show should continue and the White Horse Show Trust was established in order to distribute the hard-earned funds to local charities and worthy causes within the three villages of Uffington, Woolstone and Baulking.

Those benefiting from the funds raised over the years have included the C. of E. school, the museum, the three churches, local sports clubs, playschool, Scouts, Cubs, Beavers, Brownies, the Jubilee Field and the community minibus.

The achievements of the show are all the more remarkable when you realise that, while it is probably the largest and longest-running show of its kind, it is organised and run entirely by a team of volunteers who work tirelessly to make the event a success.

Some interesting facts about the participating events and trade and craft stalls at this year's show follows:

The Flyer Yak – Introduced in 1995, the Yak Flyer almost instantly became one of the most spectacular solo display acts of the season, winning acclaim from the organisers and the public for the spirited content and entertainment packed into a ten-minute sequence. The aircraft's livery is that of its sponsor, *FLYER* magazine.

First produced in 1976 as a world-class competition aerobatic aircraft, the Yak-50 went on to win the World Aerobatic Championship in that year. The Yak-50 is powered by the growling 360 hp supercharged Ivchenko engine coupled to an experimental Hoffman three-blade propeller providing stunning performance.

Starting with a dive on the crowd at 270 mph, pulling up from 200 ft at plus 9 G into a vertical roll and through three spins in all three axes ending in an inverted flat spin. This display has experienced pilots asking, 'How do you do that?' In all there are over fifty different flight attitudes in this spectacular routine. Manoeuvres include rolling circles, outside Cubans, lomcevaks, stall turns, vertical rolls and many more. The display sequence is designed so that there is never more than five seconds of straight flight in any attitude.

Helicopter Pleasure Flights – This is the fourth year that Elite Helicopters have provided helicopter pleasure flights for the public. Following last year's success they will again be operating a Bell Jet Ranger helicopter at this year's White Horse Show.

The Bell Jet Ranger carries four passengers at a time and the pleasure flights will be operating between 1,000 and 1,500 feet at a speed of around 150 mph. Those on board will experience a wonderful bird's-eye view of the surrounding area. Sharon Biggs, operations manager of Elite Helicopters, says, 'Children as young as two have been thrilled by the experience and a mature lady of ninety-six years loved every minute of the flight and fulfilled a lifelong ambition.'

The flights are approximately five minutes in duration and the prices are £15 per adult, £12 per child (under fourteen years) and OAPs. A special rate for a family of four (two adults and two children) is available at £50. At the end of the flight all children receive a certificate to commemorate their flight. Elite assure us that any adult who requests a certificate will not be refused.

Western Bareback Barrel Racing – All the excitement, thrills, spills and laughs of the Barrel Race Contest. The chuck wagon sets the scene, positioning the barrels in the arena while the commentator explains the rules. A member of the team shows how it should be done, then the contestants try it – usually with hilarious results.

Prior to the performance volunteers are found from the audience to participate in a race against the clock, riding bareback around the barrels and back to the finishing point. The rider with the fastest time receives a trophy, then does a lap of honour around the arena in the chuck wagon. The Western bareback racing display was shown on the ITV 1988 *Telethon*.

Professor Crump – Step this way for fun – the overgrown professor is loose! He has been studying nonsense for years and gets up to all sorts of mischief with balloon trickery, juggling, corny jokes and crazy gadgets on his giant yellow bicycle and push scooter. His credits include the West End show *Barnum*, *The Sooty Show* on TV and BBC's *Antiques Roadshow* to name a varied few.

Stationary Engines – Since the beginning, the White Horse Show has had the support of a dedicated group of enthusiasts who spend their free time in the winter months renovating the farm machinery and power units which they come across, sometimes in ditches and often in pieces. Many originate from the early part of this century and have been brought back to their original working condition after many hours of work.

At this year's show Mr J P Miller is exhibiting a Villiers WXII made in 1926. He found it in a barn in Burford where it had lain for forty years; restoration work took around two years. Mr I J Clarke is showing two Lister 'D' engines, one of which he bought at a car boot sale. The Lion 5 hp exhibited by Ricky Hitchman was discovered in Windsor Forest running a water pump.

Mr P J Frankum will be showing no less than six exhibits. Mr M P Day has restored a Nova 'S' Type 1.5 hp dating from 1914, which is believed to be one of only three in Great Britain.

All these engines and many more can be seen at the display of stationary engines, where a full list of exhibits is available. The owners will be only too pleased to discuss their engines with you. The committee would like to thank those exhibitors who have brought their engines to this year's show for the enjoyment of our visitors.

Lawnmower Racing – The British Lawnmower Racing Association was founded in 1973 in a pub by a bunch of sporting enthusiasts bemoaning the ever-increasing costs of all forms of motor sport. This new and eccentric sport became an almost overnight success and, after just two or three events in the first years, soon became responsible for over a dozen events each season.

The main aims of the association are to provide a keen, well-organised and inexpensive motor sport in a daft sort of way. Racing includes the season-long National Championships, the British Grand Prix, the annual twelve-hour race and the World Championships at the end of the year. Social events include the annual Grand Grasscutters Ball.

Stirling Moss has won both the British Grand Prix for mowers and the annual twelve-hour race. Derek Bell, World Sports Car Racing Champion has won the twelve-hour mower race twice; mind you, he had had a bit of practice, winning the Le Mans twenty-four-hour race five times. Happy mowing!

Farm Animals – We have on display a selection of animals found on smallholdings today and in the past. Some are rare breeds which enthusiasts are working hard to preserve in this country; others are more established. There are sheep, goats and a cow. The South Oxfordshire Poultry Club are showing a wide variety of poultry, while the Didcot and District Rabbit Club have an exhibit with many interesting breeds of rabbit together with an abundance of useful information for rabbit keepers. Almost all the animals are raised for a purpose, whether for milk, wool, meat, eggs or for breeding stock.

There is wool spinning throughout the day, while the Friends of Cogges Museum have a stand demonstrating various country crafts. The Farming and Wildlife Advisory Group exhibit will be in attendance again this year. Thanks to White Horse Animal Feeds of Childrey for kindly providing feedstuff, the Lonsdale Estates of Kingston Lisle for the loan of hurdles. Please do not smoke in the animal marquee.

Island Farm Riding Centre and Donkey Rescue – During your time here today, make a point of visiting the donkeys from Brightwell-cum-Sotwell, near Wallingford in South Oxfordshire. These lovely animals have been saved either from near starvation due to neglect or bought from livestock markets where they could have been taken abroad for slaughter. This work started in 1983 with the rescue of a pony called Penny and progressed on to donkeys in 1993.

After many months of care and rehabilitation these donkeys are now fit and well, and they can give rides today to children up to seven stone. Back at the centre, special-needs schools in Oxfordshire visit with small groups of disabled children to pet and ride other donkeys.

Four donkeys whose lives have changed from starvation and near-death to TV stardom are Chocolate, Jumpin' Jack, Charlie and Fred. They spent a day filming with BBC at Thetford in Suffolk for a children's series called *The Phoenix and the Carpet*, to be shown on Sunday afternoons in the late autumn. The series is set in the early 1900s and you can see the donkeys in Episode Three, when the scene is in a market in India. Anyone wishing to visit the centre and see the work we do will be most welcome.

Again, as was normal with a White Horse Show, this was a huge success. The profit was being forecast as good; this in itself must have given the new chairman Derek Kelsey a boost of confidence. This had to be a good omen for him, as taking on this post must have been a very daunting task. Full credit must also be given to all of the committee, together with the many helpers that make a show of this size and class a success. But, again, I must reiterate the chairman's post is at times an unthankful job, as at times he must accept the decision of the majority of the committee whilst not agreeing with that decision. He then must carry on and make sure that that decision is adopted by all and sundry as the way forward for the White Horse Show. I thought that Derek was the right person in the right place and would carry out that duty as well as any person I knew.

When the wash-up meeting was held for the 1997 show a considerable number of the committee thought that by still sticking to the August bank holiday weekend they were clashing with too many other events that were being held on that same weekend. Therefore, at their next meeting they would discuss this in more detail. Although not being a member of that committee any longer I did have very grave doubts as to the feasibility of moving away from that weekend. After all, we had been running our show on this weekend for twenty-six years and had seen off all opposition during that time. The only way to keep the show going in my opinion was to have a really good star attraction and accept a smaller profit margin until the present financial situation improved. Once the general public started to get an easier time with their financial state, then the show would return to its old glory. But, no longer being a member of the show committee, I could have no say in that matter. However, being a White Horse Show Trust member, I hoped that the right decisions were made, as the White Horse Show was still a great asset to the three villages.

At the next meeting, with a considerable number of new members in attendance, the idea of moving the show to a new date away from the August bank holiday weekend was adopted. After some lengthy debating it was decided to move the show to Saturday and Sunday 4 and 5 July 1998. This of course was always my greatest fear. This again I believe was a decision that was taken without any real thought for the work pattern of the people who had patronised the show over the years that it had been running. First of all, if we look at the plight of the everyday worker at that time, in a normal week with the recession biting, if there was a chance of overtime available that was inevitably going to come on a Saturday morning; it was only natural that he was going to take the chance to earn instead of spend, whereas on a bank holiday weekend a considerable number of firms and businesses close down, which leaves the workforce with that time free and no chance of any overtime. Therefore they could still pass this free time at a show such as the White Horse Show, providing that the cost was not too great and it was good value for the money that they were spending.

I have always classed myself as being working class and I know only too well that the last two to three years that I was at work we were finding that we never had the money that we had had in the past to spare. Also, I had listened to other working people that I met in the course of my work and found that I was not the only person feeling the recession. But still the news media was trying to tell everybody that we were wrong and the country was not going to go into recession. With quite a number of firms increasing their hire costs and charges, this was quite different to the news media's thoughts on the real situation. When one was looking at the increasing costs of putting on the White Horse Show it was plain to see.

When it came to cutting our costs I still believe that the wrong attitude was adopted by a few. They expected that we could cut costs by having cheaper events taking part. They assumed the public would not notice this fact and the profits would still roll in, but how wrong they were. This was coupled with the fact that other shows in June and July were all specialist shows. These did not cover such a wide range of interests as the White Horse Show, but nevertheless were long-established shows of specialist subjects over a very long period of time. The exhibitors of these shows were not going to forsake the shows that they had attended over that period of time.

The thought that went through my mind at the time was the same it had been for a long time – that this was a bitter pill that we must swallow. That bitter pill was to maintain a good class of all-round show that interested a large cross section of the public and thus would keep the White Horse Show on the road, with a reduced profit. In this way, when the economy picked up, which inevitably it would, the White Horse Show would still be there to carry on benefiting the local communities as before. Still being an active member of the White Horse Show Trust I would be able to watch this change taking place. Also I would be in a position to see the financial gains or losses that would occur when this change took place. I still sincerely hoped that the show committee would make the right decision in this field, but still had very grave doubts.

But, going back to the 1997 show, it was very pleasing to see that we had made a profit of £8,000. After all, the preaching of doom speaks for itself. But again I must reiterate that I still had faith in the new chairman being able to hammer in new policies and keep the show on the road if changing the date of the show failed. This was, in my own opinion, certain to happen.

1998

I will list again the whole committee for the 1998 show. They were as follows: chairman, Derek Kelsey; secretary, Ann Kelsey; treasurer, Ray Avenell; field director, stationary engines, tractors and arena events, Paul Armishaw; other events, Nigel Tilling; field services, Bill Mattingley; publicity and programme, Mike Thomas and Cuan Ryan; safety and security and the hunt, Clive Avenell; trade stands and local crafts, Jill and Malcolm White and Tina Monk; historic vehicles and catering, Derek Kelsey; helicopter and show control centre, Ann Kelsey; heavy horses, Debbie Wallis; animals, Tony Parsons; pony parade, Brian White; parking, camping, evening events, Christine Holley; stewards, Viv Boaler, Stewart Lovelock, Gareth Armishaw, Damien Wilson, Dick and Gwen Allen.

Special thanks must also be forwarded to Mr Jim Soden of Sower Hill Farm and to Mrs Marcella Seymour of Britchcombe Farm for making the fields available for the White Horse Show in early July. This was some eight weeks earlier than before. When you realised some of the worry we had had in the past as to whether the fields we were requiring would be ready in time for the show to go ahead on the scale as planned, that was some achievement. I knew only too well some of the headaches and sleepless nights we had had in the past on this subject and what a worry it was.

One year in particular springs into my mind on this subject. It was when we were using the sports field in the Fawler Road as the main show site. Mr Jim Matthews had given us permission to use his fields on the opposite side of the road for the car parking. These fields were in fact full of standing wheat but, at the time of the permission being given to us, we assumed in normal circumstances this would be harvested with time to spare. But this year turned out to be anything but normal; the first three weeks of August were a very trying time for farmers. The weather was not exceptionally wet but it was messy, which was enough to severely delay the combining of these crops. The result was that Mr Jim Matthews was still combining in the car park until late on the Saturday night prior to the show on the very next day. But luck was on our side in the end: Mr Matthews managed to finish one whole field and cut a track through the next field to give cars access to another field where parking could take place. This in itself was a very commendable act to enable the White Horse Show to take place. The whole of the committee at that time were extremely grateful for that act. I think that our chairman at that time had no sleep for the fortnight leading up to the show. Of course, John Little, being the founder of the show, was used to losing sleep over the event. In all honesty I believe that that year was the nearest we ever got to having to call the show off.

This near tragedy occurred in 1977; at this time we were only approaching our sixth birthday and what the consequences of cancellation would have been is too catastrophic to think about. The possibility was that there would not be another White Horse Show for the benefit of the communities.

But now back to the 1998 show. Another fear that I had with the date alteration for the show was the extra financial burden of advertising and publicity that would have to be borne by the show to inform everybody of that date alteration. After all, the show had been running on the bank holiday for twenty-six years and that date would be firmly in the mind of people who had patronised the White Horse Show over that period of time. But, nevertheless, I still wished the committee all the success possible in the bold move that they were making. A fair programme of events was planned over the weekend of 4 and 5 July 1998. This was as follows:

Saturday 4 July	Sunday 5 July
11.10 First Aid Demonstration	11.10 First Aid Demonstration
11.35 Island Farm Donkeys	11.35 Island Farm Donkeys
11.50 Gamegoer Gundogs and Falconry – Display 1	11.50 Thamesdown Bus Company
12.00 Mrs Jenny Pitman to open the show	12.20 Gamegoer Gundogs and Falconry – Display 1

12.30	Strawberry Fayre Majorettes	13.00	Strawberry Fayre Majorettes
13.00	Monster Action Stunt Display – Part 1	13.30	Monster Action Stunt Display – Part 1
13.35	Gamegoer Gundogs and Falconry – Display 2	14.05	Gamegoer Gundogs and Falconry – Display 2
14.15	Parade of the Old Berks Hunt	14.45	Tractor Parade
14.45	Monster Action Stunt Display – Part 2	14.15	Parade of The Old Berks Hunt
15.15	Pony Parade Winners Presentation	15.15	Monster Action Stunt Display – Part 2
15.45	Historic Motorcycle Parade	15.45	Three Counties Egg Throwing Competition
16.30	Strawberry Fayre Majorettes	16.15	Historic Vehicles Parade and Presentation
		17.00	Strawberry Fayre Majorettes

Wantage Gymnasts will perform near the committee bus.

The heavy horses show will take place throughout the day in its own arena.

The committee would like to extend their thanks to the following who make this show possible:

The British Red Cross (Oxfordshire Area) for their valuable help in providing first-aid cover; Thames Valley Police for their assistance with traffic and security; Uffington Youth Club for selling programmes; Stanford-in-the-Vale Scouts for clearing the litter; Uffington PTA and Village Hall Committee for providing car park attendants; Faringdon Scouts for organising exhibitor car parking; Mattingley & Sharps for the public address system; Simon Stafford for producing all the artwork; Bertrand Faure for their most generous donation towards the cost of pre-show publicity; Mr Michael Green, MFH, Mrs J Whittington, MFH, and Mr Marcus Armitage, MFH, for their contribution to the show with the Old Berks hounds; Uffington Garage, Uffington School, Uffington Shop, Buckell & Ballard (Wantage) for ticket sales and support; Geoffrey Bailey Shoes (Wantage) who in addition kindly made a display facility available, and Uffington

School children for creating the display; Clarks of Wantage for trailer provision; Cottage Farm Eggs for supplying the eggs for the Three Counties Egg-Throwing Competition.

The committee extends thanks to Ken Freeman, Charlie Walters, Jim Matthews and Lonsdale Estates for their assistance and cooperation in putting on the show, and all those many individuals from the area who put in so much time and hard work to make the show a success.

The committee also offers sincere thanks to all those companies who have generously supported the show through programme advertising and sponsorship of events.

Police message – Amongst the new attractions at this years show will be a 'Real Ale Bar'. But please remember: if you drink, don't drive.

The committee is especially grateful to the following people who have generously agreed to become patrons of the White Horse Show: Mr N Bird, Mr R Bracey, Mr B J Cale, Mr J Lane, Danetree Veterinary Surgeons, Col. P G Rosser and Sir Adrian Swire.

If you are interested in becoming a patron, please enquire at the committee bus or contact Ray Avenell for further details.

The Three Counties Egg-Throwing Championship – We have been holding an egg-throwing contest in the village for many years at school fêtes etc. but at the 1998 White Horse Show we want to turn it into a *megga* event. It's cracking good to watch and even more eggciting to join in. And it's so simple. The competition takes the form of partners facing each other to form two rows of people 6 ft apart. The idea is to throw an egg (raw) to your partner who will hopefully catch it. After each throw both rows of people step back and repeat the procedure. Each time an egg is broken, the couple drop out until only one pair is left – the winners, who will be presented with a smashing trophy. In case you're in any doubt, there will be a short demonstration by a team of eggsperts in the main arena about an hour before the event.

The competition will be taking place in the main arena on Sunday afternoon at 3.45 p.m. This event is open to everybody of any age. To enter just register at the committee bus before 3.30 p.m. Entry is completely FREE, but there will be a box for voluntary donations to an animal charity.

We want this to be the biggest egg-throwing competition ever seen in this part of the world (or indeed anywhere else), so don't hesitate, sign up at the bus.

Farm Animals – We have on display a selection of animals found on smallholdings today and in the past, as well as demonstrations of many crafts based on animal products. Some are rare breeds that enthusiasts are working hard to preserve in this country, while others are more common but interesting nonetheless. There are several kinds of sheep, goats, pigs and a wide variety of poultry, plus an egg competition.

Outside the marquee you can see fine examples of Belted Galloway cattle, as well as Victor the donkey and other old friends who appear regularly at the Uffington Show. Almost all the animals are raised for a purpose, whether for milk, wool, meat, eggs or for breeding stock. Please feel free to come and ask questions of the owners about anything related to raising and caring for these animals. There will be an exhibit by the Hawk and Owl Trust with several of these wonderful birds for you to see on the Sunday. We are planning demonstrations of sheep shearing during the show. In addition there will be country crafts such as spinning and again you are welcome to come and talk about these activities with the exhibitors.

Thanks to White Horse Animal Feeds of Childrey for kindly providing feedstuff and to Lonsdale Estates of Kingston Lisle for the loan of hurdles. Please do not smoke in the animal marquee.

Classic Bikes at the Uffington Show – Welcome once again to the world of classic motorcycles, a colourful and much appreciated feature of the Uffington White Horse Show.

This year has seen a change of show date, with Saturday 4 July being the prize-giving day for the old bikes. If that fourth of July date with its Yankee associations suggests that this year's competition, for five trophies, will be dominated by trendy Harley-Davidsons, nothing could be further from the truth! Just about the only 'all-American freedom machine' likely to be on show is one wonderfully well-used V-Twin, built in Springfield, Massachusetts. But its owner doesn't play favourites, and may well come on his equally 'lived in' alternative machine, a Cossack 650 – from Russia.

It is very fitting however that 4 July is Independence Day, because independence is what a British motorcycle, anything from a Frances-Barnett to a Norton, must have meant to many show-goers in days gone by. So come and rekindle some memories with the sight and sound of over a hundred of these lovingly cared-for machines of yesteryear, while I and my fellow judge, ex-Castrol man Derek Guy, struggle to sort the best from the rest.

And when the time comes for the parade and the prize-giving in the main arena, let's hope that something else which changes for 1998 is the weather. We would rather not have a monsoon again this time.

Judges for the historic motorcycles will be Derek Guy and Steve Wilson. The 1998 historic motorcycle event is kindly sponsored by Laporte Absorbents (Baulking) Ltd.

Wantage Gymnasts – Wantage Gymnasts have now been going for more than twenty years. The club, which is run by Mrs Clements, is based at Wantage Leisure Centre. It has built up a membership which now exceeds sixty active participants. Most, but not all, members are girls and ages range from seventeen down to as young as four. Wantage Gymnasts have been highly successful at both county and regional levels. They took more individual apparatus medals than any other club at the last Oxfordshire championship. The gymnasts have put on many demonstrations in the last year at places as diverse as Betterton House and Christchurch Cathedral, Oxford.

They will be performing twice on Saturday in their own area near the committee bus at 14.00 and 15.30.

Double-Decker Bus Driving – Have you outgrown your Mini and want to try something bigger? As a child did you have a secret ambition to be a bus driver? Or are you just curious about what it's like to drive a bus? Well now's your chance. At this year's White Horse Show for a small fee you can try your hand at driving a real double-decker bus under the supervision of a qualified professional instructor. And, whether or not you're going to have a go yourself, be sure to watch the demonstration in the main arena of how these huge vehicles can be manoeuvred with pinpoint accuracy. Thanks to Mr Hill of Thamesdown Buses and Stagecoach.

Model Spitfire – The Spitfire Mark IX on display is a full-size replica built from fibreglass and wood, although the wheels, tail wheel, canopy and cockpit gauges are original items from World War II Spitfires. The Spitfire is owned by Derek Johnson, an aerospace technician, who has worked on the building of the Concorde. Derek has taken two years in his spare time to complete the Spitfire and, along with the Danish Royal Air Force Hawker Hunter he is renovating at Kemble Aerodrome, says that the aircraft are available for air shows, exhibitions, country shows, TV and films. Derek would be pleased to hear from enthusiastic volunteers to help with the Hunter.

Monster Action Stunt Display Team – Probably the most exciting show of its kind, Monster Action has really come up trumps this year. The show consists of a mixture of new and traditional stunts including an entrance that will leave you breathless. Monster Action boasts more variety and content than any other show of its kind in the world. The first half of the show includes such things as firewalls, human torch, the high stool, two-wheel driving on a quad and a motorcycle combination, BMX jumps and clever antics with a truck.

The second half of the show involves a very slick and smooth car-jumping routine. Lots of rival acts jump cars but not quite as Monster Action do! They jump them with rollerblades, BMX bikes, motorcycles, motorcycle combinations and a quad bike, and not always just one at a time!

The team have been selected and professionally choreographed by top TV stuntman Steve Griffin, who has over 500 film and television appearances to his name. These include, *Braveheart, Goldeneye, In the Name of the Father, London's Burning, The Bill* and *Peak Practice*.

The Classic Car Parade – In previous years the classic car display has been held on the Monday of the August bank holiday. This year it is being held on the Sunday of an ordinary weekend. That means that the owners of the cars have one less free day to polish them.

Not that a couple of hours with a tin of Simoniz will greatly affect the outcome of the competition when it comes to overall condition. The quality of presentation of a classic car comes either as the result of years of careful and loving maintenance, or of many hours, sometimes stretching into weeks and months, of painstaking restoration. The final polish is only the icing on the cake. We hope that you will find the large variety of classic cars on display today – ranging from the antique to the comparatively modern, from vintage tourers to 1970s sports cars – of great interest and enjoyment. You will find the owners and drivers are as varied, and in some cases as old, as the cars themselves! Any of them will be only too pleased to talk to you about his or her particular pride and joy.

The Classic Car Parade has been generously sponsored by TWR (Jaguar) Ltd.

As can be seen, the committee had booked a full programme for the show, with all of the supporting sideshows. But I did think that at least one star turn each day, which they could have really publicised in their advertising, would have helped the change of weekends. I talked to a lot of people about the change of weekends, and I was getting the same feedback – it was a big mistake, but one that the committee was perfectly entitled to make. It also came to light during the run-up to the show that it was still going to clash with other well-established shows; the only thing we could do was to wish them luck and keep our fingers crossed, with the hope that the weather would be on its best behaviour for the show's sake.

But – alas! – over the two days of the show the weather was not on its best behaviour and the crowds did not turn up in their usual numbers; in fact numbers were well down on other years.

On the financial side it was quite a disaster: the show was going to show a loss of £995. OK, this was a great disappointment for the committee, but on the other hand it was not the end of the world, and certainly not the end of the White Horse Show. Members of the committee that I talked to after the event were all adamant that the show would go on in 1999. However, they would be looking at the opportunity of reverting to the August bank holiday weekend at their next meeting.

One thing that had to be in their favour was the fact that the present chairman Derek Kelsey was going to remain at the helm. If anybody could pull this show out of the doldrums it was Derek. I knew that he had the greatest regard for John Little and the all-round benefit that the show had created for the three villages over its period of time, and I was equally sure that Derek would, as the saying goes, move heaven and earth to achieve just that. As I have said so many times in the past, to be committed to the show you must have the support of your partner to succeed in your commitment to this type of work. Derek had this without a shadow of doubt, as his wife, Ann, would be continuing with the secretary's duties. I hoped that this great teamwork would carry on for the foreseeable future. One other person I feel I must also give praise to is the treasurer, Mr Ray Avenell. I did not think that this one little setback would worry Ray too much, as he knew White Horse Shows of the past and their potential for the future. He also knew that he was working with a great team. It, of course, might take more than one show to pull back to the shows of old, and it could not be forgotten that the recession-that-never-was was not over just yet. It had to be also borne in mind that, although the loss on the 1998 show was £995, the disaster fund would drop considerably more than this sum. This was because the show committee would have to have a cash-flow situation before they could even think about getting started with the organisation of the 1999 show.

This of course did not mean that the White Horse Show Trust had no money to distribute to local charities; in fact that could not be further from the truth. We on the trust had some funds left from the previous year, and to add to this was the interest that was gained on the investment of the disaster fund. Thanks must in this instance go to our treasurer, Mr Peter Erskine, whose judgement on investment was certainly second to none. Each year he always managed to gain considerable interest on this for us the trustees to distribute. At the trust meeting that was called to deal with the situation arising from the loss at the 1998 show, we had before us a letter from the chairman of the show, Mr Derek Kelsey. This was simply a request from the show committee regarding distribution of funds in this year. Their request was for us to give serious thought as to whether we ought in fact to distribute any grants at all after the loss made at the 1998 show. The show committee were understandably worried that if grants were awarded after a show loss, this could in fact give a false impression to some of the beneficiaries within the three villages. Being involved with money-raising in the village for thirty-eight years, I thought that the request carried a certain amount of common sense. But not all of the trustees thought the same way; in fact their thoughts were turning to the possibility that we as trustees were being interfered with by the show committee. This of course was not true. Having been a show committee member for many years I was always interested to know where the money that our hard work had produced was going, even before I had become a trustee. I also knew at that time, that by rules of the charity commissioners and HM Inspector of Taxes it was the sole responsibility of the trustees registered to the charity commissioners to distribute the profits of the show in grants to the registered beneficiaries within the three villages. That had always been the case in the past, but what seemed to be falling down at the present time was the communication between the two bodies.

This hiccup between the two bodies was quickly cleared and put behind us all. We undertook that the full White Horse Show Committee would see the trustees' recommendation before any monies were distributed, and any thoughts for or against would be listened to in the feedback from the show committee. Therefore, with this behind us, the trustees decided that the White Horse Show Committee were in fact right to make their request that no grants would be distributed this time. It was therefore decided at the trustees' meeting that we would wait to see further developments of the financial position of the show in preparation for the following year. After all, the show committee would have to be falling back on the disaster fund to start to finance the next show, which by this time they had already committed themselves to do. With my own experience and involvement with this project right from the very beginning, it was the only sensible thing to do. If we had not gone down this path we could well have given some people the idea that even without a White Horse Show there would always be some money to distribute. That seems to be an odd thought, I know, but having had to battle against narrow-minded people in the past who thought that funds just fell out of the sky, it was the only path to take.

My commiserations at this time went to the White Horse Show Committee, who at that time had made a very brave decision to alter the date of the show in the hope that it would improve the attendance and the profitability of the show. Then, to put all the work into that decision and see that they had in fact at the end of the day incurred a loss must have been very heartbreaking. This, together with the knowledge that for the 1999 show they would be changing the show's site, which always involved extra work and headaches galore, must have been a very daunting thought to all the committee.

1999

The surprise that was to follow was that the show committee again decided that they were going to stick to 3 and 4 July as the show weekend. That was their prerogative and they were perfectly entitled to make that decision. The only thing that I could do was to wish them all the luck possible, but nevertheless I still had very grave doubts as to the feasibility of a successful show at this time of year.

The new showground was to be in fields belonging to Mr Richard Whitfield at Fawler Farm. Once more I can only reiterate the extra problems that face the field organiser when the show moves to a new site. That person has the headache of deciding where everything is going to be sited, together with the question of how many gates are needed. Also, what material do we need? Can we manage the work ourselves? How long will it take us to perform this work? When can we start? And, of course, how long have we got the fields for? All this work and worry would be falling on the shoulders of the field director, in this case Mr Paul Armishaw. The committee could count their blessings in this direction, as in Paul they had a very capable member for this work; likewise he had the backing and the assistance of a very capable chairman in Derek. But nevertheless, this was always a very big and unthankful task to have to face, and at the end of the day you had to get it right. Bear in mind that you were expected to have a showground plan ready for discussion with the committee, sometimes up to a month in advance of the show. This far back from the show it was not unknown that you would still be trying to find out how much room certain people needed, and what in fact was coming to the show. Paul certainly had my sympathy, and I could only wish him luck in this field.

The show committee requested funds from the disaster fund to finance the start of the 1999 show, which of course was not questioned. After all, this was what this fund was all about. It was started for just this purpose and at times extra money was invested in it, as the cost of running the show was forever increasing as the years went by. It was now going to prove that that shrewd idea was invaluable in allowing the 1999 show to get off of the ground. As the run-up to the 1999 show grew closer, it was apparent that the committee was very reluctant to pay out for any real first-class events. They thus committed their budget cost of running this show as low as they possibly could, which was, I thought, very prudent thinking. Nevertheless, they had a good and varied programme put together for the two days, as follows:

Saturday 3 July

12.00 Stagecoach Bus Driving Competition
12.30 The Eagle and Vulture Show
13.05 Tricky Tykes Terrier Racing
13.45 The GWR Majorettes
14.10 Parade of the Old Berks Hunt
14.35 The Eagle and Vulture Show
15.10 Parade of Historic Motorcycles
16.00 Tricky Tykes Terrier Racing
16.40 Stagecoach Bus Driving Competition Final
17.25 The GWR Majorettes

Sunday 4 July

11.00 The Eagle and Vulture Show
11.35 The Romford Drum and Trumpet Corps
12.00 Tricky Tykes Terrier Racing
12.40 Parade of Vintage Tractors
13.00 The Eagle and Vulture Show
13.50 The Three Counties Egg Throwing Championship
14.30 Parade of Heavy Horses
15.00 Tricky Tykes Terrier Racing
15.40 Historic Motor Vehicles Parade
16.30 The Romford Drum and Trumpet Corps

The Heavy Horse Show will take place in its own arena and will commence at 10.30. Judge, Mr R M Gifford; ring steward, Mr Bob Brickell; collecting steward, Mr Ken Freeman.

The committee are most grateful to the following for their very kind sponsorship of the classes in the heavy horse show.

Class 1 – Mr John Bosley, Uffington; Class 2, Churn Stables, Blewbury; Class 4A, The Woolstone Stud, Woolstone; Class 7, Lord Faringdon Farms and Gardens, Buscot Park; Class 9, The Horse & Jockey, Stanford in the Vale; Class 12, The Blowing Stone Inn, Kingston Lisle.

At one time almost all of Britain's land was worked by horses ploughing, drilling seed, raking, turning and carting hay.

In the 1950s and 1960s, the introduction of mechanised farm implements and tractors meant that the need for horse power on land was reduced. It seemed as though the heavy horses were becoming redundant. Their numbers were sadly in decline. Fortunately, these magnificent creatures had many supporters and today their future is assured. It is a stirring sight to see a parade of heavy horses on show.

An average heavy horse weighs around a ton and is capable of pulling enormous weights. Horses are measured in 'hands'. Each hand is equivalent to four inches. The measurement is taken from the ground to the top of the shoulders (withers). The long hair on the lower leg is known as 'feather'.

Schedule of Classes:

Class 1 – Best Barren Mare in hand three years upwards – Isis Construction Perpetual Challenge Trophy

Class 2 – Best Gelding in hand three years upwards – Jewson Perpetual Challenge Trophy

Class 3 – Best Suffolk/Clydesdale/Percheron/any breed other than Shire, any age, any sex – The White Horse Show Perpetual Challenge Trophy

Class 4 – Fillies/Colts/Geldings one year – R J Brickell Perpetual Challenge Trophy

Class 4A – Fillies/Colts/Geldings two years – White Horse Show Perpetual Challenge Trophy

Class 5 – Brood Mare with foal at foot – T Calder Perpetual Challenge Trophy

Class 5A – Foal-produce of heavy horse stallion and mare – Mobac Site Services Perpetual Challenge Trophy

Class 6 – Novice of any age, breed or sex, never having won a first prior to the day of the show – Clarkes Mill (Wantage) Perpetual Challenge Trophy

Championship – first & second of above classes – Fawley Stud Perpetual Challenge Trophy

Champion qualifies for the West of England Heavy Horse Championship final 1999

Class 7 – Harness Class (show) – 75% harness/25% horse and presentation. This Class is a qualifier for the West of England Heavy Horse Championship – Harold Hyde Memorial Perpetual Challenge Trophy

Class 8 – Harness Class (agricultural) – 75% harness/25% horse and presentation. No chrome chains or patent leather – Mr and Mrs K Freeman Perpetual Challenge Trophy

Class 9 – Best single turnout, trade only – D Herring Perpetual Challenge Trophy

Class 10 – Agricultural turnout – any horse-drawn machine/cart etc. used for agricultural purposes – R J Brickell Perpetual Challenge Trophy

Class 11 – Best pair of horses in harness – P White Perpetual Challenge Trophy

Class 12 – Best pair, unicorn or team turnout, trade or agricultural – White Horse Show Perpetual Challenge Trophy

As can be seen, to organise and run a heavy horse show of this magnitude takes time, patience and a lot of hard work and worry. For this, the committee and the public must thank Debbie Wallis.

At this year's White Horse Show you will find dozens of craft stalls catering for every possible interest. There are too many to list but they include: hand-decorated china, wood craft, pyrography, candles, peg bags, waistcoats, cuddly toys, mirrors, pots, hats and scarves, quilted cushions, ceramics, greetings cards, key rings, glass painting, trinket boxes, Asian wood carvings, wrought-iron furniture, watercolours, bird boxes, jewellery from Mexico, South Africa and England plus lots more.

With all of this for the public to savour, our typical English summer had to have the final say in the profitability of the show. The week leading up to the show was fairly wet, and over the two days it could only improve to give frequent and heavy storms. This of course had a large effect on the volume of attendance over the entire duration of the show, coupled together with the fact that there were other long-running shows going on in opposition. When all these things were taken into consideration it was not surprising that it looked that this show would again show a loss. In fact, when all the income and expenditure had been cleared for the 1999 show it was showing a loss of £1,300. This in itself would not be enough to kill the White Horse Show, as the disaster fund was still there for these types of setbacks, which goes to prove what a good thought it was to set up such a prudent idea as the disaster fund. On the other hand, what thoughts were going through the minds of the committee members who worked so hard to put the show on, only to be defeated by the elements? It is these people who deserve some sympathy in times like this; yes they made the decision to alter the date of the show, but they certainly deserved better luck than this. However, I was sure that they would be strong enough to give the millennium-year show their all. I am equally sure that the chairman Derek Kelsey would be more determined than ever to make the twenty-ninth White Horse Show a success.

2000

After the committee had got the wash-up meeting out of the way from the disastrous 1999 show they were committed to going away and coming back to the next meeting with new ideas for the 2000 show. They came back to the next meeting with more determination than ever before, and not one single resignation was tendered. It is this grit and determination that makes the White Horse Show Committee such a great team: that is why the White Horse Show has been going for such a long time. They make decisions and stick to that decision right or wrong; if it's wrong they are strong enough to reverse that decision and get it right the next time. That is what good committees are made of; if it was not the show would not be entering its twenty-ninth year.

The best news to come out of the first meeting for the show in the year 2000 was, I believe, that the committee had overwhelmingly decided to revert to the August bank holiday weekend. But, rather surprisingly, they had also decided that they would try to have a three-day event. This would of course be the first attempt at this since our first show in 1972, under the chairmanship of the late John Little. Again I could only wish them luck in this field, as we had found the workload just too much to cope with at that time. But one thing in their favour now was that they had a much larger committee, and this could generate a greater workforce.

It was intended that the Saturday would entail a pony show together with a large car-boot sale. But prudence would again have to be a priority on the expenditure side, to try and claw back the losses of the last two years. But at the end of the day they had put together a reasonable programme of events for the next show. That programme was as follows:

> It is confirmed that the Saturday entertainment will be a pony show. This would take place in Arena 1 from 10 a.m. to 5 p.m.

This has been put together by Mr Brian White, with the help of his wife and daughter, who have worked tirelessly to organise this event. The event will take the pattern of a gymkhana for youngsters. It will centre on light-hearted competitions which are intended to be both entertaining for those watching and good honest fun for those taking part.

With a little bit of luck we can have a sporting afternoon for equine-minded youngsters where the timekeepers and judges can give their verdicts without being set upon by irate youngsters, or, more terrifying still, their mothers.

The committee wishes to thank those companies and businesses who have so generously sponsored this event.

The car boot sale is being organised by Mr Tiggy Packford and his wife Polly. This will take place in the historic car area and will operate from 12 noon until 5 p.m., unless everyone sells out beforehand.

On Sunday 27 August 2000, the show would be taking a different pattern than in the past, as the heavy horse show would be the main event. This would take place in the main arena, Arena 1, from 10.30 a.m. to 5 p.m. This would of course encompass all of the usual classes of the heavy horse section.

Thanks must go again to Debbie Wallis for her hard work and worry in organising this event. Thanks also go to the following: judge, Mr A Bull; ring steward, Mr Bob Brickell; collecting steward, Mr Ken Freeman; commentator, Mr Peter Davies.

During the lunch-break of the heavy horse show, Arena 1 would be utilised as follows:
  12.30 to 13.00: Presenting Island Farm Donkeys
  13.00 to 13.30: Parade of the Old Berks Hunt

In Arena 2 the programme was as follows:
  2.00 to 2.45: Historic Tractor Parade and Presentation
  2.45 to 3.30: Historic Motorcycle Parade and Presentation

At all other times during the day, Arena 2 would be occupied by bus-driving tuition given by Stagecoach.

Monday 28 August 2000 would carry on as in the White Horse Shows of the past. The programme as follows:

10.30　Carriage Driving – In Hand
11.00　Egg Throwing Demonstration
11.15　Presenting Island Farm Donkeys
11.30　Carriage Driving – Exercise Cart Class.
12.00　Vander Brothers Aerial Artists.
12.30　Carriage Driving – Demonstration of putting pairs into a vehicle. This is an opportunity for the public to experience 'hands-on driving'
13.00　Horsemen of the Apocalypse
14.00　Egg-throwing competition
14.30　Carriage Driving – Obstacle cone course
15.00　Vander Brothers Aerial Artists
15.30　Historic Car Presentation
16.00　Ladies Hat Parade
16.30　Carriage Driving – Grand Parade

Stagecoach Bus Driving Tuition throughout the day in Arena 2.

The committee were again thankful to Mr Richard Whitfield for the use of Fawler Farm fields.

At long last the weather had been kind to the committee for this show, and I am sure this was appreciated by all concerned. It was certainly welcomed by the general public, who supported the show in greater numbers than in the previous two years. This fact was reflected in the profitability of this show which, together with the prudence in planning and expenditure, was expected to return a fair profit at the closing of the show on the Monday evening. News like this so early, I know from past experience, gives everyone involved a feeling of satisfaction. Even after all the hard graft you feel that, yes, we got it right. I would also like to think that returning to the August bank holiday weekend played a part in the success.

At the wash-up meeting of this show it was forecast that a profit in excess of £5,000 would be returned. During the coming months, after all expenditure and income had been dealt with, the final profit of the 2000 show was revealed to be £7,035. This was great news: at last the White Horse Show was back on the road again. This could only be due to the extremely hard work and resilience of the committee and their leader, Derek Kelsey. Therefore, the benefit of this hard work could again be shown in grants within the three villages. I am sure this was appreciated by the recipients.

2001

With all this behind the committee, it was nice to learn that planning for the 2001 show was taking place. This was again having its hitches, and big headaches were thrown at the committee in the fact that the dreaded country disease of foot and mouth among cattle hit epidemic proportions during the winter of 2000, and lasted well into the spring of 2001. This of course caused major problems with the planning for the 2001 show. When one takes into account that the show in itself requires a considerable number of farm fields to take place in, how could the committee go about making firm bookings for the show when the restrictions that came with this disease were rigidly enforced? Anyone who has seen, or anyone who realises even, the consequences the disease has for farmers, would realise the reluctance of the farming community to get involved in any commitment that allowed access to their property. Even as early as January this was causing real problems for a new member of the committee who had been brave enough to take on the responsibility of running and organising the animal tent. Therefore, I expect that Mr Vern Dunkley began to wonder what he had walked into, but I was equally sure that he would have the support of the committee come what may.

By mid-March, certain decisions had to be made. As some country shows were already being cancelled, it was therefore more important than ever that, if it was at all possible, the White Horse Show would go on. By late April, the foot-and-mouth epidemic had eased a little, which made looking forward to the end of August a little easier. During May, advice was sought from the Ministry of Agriculture. Of course it was hoped they would at least have some of the answers to the questions that the committee wanted to put, together with any advice that was appropriate to the situation the show committee were in. However, I suppose that was too much to ask for. We were told that if the restrictions on the movement of animals had not been lifted it would not be possible to have this type of animal at the show. It would therefore be the responsibility of the farmer to ensure that anyone entering his property stayed rigidly within the law.

After talks with the farmer, Mr Richard Whitfield, it was decided that they should carry on planning the show without bovine animals. But he would have to insist that each gateway had a disinfectant and straw barrier even after the restrictions had been lifted; he was sorry, but he would have to insist on this as an added safeguard to his own stock. To allow the show to go ahead on his land was an extremely brave decision to take. I therefore think that all who attended the show in 2001 owed a great deal of thanks to Mr Richard Whitfield for allowing the show to continue. I know in fact that the chairman and committee realised this and made their feelings plain to all and sundry. The magnitude of that decision would in years to come be even more plain to see.

The programme for the 2001 show carried a statement about these problems on page 4; it read thus:

> The committee would like to extend a very warm welcome to exhibitors, performers and visitors at this year's show.
>
> The foot and mouth epidemic has made 2001 a terrible year for farmers and people who earn their living from the countryside. We send our sincere sympathy to all who have been affected by this awful disease, including those country shows that have been forced to cancel. The White Horse Show has been fortunate in having a regular August bank holiday date which, being relatively late in the season, meant we could press ahead with our preparations in the hope that the worst would be over before our show.
>
> Our gamble has fortunately paid off and you will see that we have succeeded in putting together a programme of events every bit as good as last year. Not only are our regular attractions such as historic vehicles and country pursuits at full strength, but we have also filled our animal tent with some different and interesting animals and got an action-packed schedule of arena events. We are particularly pleased this year to welcome again the beautiful heavy horses.

The Horsemen of the Apocalypse made such a sensational debut at last year's show, attracting a six-deep audience round the arena, that we have asked them to do an encore this year. We've added an exciting new motorcycle display, the Honda Imps, and the Rockwood team will enthral dog lovers. Something very special and innovative this year will be a show of miniature horses, and the National Hunt Jockeys' Gymkhana promises to be hilarious – as well as raising money for a very worthy cause, the Injured Jockeys' Fund.

The White Horse Show has a charitable trust and all proceeds from the show are used to help local charities and community organisations. This year we are celebrating our Pearl Anniversary, thirty consecutive years of fundraising for Uffington and the neighbouring villages. These years have resulted in a new village hall, a community minibus and financial assistance for the school, the church and many other good causes. We thank you for your support, which will enable us to continue this work, and we hope you have a very enjoyable show.

It leaves me and one or two other people to thank our lucky stars that the committee decided to revert back to the August bank holiday weekend for the show, because if they had not it would have been virtually impossible to have run the show early in July. It is a known fact that once you have to cancel a show of this type and size, it takes a long time to get started again, if ever you do in fact manage to get back to a large and profitable size. To lose this show after all this time would be a large blow to the local community. However, a little more on some of the attractions at this year's show.

Horsemen of the Apocalypse – This act was a sensational hit at our 2000 show. It was the brainchild of Ian van Temperley, who has been riding and working with horses since a very early age. A registered Equity Stuntman, Ian now has a long list of film and TV credits to his name, including *Merlin*, *Sleepy Hollow*, *Jason and the Argonauts*, *The Visitors*, *Sharpe* and *Extremely Dangerous*. He was introduced to the world of films by Gerard Naprous, a stunt coordinator, and worked all over the world with him in the Devil's Horsemen. The Horsemen of the Apocalypse is an exciting new adventure set up in 1999, using highly skilled stunt horsemen with a wealth of experience. The same team are so versatile that they can also put on other shows such as 'Wild West' or 'Cossack'. However, Horsemen of the Apocalypse is a new style of show offering something very original and appropriate to the start of the twenty-first century, and incorporating costumes and effects which you won't see in any other show. The theme is really unusual and the unique script, together with the high standard of horsemanship, make an exciting combination that you won't forget in a hurry.

Jockeys' Gymkhana – Following the cancellation of this year's Cheltenham Festival, the jockeys have been seeking a suitable alternative to show off their considerable riding skills. We believe that this is the event. It will take place in Arena 1, at 4 p.m. on Sunday, after the parade of heavy horses. Don't miss it! Yes, come and watch in awe as these brave men take part in a fun gymkhana in aid of the Injured Jockeys' Fund. See man and beast become one as they strive to be first past the post.

It may be light-hearted but one thing's for sure, the jockeys will be out to win. It's A CERTAINTY!

The Jockeys – Mick Fitzgerald, Timmy Murphy, Carl Llewelyn, Jim Culloty, Tony McCoy, Andrew Thornton, Sean Curran, John Kavanagh, Adrian Maguire, Seamus Durack, Glen Tormey, Graham Bradley.

Commentator – Richard Pitman, BBC racing presenter.

Many thanks to Lynda Froud of White Horse Animal Feeds for kindly sponsoring this event.

The Injured Jockeys' Fund chairman – Lord Oaksey.

The Injured Jockeys' Fund was established in 1964 and is governed by a trust deed. The prime purpose of the IJF is to provide assistance, financial and otherwise, to those jockeys who are injured and are unable to ride. The beneficiaries, their families and dependants receive pastoral care from the IJF almoners and financial assistance. The IJF has nearly 800 living beneficiaries on its books.

Grateful thanks to Richard, the jockeys, the children and of course their ponies.

The Honda Imps – Making their first appearance at our show, the Honda Imps are Britain's largest motorcycle display team, with forty young riders. Their impressive track record includes UK appearances at the Edinburgh Military Tattoo, VE Day Celebrations in Hyde Park, the Royal Bath & West Show, and the

International Air Tattoo. They have also performed overseas at the Nova Scotia International Tattoo in Canada, the Chingay Procession and Bukit Turf Club in Singapore, as well as Belgium and the Netherlands.

The Imps are not a stunt team, but a highly skilled display team with a family appeal, for whom public safety is a priority. Their non-stop performance includes intricate formation rides, pyramids, comedy, tricks, jumps and a lot more.

Formed in the early 1970s, the Imps are the display team of the Impstart Trust, a charity dedicated to helping children grow to full maturity through structured, adventurous experiences. The children are led by unpaid voluntary leaders and enjoy every minute of what they do. The Imps are sponsored by Honda.

At this year's show we would be using two arenas. The programme for Sunday 26 August was:

Arena 1

10.00–13.00 Heavy Horses
13.00 Hounds of the Old Berks Hunt
13.30 Heavy Horses
15.15 Parade of Heavy Horses
15.30 Heavy Horses
16.00 Jockeys' Gymkhana

Arena 2

11.45 Island Farm Donkeys
12.00 Ray Prior Falconry
12.30 Rockwood Dog Display
13.30 Miniature Horses Show-jumping
14.30 Rockwood Dog Display
15.00 Ray Prior Falconry
15.45 Historic Motorcycles Parade

The arena timetable for Monday 27 August was:

Arena 1

11.00 Presenting Miniature Horses
11.45 Presenting Island Farm Donkeys
12.00 Egg Throwing Demonstration
13.00 The Honda Imps

Arena 2

Driving tests will be held in Arena 2 on Monday until 14.30.

At 14.45 there will be a parade of historic tractors, followed by the parade of historic cars at 15.00.

	Motorcycle Display
14.00	The Horsemen of the Apocalypse
15.00	Three Counties Egg Throwing Championship
15.30	The Honda Imps Motorcycle Display

Arena events at this year's show were generously sponsored by Fish Brothers.

The Animal Marquee – In this marquee and in the near vicinity we have a wide range of interesting animals and birds and crafts associated with animal products and the countryside. Take time to linger and chat with the exhibitors, who will be delighted to share their knowledge and enthusiasm with you.

The foot and mouth outbreak this year has had its impact on the animal marquee, which has urged us to find alternative animals to interest and delight – hedgehogs, tortoises, rabbits, snakes, hens and guinea pigs.

We will also be having demonstrations of activities such as felting, lace making, weaving and making rope from hay. Remember – for the safety and well-being of the animals – smoking is not permitted in the marquee.

Other country pursuits that will be taking place throughout the show are as follows:

Clay Pigeon Shooting (not competition) – Come and try the ultimate sport for hand and eye coordination. Expert tuition available throughout the weekend on our 'have a go' stand for those of you who have never tried this exciting sport. All safety equipment supplied. A selection of guns to suit men and women, young and not so young.

Archery – Have a go with a long bow. A test of steady hand and true eye – can you put six arrows in the gold? No? Then trust the expert tuition of Gerald Mills and his team from Bampton Archery Club. All equipment provided.

Air Rifle Target Shooting – Test your skills with these most accurate weapons on the six-metre target range. Air rifles supplied and expert tuition on hand throughout the weekend from some of the best shots in the country.

Terrier Racing – Bring your own terriers, lurchers, whippets, or even the good old family pet and see how fast they come out of the trap in pursuit of a simulated quarry.

As anyone can see, running a show as large as the White Horse Show takes a considerable amount of planning and organising. Of course the amount of sheer hard work to build the showground to fit everything in is a mammoth task also. But everybody must surely congratulate the committee and helpers even more this year because of the foot and mouth epidemic. This in itself gave all persons involved a very worrying time, with the uncertainty of whether there would be a show or not. But the determination of all concerned to put the show on means that it must go down as one of the most satisfying of all time. Leading up to this show, every time you listened to the news or read the newspapers, shows and events of this type were being cancelled right up to within a few weeks of the White Horse Show. When the Cricklade Show was called off it was no surprise, as being predominately a cattle show these were the first types of events to fall. I felt real sorrow for the organisers of these shows, knowing the amount of work, thought and worry that must have been put into them. To be defeated in the end by this disease must have been heart-breaking.

But, as the saying goes, it's an ill wind that doesn't do somebody some good. I believe that by making sure they had the alternative events ready and by really good planning it all came right for the White Horse Show. In that way, if the public could not go to their usual bank holiday entertainment they came to the White Horse Show. This the committee found to be a fact at their wash-up meeting when the profit from their hard work and worry was forecast to be in the region of £20,000. When this news was released to the public it certainly caused a stir among the critics of old. I, for one, was not behind in reminding one or two of the old adversaries that the show had taken off again in a big way. When the accounts were finally published for this, the 2001 show, it projected a profit of £21,908.

Village sign funded by trust

As always, though, as great as the feeling was within the committee, thought, planning and work had to be directed towards the 2002 show. As it was the Golden Jubilee of HM Queen Elizabeth II, an extra programme of events would have to be held in the village to mark that occasion. As usual some of the show committee would undoubtedly be involved with those celebrations and planning. It had already been decided that a special village sign would be erected in the Jubilee Field during these celebrations, costs of which would be borne by the profits of the 2001 show.

With the White Horse Show once more back into the profit-making of old at the 2000 show, it was with much pleasure that we were able as trustees to sit down at our meeting on Wednesday, 21 November 2001. We were happy in the knowledge that we could look at the grant applications and be able to make recommendations on the surplus funds from the show of 2000.

Although that show had in fact returned a surplus of £7,035, the trustees had considerably less than this to recommend for distribution. This was because the White Horse Show Committee had made a very sensible and shrewd decision. The funds that had been used from the disaster fund over the previous two years of show losses were to be reimbursed from that surplus back into the disaster fund to cover any further disasters that the show might encounter in the future. In this way, providing that there would always be sufficient volunteers to organise and run the show, it would be able to continue, hopefully well into the future.

But – alas! – this meeting was in no way going to be normal: the first three grants were straightforward and did not cause any problems whatsoever, but the next certainly made up for this. The Sports and Social Club made a request for a grant to replace an old garage that had become unsafe and dangerous; their request was for £5,000. The size of the grant request was somewhat large to begin with, therefore we had to have a lot more information before we could make any grant at all. It was decided, therefore, that we must have a considerable amount of information and explanation as to why a replacement garage was going to cost so much. The three main questions that we as trustees were asking were, firstly, were they, the members of the Sports and Social Club, prepared to undertake the work or a part of the work? Secondly, was the club putting their own funds to use on this project? Third and foremost, had they applied for any grants from any other grant-giving bodies, for example any other sporting associations that give grants to projects such as this, and of course had they applied to the Vale of White Horse District Council?

The answer to the third part of this, concerning a grant from the Vale of White Horse District Council, was answered promptly by our chairman of trustees, Mr V Boaler. He informed us that in fact the Sports and Social Club had made an application to them for a grant, but this had been unsuccessful, in as far as a straightforward answer to their application was concerned. We were informed that in fact the council had made enquiries to the sports club. They wanted to know what size of grant the White Horse Show trustees were going to make to them before they could make their grant. Their explanation for this attitude was that they had other grant applications for projects from other villages that did not have additional funds as our three villages had. Therefore, they would have to look more in favour of villages that had not tried to raise funds on their own.

This attitude from a council that was elected to represent all people within their boundaries I found disgusting. To say that this information made me irate was very much an understatement and I was certainly not backward in saying so. I therefore raised the question: were we citizens in the villages of Uffington Woolstone and Baulking paying less council tax in the same bands as other citizens in the Vale of White Horse? Or was this just another good kick in the teeth for working hard over a great number of years trying to help our own community? If this was the case then the people of the three villages might just as well sit down and wait for the handouts to come our way for nothing. Then, thinking of all the tremendous hard work that had been put in to raise funds over the last forty-one years, I was not prepared to let this happen. To do so would not have been fair or have done justice to all of the people who had participated in the past and had now left the area or died in the meantime. However, this item was left in abeyance until we had answers to the questions we had asked.

It was at this point in the meeting that I thought it was the right time to disclose to the other trust members the decision that my wife, Myra, and myself had made. It was the most difficult decision that we had ever made, but with Myra's health problems it was the only one that we could make in the end. I therefore informed them that it was with very deep regret that we had decided to leave Uffington to live in Kidderminster, as we could see no prospect of a bungalow coming on to the market in the Uffington area in the foreseeable future. Therefore, with our daughter and her family living in Kidderminster, and Myra's ability to negotiate stairs becoming worse by the day, it was the only decision we could make. I of course informed them that I would confirm the decision in writing in due course. This I did as promised, with a letter to each trustee; the effective date of my resignation was 31 October 2002. It certainly gave me no pleasure to resign, as I had been involved with the whole project from the beginning in April 1960, a total of forty-two years and six months. Throughout that time, through thick and thin, through all the arguments and disagreements and of course the laughs and fun times, I always had the feeling of satisfaction that we had together achieved a great deal. It is one thing in my lifetime that I would not have missed for anything else.

A further item on our agenda at this meeting was whether it would not be a more sensible thing for us to consider extending the size of the trustees to seven members. This was given due consideration, with the outcome being 'certainly'. With this item discussed in full it was decided to ask Mr Derek Kelsey to join us. This I thought was a very good idea for two reasons. Firstly, we would be able to have a broader look at requests for grants with seven people's views on any subject that might come before us as trustees. This in my opinion had got to be the right way of looking at requests. Secondly, and foremost, Derek was the chairman of the White Horse Show Committee and would certainly have first-hand knowledge on two very important points. The first one was: had the organisation requesting a grant taken an opportunity to be at the show raising funds? The other was: what were the thoughts of the other people on that committee? Knowing and having worked with Derek over a number of years I knew that he would understand that he would only have exactly the same power as all the other trustees. It was therefore with pleasure that I could be at the meeting that he came to and accepted the invitation to join us.

2002

At the very next meeting of the trustees it was with sorrow that we had to accept the resignation of our long-standing secretary and treasurer, Mr Peter Erskine, who had decided that it was time for him to retire from these posts due entirely to failing health. All trustees wished Peter good luck in the future, with the hope that his health would greatly improve in the very near future. As a result of this sad news from Peter it was our duty to fill those posts that had became vacant. After a very short discussion, and quite a lot of pressure from all present, Derek succumbed and accepted these posts. This I believe was a really good outcome, as by filling these posts Derek would in future knit the trustees and the White Horse Show Committee to a very close understanding with each other. This would also still be in line with the charity commissioners' rules and regulations.

At the next meeting of the trustees, we heard that the Vale of White Horse District Council had at long last made a grant to the Sports and Social Club. This in itself allowed us to make our grant regarding the replacement garage, as members of the Sports and Social Club had undertaken to perform as much work as possible with their own labour.

The 2002 show would again be a three-day event, with the Saturday being a pony gymkhana that would take place in Arena 1 from 10 a.m. to 5 p.m. This was thanks to the organisation of Brian White who, together with his wife and daughter, worked tirelessly to make this event possible for youngsters. Thanks must also go to the following companies for their sponsorship of this pony fun day and display:

Warman Trophies of Wantage, Carter & McArthur, Graham Fletcher, Kelly Brother Builders, Clarks (Wantage) Ltd, Uffington Sports Club, Vale and Uffington Garages, Wallis Dairy Uffington, Mervyn Richings Farrier, The White Horse Woolstone, I & J Mildenhall Builders, M & S Sound Systems, Vicky White and Pip, White Horse Transport, Wantage Tyre

Services, Wantage Building Supplies, Faringdon Roofing Services, M R Wallis Roofing Contractors, Adrian Holley General Builders, Ann and Derek Kelsey.

At this year's show we would be using two arenas. The programme for Sunday 25 August was as follows:

Arena 1

- 10.30 Heavy Horses
- 13.00 Parade of Old Berks Hunt
- 13.30 Heavy Horses
- 15.15 Parade of Heavy Horses
- 15.30 Heavy Horses
- 16.00 Jockeys' Gymkhana

Arena 2

- 11.00 White Horse Kites
- 11.15 Ray Prior Falconry
- 11.45 Rockwood Dog Display
- 12.15 Island Farm Donkeys
- 12.45 Kangaroo Gymnastics
- 13.15 Miniature Horses
- 13.45 Ray Prior Falconry
- 14.15 Rockwood Dog Display
- 14.45 Island Farm Donkeys
- 15.15 Kangaroo Gymnastics
- 15.45 Historic Motorbikes

The timetable for Monday 26 August was as follows:

Arena 1

- 11.00 White Horse Kites
- 11.30 Karate Display
- 12.00 Adams Axemen
- 12.45 Egg Throwing Demonstration
- 13.00 Kangaroo Gymnastics
- 13.30 Adams Axemen
- 14.00 Break for Spitfire
- 15.00 Three Counties Egg Throwing Championship
- 16.00 Kangaroo Gymnastics

Arena 2

- 11.15 Island Farm Donkeys
- 11.45 Ray Prior Falconry
- 12.30 Tomorrow's Gun Dogs
- 13.15 Island Farm Donkeys
- 14.00 Break for Spitfire
- 14.15 Ray Prior Falconry
- 14.45 Tomorrow's Gun Dogs
- 15.15 Historic Tractors
- 15.45 Historic Cars.

Arena events at this year's show were generously sponsored by Fish Brothers.

Jockeys' Gymkhana – This event was a great success at last year's show, raising £2,800 in sponsorship for the Injured Jockeys' Fund. The jockeys are back again this year for some more fun as well as raising more funds for their charity. Make sure you come along to Arena 1 on Sunday at 4 p.m. The action will be fast, furious and very funny.

Everyone knows about Tony McCoy's record-breaking season, and that Jim Culloty rode Best Mate to win the Cheltenham Gold Cup and Bindaree to win the Grand National; but racing is a dangerous sport. Earlier this year Seamus broke his leg for the second time, Jim broke his arm, Mick broke his wrist and Adrian suffered a broken neck. Thankfully they are all fit again, but some jockeys are not so lucky.

The jockeys – Mick Fitzgerald, Timmy Murphy, Carl Llewellyn, Jim Culloty, Tony McCoy, Andrew Thornton, Sean Curran, John Kavanagh, Adrian Maguire, Seamus Durack, Tom Doyle, Sarah Bosley, Matt Batchelor, Noel Fehily.

Commentator – Martin Bosley.

WWII Spitfire – At this year's White Horse Show something very special will be happening at 2 p.m. on Monday. Last seen over Uffington at our VE Day celebrations, we are delighted that this year we shall again be able to view at very close range the most famous and charismatic British plane of all time. We are indebted to the Battle of Britain Memorial Flight 2002, which has kindly agreed to provide a Spitfire flypast at our show.

The prototype Spitfire flew from Eastleigh Airport, Southampton, on 5 March 1936. The advanced aerodynamics and construction techniques stemming from the Schneider Trophy racing aircraft were incorporated in the Spitfire's design by R J Mitchell. Developments of the aircraft were to establish and maintain the air superiority so vital to the defence of the United Kingdom and hence ultimate victory throughout the war that followed.

The first aircraft was delivered into service with the Royal Air Force in August 1938, and by the beginning of the Battle of Britain nineteen squadrons were equipped with Spitfires. The total number built exceeded 22,000 in thirty-six separate marks. Such was the vision of the designer and the potential of the aircraft that it progressed from the prototype – weighing 5,400 lbs with a 1,050 hp Merlin engine – to the Seafire Mk 47 – weighing 12,500 lbs with a 2,350 hp Griffon engine. All this was accomplished in essentially the same airframe with relatively minor modifications.

Songs of Praise at the Show – Our peripatetic parish priest, the Rev. John Gawn-Cayne, will be conducting a short service of hymns and prayers from various points around the showground, starting at 10 a.m. on Sunday. Please join him and fellow parishioners in offering praise and thanks for our community, our beautiful countryside and the many gifts with which we have been blessed. You are most welcome to accompany Father John as he visits our marquees and attractions, or to listen to the service, which will be broadcast over the public address system.

The Adams Axemen – The Adams Axemen from Dorset were formed in 1966 as the New Forest Axemen, the first axe-racing team in Great Britain (and they're still the best). They appear across the UK at more than fifty events each year. Last year they had another busy season performing at many shows around the country, including the New Forest and Hampshire, Royal Welsh, Royal Cornwall and Devon County Shows. They have taken their act to Australia, New Zealand, America, Europe and Canada as well as performing on TV. The Adams Axemen are a team of professional showmen who love their business and who present a fast, fun show of strength, skills and rustic humour. Their aim is to provide demonstrations of the skills of the forester and lumberjack in a manner that is both entertaining and educational to the public and enjoyable to themselves. The demonstration consists of all aspects of log axing, springboard chopping and cross-cut sawing.

They did in fact perform at an earlier White Horse Show when they were still known as the New Forest Axemen. At that time they held the crowd in wonderment and awe; we have no doubt that they will do the same again, so do not miss them. They are performing twice in Arena 1 at 12 p.m. and 1.30 p.m. on Monday.

Models – We are very grateful to Mr J Scutts and friends from Swindon, Witney, Bourton-on-the-Water, Newbury and Faringdon who have assembled a magnificent display of models in one of our marquees. Their exhibits include a farmyard, gypsy encampment, canal boats, soldiers, aircraft, caravans and horse-drawn vehicles, steam engines and a circus, a scrapyard, transport in punch embroidery and early yesteryear toys.

Kangaroos Gymnastic Team – The Kangaroos Gymnastic and Trampoline Display Team is now generally recognised as the best of its kind in Britain. The first team was formed in 1981 and over the years it has matured and developed the highest levels of performance. They have given presentations in many types of venue from Wembley Stadium to prestige office blocks; from village halls to television productions; from many charitable functions to the worlds of advertising and military tattoos. Major appearances include the FA Cup Final, England vs. Germany, two Grand Nationals, the Rhine Army Show and the Guernsey Battle of the Flowers.

Other performances have included the Derby Military Tattoo, the Taunton Flower Show, the RAF Cosford Air Show, the Wiltshire Show, the North Somerset Show, the Metropolitan Police Gala and many, many more. The Kangaroos have been seen on television on numerous occasions, including a display before Her Majesty the Queen at the Broadgate Centre, *You Bet!*, *Blue Peter*, the Sheffield Special Olympics and *Britain's Strongest Man*.

The Kangaroos hold several performance world records. One for the longest and highest continuous vaulting move – 223 feet long, with nineteen performers in the air at the same time. Another is 43,629 somersaults in twenty-four hours performed for *Children in Need*.

The team comprises thirty boys aged from twelve to twenty-one. Most are pupils at Polesworth High School near Tamworth. They are trained by their founder, Mr Bruce Gracie, who is a teacher at the school. Initial training can take up to three years, depending on the complexity of the moves. Says Mr Gracie, 'The kids who come to us are not gymnastic experts or spring coils; they are normal lads who take an interest in the sport. They have to work hard and they know if they have the commitment and determination they are always welcome.'

The Kangaroos' display consists of seven increasingly difficult and more spectacular moves, with over 200 somersaults including many doubles. If conditions are right they may even do some triple somersaults, not performed by any other team in the UK.

The highlights of the display are multiple somersaults over a car or motorcycles, and the final 'Big Move', which is the longest, highest and most spectacular continuous vaulting move performed possibly anywhere in the world.

As can be seen from this very full programme of events over the period of the show, it was designed and planned to capture as wide as possible interest and to attract a very wide cross-section of the general public. Given the weather over the length of the show, it couldn't fail to attract a good crowd. It still must not be forgotten that a bigger crowd also spells more hard work and worry for the committee and the old faithful helpers.

When the final balance sheet was to hand for the 2002 show it again turned in a fantastic profit margin of £20,289. Although slightly down on the figure for 2001, it still had quite a number of people absolutely speechless. With these profit margins well to the forefront of the committee's publicity campaign, they could only benefit from them in the future if the hard work and unison within the committee continued as in the past.

As a direct result of the huge success of the last two White Horse shows, the trustees were able to award grants to local organisations as follows:

Uffington Sports Club, £4,700; to the erection of the village sign, £2,260; senior citizens' Christmas lunch, £82; Thomas Hughes Memorial Hall, £1,443; Uffington Players (amateur dramatics), £2,356; Thomas Saunders Foundation, £400; Uffington Youth Club, £162; Tom Brown's School Museum, £1,000; Uffington Afternoon Club, £200; St Mary's Church, Uffington, £750; Uffington Christmas-tree lights, £946; Uffington Primary School PTA, £1,000; Uffington Bus Shelter, £500; for the third new UBW community minibus, £6,000; White Horse Preschool, £300; Uffington Short Mat Bowls Club, £75. This made a total of £22,174 that had been allocated in grants for 2002.

The trustees were pleased to confirm that these grants would bring the total of grants awarded since the formation of the White Horse Show Trust in 1982 to almost £150,000. This of course would not have been possible without the support and hard work of the White Horse Show Committee. This is of course a terrific amount of money to be raised by voluntary workers over this period of time. What the total of funds raised by the local organisations themselves at these shows had been was at this stage a question to which there was no answer. To guess would be rather fruitless, but the total must be very large indeed. It leaves me to wonder what some of the old time knockers would say now. After all, if any notice of their preaching of doom in the past had been taken, the White Horse Show would not be in existence today.

2003

While all of this was taking part, the show committee had been as busy as usual with the planning and bookings for the 2003 show. Whilst this show was being planned, some very important news came through to the show committee. This was that their chairman, Derek Kelsey, had been awarded the MBE in the Queen's Birthday Honours list. Well done, Derek; you certainly deserved the recognition for lifting the show back to life after the two years in the doldrums making a loss. It only came back entirely through your own shrewd judgement and hard work, together with winning the backing of the entire show committee. I can only reiterate that your good wife, Ann, must also take credit for the support that she has given you through thick and thin since you accepted the chairmanship of the show. It also goes to show that, at long last, the great work over a very long time by ordinary people prepared to work for the betterment of the local area has at long last been recognised. I can only hope that the beneficiaries and all the local people will appreciate the hard work by the committee and your guidance over the years. Again it is a great honour truly earned by yourself, Derek, and all members who have served on the White Horse Show Committee over the years.

Thus back to the 2003 show, which again would be a three-day event on the Saturday, Sunday and Monday of the August bank holiday weekend. Thanks to Mr Richard Whitfield it would again be held in the fields of Fawler Farm. Again I will list the faithful members of the committee, together with their responsibilities within the show: chairman, Derek Kelsey, MBE; secretary, Ann Kelsey; treasurer, Ray Avenell; field director, arena events and security, Paul Armishaw; field services, Bill Mattingley; commentators, Malcolm White and Fran Walsh; publicity and programme, Mike Thomas; sponsorship, Simon Saunders; catering, litter, first aid, RAF, Derek Kelsey, MBE;

hunt, Clive Avenell; stands, Christine Holly and Annette Rayner; historic vehicles, Eric Wyard; helicopter, show control centre, Ann Kelsey; heavy horses, Debbie Wallis; animals, Vern Dunkley; pony gymkhana, Brian White; country pursuits, Martin Bowsher and Christine Holly; stationary engines and tractors, David Clarke and Ces Witchell; parking, Christine Holly; stewards, signs and support, Stewart Lovelock, Gareth Armishaw, Damian Wilson, Stephen Fisher, Viv Boaler, Lloyd Whitfield and Darren Scrivens; bar, Tiggy and Polly Packford.

This list of people and the amount of work they have to do to make a show the size of the White Horse Show a success must give the beneficiaries some idea of the amount of gratitude they should show to the show. The list, of course, does not show the old faithful volunteers who come along to help at every show, to do turns on the entrance gates, car parking, litter picking, building the showground... the list is never ending.

Battle of Britain Memorial Flight – Anyone who came to the 2002 show on the bank holiday Monday will remember the buzz of excitement as an original WWII Spitfire swooped low over the showground. This year, however, we have an even bigger treat in store, thanks to the Battle of Britain Memorial Flight (BBMF). At 3.45 p.m. on Sunday, visitors to the show will have another chance to see at very close range the most famous and charismatic British plane of all time. But this year the Spitfire will be accompanied by a WWII Lancaster. Of the 7,377 Lancasters built, only two are still in airworthy condition, and the other one is in Canada.

Lancaster PA474 was built in Cheshire in mid-1945 and earmarked for the 'Tiger Force' in the Far East. However, the war with Japan ended before she could take part in any hostilities. She was therefore assigned to photographic reconnaissance duties with 82 Squadron in East and South Africa. On returning to the UK she was loaned to Flight Refuelling Ltd to be used as a pilotless drone. But before conversion started the Air Ministry decided to use a Lincoln instead and PA474 was transferred to the Royal College of Aeronautics for trials on a new wing.

In 1964 the plane was adopted by the Air Historical Branch for future display in the proposed RAF Museum at Hendon and was flown to Wroughton, where she was painted with camouflage paint. During this period PA474 took part in two films: *Operation*

Crossbow and *The Guns of Navarone*. Later that year she was moved to RAF Henlow, then in 1965 permission was granted for her to make a single flight from Henlow to RAF Waddington, where she joined 44 Squadron, the first unit to have been equipped with Lancasters.

At Waddington a programme of restoration was begun and by 1967 PA474 was allowed to fly regularly, eventually joining the BBMF in 1973. Restoration work has continued ever since, including the addition of a mid-upper turret discovered in Argentina and fitted in 1975, the year the plane was adopted by the city of Lincoln. Its current 61 Squadron livery was applied in 2000, representing EE176 'Mickey the Moocher', one of the great Lancaster Centurions who flew and survived over 100 missions.

New Thomas Hughes Memorial Hall built with proceeds from the early shows

The Thomas Hughes Memorial Hall is located on the Jubilee Field in the centre of the beautiful village of Uffington. The new hall was completed in 1975, replacing a wooden and corrugated iron hut that was in a very poor state of repair and dated back to just after World War I. It was built with funds raised in various and numerous ways from 1960 until 1972, when the White Horse Show came into being and funded the final push for completion, together with a very generous gift from Professor and Mrs Seton-Lloyd of Woolstone. In 1981 a further phase was completed, consisting of an additional smaller hall, again funded by proceeds from the show. The show continues to support certain elements of the hall's upkeep.

The hall has very good facilities and includes a very well-equipped kitchen, warm-air ducted heating, disabled toilet, baby-changing facilities and a large car park. The hall is used extensively by numerous local organisations, including badminton, mothers and toddlers, nursery school, indoor bowls, senior citizens, Brownies, Youth Club and martial arts. It is also available for hire to persons living outside the local parishes.

On Saturday 23 August the pony gymkhana took place in Arena 1 from 10.00 to 17.00.

At this year's show, two arenas were used. The programme for Sunday 24 August was as follows:

Arena 1	Arena 2
10.30 Heavy Horses	11.00 White Horse Kites
13.00 Tae Kwon Do	11.15 Ray Prior Falconry
13.15 White Horse Kites	11.45 Tomorrow's Gun Dogs
14.00 Heavy Horses	12.15 Cumberland Giants
15.30 Parade of Heavy Horses	12.45 Adams Axemen
15.45 Spitfire & Lancaster	13.30 Merlin Engine
16.00 Jockeys' Gymkhana	13.45 Tomorrow's Gun Dogs
	14.15 Ray Prior Falconry
	14.45 Cumberland Giants
	15.15 Adams Axemen
	15.45 Historic Motorcycles

The committee were very grateful to the Fish Brothers Group for their generous sponsorship of this year's arena events.

The timetable for Monday 25 August was:

Arena 1

11.00　White Horse Kites
12.00　Adams Axemen
12.30　Old Berks Hunt
13.00　Cumberland Giants
13.30　Mighty Smith
14.00　Adams Axemen
14.45　Egg Throwing Demonstration
15.00　Three Counties Egg Throwing Championship
16.00　Cumberland Giants

Arena 2

11.15　Mighty Smith
11.45　Ray Prior Falconry
12.30　Tomorrow's Gun Dogs
13.15　Merlin Engine
13.30　Army Cadets Mock Battle
13.45　White Horse Kites
14.15　Ray Prior Falconry
14.45　Tomorrow's Gun Dogs
15.15　Historic Tractors
15.30　Historic Cars

About some of the events and participants at this year's show:

The Mighty Smith Show – Performing at the White Horse Show for the first time this year, Adrian Smith – the 'Mighty Smith' – has won the UK's Strongest Man title a record three times. He gained a highly creditable fifth place in the World's Strongest Man and has represented the UK all over the world in international strong-man events. He now presents a show geared towards family fun with visual humour and audience participation. His act includes tearing up telephone directories, bending six-inch nails with his teeth, walking on a bed of broken glass and presenting a tug-of-war using four strong men pulling on a rope tied around his neck. He can hold a chair with a lady seated on it between his teeth and does a comedy tug-of-war with loads of children. These, along with some more serious feats of strength, combine with a £1,000 challenge to anyone who can duplicate them.

Barrow of Booze – As you walk round the showground you may meet someone pushing a wheelbarrow full of whisky, wine, bubbly, beer and other alcoholic beverages. This is not a mobile bar! (Tiggy will be very happy to serve you in the beer tent if you are feeling thirsty.) On show Sunday and Monday we are raffling the barrow and its contents to raise money for a Christmas lunch for Uffington's senior citizens. Just buy some raffle tickets from the 'pusher' and all those lovely drinks could be yours – plus a barrow to push them home in.

Craft, Trade, Charity and Information Stalls – The White Horse Show is very pleased to welcome all those running the wide variety of craft stalls catering for every possible interest. As always there are too many to list but they include: needlecraft, paintings, pets in pots, 'crystal waters', toys, hand-made hats, fine fashion jewellery, pyrography (the art of burning on wood), clothing, dolls' clothes, hand-decorated china, garden furniture, hand-carved walking sticks, plants, bulbs, household goods, silk-flower cards and arrangements, glassware and candles.

For children there is face painting, amusements and a number of stalls selling toys.

Several charity and information stalls will also be running at this year's show. These include St Mary's Church, Uffington, Wantage and District RAFA, Prospect House Lottery, the October Club, Cats Protection League, the Samaritans and the Countryside Alliance.

Also of interest: the lace-making stand and display by Tom Brown's School Museum and dog grooming.

This year we are once again delighted to welcome Fish Brothers (Swindon) Ltd, who will be displaying a selection of vehicles from their Peugeot, Toyota, Honda and Mitsubishi ranges.

We particularly recommend that you visit the following stalls: Barbara Goodbun, semi-precious and gemstone-beaded jewellery; K McGee, Mists of Time, unique and unusual glassware; John Curtis, hand-carved walking sticks and shepherds' crooks; James Hart, J S Candles, hand-made candles; Euard Grandy, socks, underwear and children's wear; Michaela Greensmith, Wayland Crafts, hand-made and 'art to wear' clothing; the Dog Studio, dog grooming, horse livery, stone jewellery; Margaret King, Kings Kreations, hand-made jewellery; Kevin Rochlin, Ann Harries, Mexican jewellery; Cherry Bezencenet, S Pots, terracotta cookware from Catalonia; West Cookers, central-heating range cookers; Kenan Harrison, Fish Brothers, Honda Cars; Linda Ashwell, Ramblers Association, Promoting walking.

There will be awards for the best indoor and outdoor stalls at this year's show. The judges of this competition will be Stella Mattingley and Derek Kelsey.

Fairground Organ – We are delighted to welcome back Mr Read with his magnificent fairground organ. Capable of playing a huge range of tunes from marches to the Beatles, this remarkable instrument adds really tremendous atmosphere to our show. You can hear it play two hymns on 'tapes' commissioned by the show committee in our service at 10 a.m. on Sunday.

With the show committee again putting together another big and varied spread of good and interesting entertainment over the entire show, it was little wonder that yet again the attendance had risen. The gate takings had increased from £33,934 in 2002 to £42,743 in 2003. Also increased was the rent from trade stands from £3,920 in 2002 to £6,186 in 2003. But what must be fully understood by all is that the expenses also increased over the same time. On the other hand it does not put any shadow over the show committee whatsoever, because yet again they had increased the profitability of the show from £20,289 in 2002 to £30,163 in 2003. Congratulations to the committee for a very momentous achievement. This must have given them all a great feeling of satisfaction. But, at the same time, they must have had feelings for their treasurer, Mr Ray Avenell, who had quite a few headaches over this period of time. However, at the end of the day he must also have had a great feeling of satisfaction.

The shrewdness of the committee in keeping their eyes firmly on the rise of inflation, together with keeping the interest as widespread as possible with the entertainment within the show, helped to draw the crowds to the shows.

The only fear that I had over the successful turnaround from loss-making to the large profitability the show had now, was that complacency might develop within the beneficiaries of the shows. But somehow I did not think that would be allowed to happen. After all, the trustees and the show committee now had a very good and close relationship with each other. Thus, I believed, in the long run they would be looking very closely at the money-raising work that each applicant for grant had attempted prior to making a grant. I also believed that Mr Derek Kelsey, MBE, would not allow complacency to creep in anywhere after the hard work that was done by him and the show committee to recover the profitability of the shows.

The White Horse Show Trust were pleased to publish the following grants made by them in 2003. These received the blessing of the White Horse Show Committee: Uffington Sports and Social Club, £850; Uffington Players (Dramatics), £500; Thomas Saunders Foundation, £400; Uffington Afternoon Club, £200; St Mary's Church, Uffington. £1,124; Uffington Primary School, £4,000; Uffington Area Parents and Toddlers, £48. Making a grand total for 2003 of £7,122.

The trustees were Mr C P Avenell, Mr V J Boaler, Mr R D Kelsey, MBE, Mr J J Matthews, Mr W W T Mattingley, and Mr W H Mitchell.

In true White Horse Show style, before the 2003 show had taken place, the 2004 show was being planned. It had to be undertaken in this way to ensure that they were in time to book really good acts to come and perform. It is at times like this that things start to get really hectic. After all, some of the things relating back to the 2002 show were still being dealt with. Spare a thought for the poor treasurer. After all, Ray Avenell is still only human. Dealing with three shows at the same time, I can assure anybody, does happen and has happened ever since the shows really took off into the 'big time' in the early 1970s.

2004

The 2004 show would be commemorating and highlighting the sixtieth anniversary of D-Day, and surely everyone should know what this day is all about. To me, it was the beginning of the end of the Nazi regime in Germany, and the freedom of Europe. The success of this day in 1944 gave us all the freedom that we enjoy today. But, sadly, at terrible cost of life to the military forces that took part.

Remembering that day at this year's show we were all extremely grateful and privileged to have the Band of the Dragoon Guards and the Pipes and Drums of the Royal Scots Dragoon Guards performing for us in our main arena on Monday. It had been some years since we were entertained by a top military band, so having two was really special. The bands would be supported by a muster of the Royal British Legion and several regimental associations, together with a special muster from the Royal Hospital at Chelsea, as well as a display by the Army Cadets.

It was with deep regret that we had to report that Jumbo Read passed away shortly after last year's show. For many years Jumbo's fairground organs had been an attractive feature of our show and latterly provided splendid support for the hymns in the service with which our show opened. Our condolences went to all his family. We were delighted, however, that Jumbo's son Colin had kindly agreed to bring along the large fairground organ to this year's show.

At last year's show we said farewell to our vicar, Rev. John Gawn-Cayne, but the show service of thanks and praise that he instituted would be continued this year by Sue Saunders and the other members of the ministry team (10.00 on Sunday).

Finally, we said goodbye and thank you to Malcolm White and his family, who moved to the Isle of Wight. Malcolm and Jill had looked after the trade and craft stall at the show for the last few years, after which Malcolm did a fine job as a commentator for the main arena. We welcomed Mark Leahy, Adrian Dunn and Chris Rayner to the commentary team.

Thanks also went to Debbie Wallis, who had run the Heavy Horse Show in recent years and was now leaving the committee. We therefore extended a very warm welcome to Kerri Mack and Bernie Jones, who had taken on this responsibility, and we wished them good luck.

Pipes and Drums of the Royal Scots Dragoon Guards (Carabiniers and Greys), 2004

We also welcomed back, to organise the military and the pageant to commemorate the sixtieth anniversary of D-Day, a gentleman who was no stranger to White Horse shows – Colonel Tony Bateman (retired). It was great to see him back.

There follows a brief history of the military bands appearing at this year's show.

The Pipes and Drums of the Royal Scots Dragoon Guards (Carabiniers and Greys) – History: the Pipes and Drums of the Royal Scots Dragoon Guards have their origin in the small pipe band that came to the Royal Scots Greys in 1946 as a result of the demobilisation of certain Scottish Territorial Armoured Corps units. This was the Scots Greys' first official pipes and drums band. However, prior to this time there had been smaller and quite unofficial pipe bands in the regiment, including one in India in the 1920s which performed mounted.

The late King George VI took a great interest in the Pipes and Drums of the Royal Scots Greys and personally designed much of their uniform. It was King George VI who granted the Pipes and Drums the privilege of wearing the Royal Stewart tartan.

Pipes and Drums of the Royal Scots Dragoon Guards (Carabiniers and Greys), 2004

Dress: with the Royal Stewart kilt and plaid, the pipers wear a dark-blue doublet. The sporran is of grey horse hair (reminiscent of the grey horses), with tassels of black and red similar to the jowl plumes hung from the officers' bridles. The feather bonnets have the yellow Vandyke band and a white feather plume. The plaid brooch bears the White Horse of Hanover. The Eagle and Carbines badge is worn as a plume clasp in the feather bonnet and on the sporran cantle. In full dress uniform the drummers wear the regimental uniform of a bearskin hat, scarlet tunic, blue overalls, George boots and spurs. Not being classed as bandsmen, who wear a red plume in the bearskin, the drummers wear the normal white plume. The bass drummer, however, wears the distinctive white bearskin with a red plume. The white bearskin was given to the regiment by Tsar Nicholas the Second of Russia in 1894, on his becoming Colonel in Chief of the Royal Scots Greys.

Pipes and Drums of the Royal Scots Dragoon Guards (Carabiniers and Greys), 2004

Recent times: today, the Royal Scots Dragoon Guards' horses have long since been replaced by tanks and other armoured vehicles. Most recently the regiment has the honour of being the first in the army to be equipped with the new Challenger 2 main battle tank. All members of the Pipes and Drums are first and foremost fully trained tank crew members. Skills range from newly trained drivers and gunners of the younger band members, through to the combat-experienced first-class crewmen of the older members.

Many members of the Pipes and Drums served on active duty in the 1991 Gulf War and in more recent times as part of the NATO-led Stabilisation Forces helping to keep the peace in the former Yugoslavian states of Bosnia and Kosovo. Most recently the Pipes and Drums served in the Gulf in 2003, where the regiment played an instrumental part in the liberation of Basra.

'Amazing Grace': the Regimental Band and the Pipes and Drums enjoyed great success with the release of 'Amazing Grace' in 1971, particularly for their unique brand of combined music. The 1971 recording of 'Amazing Grace' became a worldwide multi-million-pound seller and was number one in the British pop charts for five weeks. Now, after twenty-five years in the public eye, 'Amazing Grace' is as popular as ever. The Pipes and Drums have just celebrated their fiftieth birthday and in that time they have played at many prestigious events worldwide, including the Edinburgh Military Tattoo.

The Pipes and Drums appear by kind permission of Lieutenant Colonel B P Edwards and are led by Pipe Major Derek Potter and Drum Major Gary Riley.

The Band of the Dragoon Guards – Wearing striking scarlet tunics, distinctive brass helmets and white plumes, the Band of the Dragoon Guards is renowned for the quality of its music, visual splendour and precision drill. On the concert platform it enjoys a similar reputation, ensuring its continuing popularity with concert audiences. The band's concert repertoire embraces a wide range of music, including popular classics, music of the Big Band era, exciting contemporary works and humorous features; these combine to produce programmes that are both entertaining and spectacular.

The band was formed on 1 August 1994 in Paderborn, Germany, following a major reorganisation of British Army music. After six successful years in Germany, the band moved to Swanton Morley, Norfolk, where its primary role remains the provision of musical support to the three historic regiments to which it has the honour to be affiliated: 1st The Queen's Dragoon Guards, the Royal Scots Dragoon Guards and the Royal Dragoon Guards.

In addition to supporting its affiliated regiments, the band travels extensively, providing quality musical entertainment to military and civilian audiences alike. Tours undertaken recently include Pakistan, Cyprus, Austria and Germany.

All members of the band are trained medical attendants and it is in this role that they serve in times of hostility. The band has only recently returned from the Gulf region, having served with 1 Close Support Medical Regiment on operations in the recent conflict in Iraq.

The band has produced two recordings, *Sounds European* and

its most recent offering *In Concert with the Band of the Dragoon Guards*. Both feature a wide selection of popular concert favourites. *In Concert with the Band of the Dragoon Guards*, in conjunction with other band memorabilia, is available from the band shop.

Acknowledgement: the Band of the Dragoon Guards appears by permission of the colonels, the Royal British Legion and Dragoon Guards Regimental Associations.

Normandy Muster, The Royal British Legion – The Royal British Legion is the leading charity looking after the welfare needs of the serving and ex-service members of the armed forces and their families. Within Berkshire and the Vale of White Horse, Oxfordshire and Wiltshire, the Royal British Legion branches in our community are exceptionally busy assisting with the rising demand for welfare assistance. This can range across all aspects of our work from providing powered scooters and wheelchairs, to help with bills or to break in one of the Royal British Legion homes.

The local communities in which we live continue their most generous support to the Poppy Appeal, which remains the main funding for all welfare assistance. In this, the sixtieth anniversary of D-Day year, the public has shown an incredible appreciation of our ex-service community and an understanding of the challenges and dangers faced by our current armed forces. The White Horse Show is therefore very pleased to welcome representatives of the county branches of the legion.

Taking the Salute: Mr J G H Champ, CBE, CEng, MI Mech, county vice-president of Berkshire and the Vale of White Horse, and past national chairman. He joined the Oxford and Bucks Light Infantry in the early 1950s and served in Egypt and Germany.

Exhortation: Col. (ret'd) A J Bateman, OBE, vice-president, Royal Scots Dragoon Guards Regimental Association; White Horse Show.

Kohima Epitaph: Mr R Good, county chairman of Berkshire and the Vale of White Horse Royal British Legion. He was born in Northern Ireland and served with the Irish Guards for twenty-two years, leaving with the rank of colour sergeant. Since joining the Royal British Legion in 1981 he has worked within his branch as treasurer and Poppy Appeal organiser and then as county treasurer and county recruitment officer.

The muster will be coordinated by the Berkshire County ceremonial officer, Mr Ray Lancaster, MBE. He joined the Grenadier Guards in 1954 and served for twenty-two years all over the world. He held the office of Legion National Parade Marshal until 2002 and was awarded his MBE in this years Queen's Birthday Honours.

The Regimental Associations – 1st The Queen's Dragoon Guards, the Royal Scots Dragoon Guards and the Royal Dragoon Guards.

These associations will be represented at the muster by their banner parties and members. Regimental associations seek to maintain contact between past and present members of their regiment, foster mutual friendship and provide social gatherings. They foster *esprit de corps*, comradeship and the welfare of their regiment, and preserve its traditions. In concert with the Army Benevolent Fund and SSAFA, they also support members and their families who are in need or distress.

These three cavalry regiments all have their origins in the late seventeenth century. They represent the amalgamation of regiments that were raised in the 1680s, during the protracted contest for the throne between James II and William of Orange. Throughout their long history they have a distinguished record of service, under the Duke of Marlborough at Blenheim, Ramillies and subsequent battles, and under the Duke of Wellington, notably at Waterloo. As the Union Brigade, they again earned distinction in the Crimea and thereafter in numerous campaigns, including the Boer War. For much of the 1914–18 war the regiments fought mainly as infantry, but there were notable instances of cavalry action and many examples of outstanding individual heroism. They were mechanised at the start of World War II and fought with distinction in Burma, North Africa and, most notably, in the Normandy campaign. Since the end of World War II, the regiments have served all over the world, especially in Germany, but also in Kosovo and in both Gulf Wars. Today all three regiments are serving in Germany as part of the Royal Armoured Corps: the Queens Dragoon Guards are a reconnaissance regiment, and the Royal Scots Dragoon Guards and the Royal Dragoon Guards are both equipped with Challenger 11 tanks.

The Army Cadets – The Oxfordshire Royal Green Jackets Battalion Army Cadet Force will be putting on a display in our arena this year. This will simulate a section attack on an enemy position. The cadets will also be tackling an assault course, displaying some military vehicles and will be happy to talk to you about the benefits of being an Army Cadet.

The 2004 White Horse Show certainly had a military atmosphere about it, which I think was justified in commemorating the sixtieth anniversary of the Normandy landings and the liberation of Europe.

On Saturday 28 August the pony gymkhana took place in Arena 1, from 10.00 to 17.00.

The programme of events for Sunday 29 August was as follows:

Arena 1		Arena 2	
10.30	Heavy Horse Show	11.00	Ray Prior Falconry
13.00	Tae Kwon Do	11.30	Tomorrow's Gun Dogs
13.15	Parade of the Old Berks Hunt	12.15	Van Buren – Illusionist
		13.00	Ray Prior Falconry
13.30	The Mighty Smith	13.30	Tomorrow's Gun Dogs
14.00	Heavy Horse Show	14.00	Van Buren – Illusionist
15.30	Parade of Heavy Horses	14.30	Parade of Historic Tractors
16.00	Jockeys' Gymkhana		
		15.00	The Mighty Smith
		15.45	Parade of Historic Motorcycles

The timetable for Monday 30 August was as follows:

Monday 30 August, Arena 1		Arena 2	
11.00	White Horse Kites	11.00	Ray Prior Falconry
12.00	The Mighty Smith	11.45	Tomorrow's Gun Dogs
12.45	Merlin Engine	12.30	Van Buren – Illusionist
13.00	Pipes and Drums of the Royal Scots Dragoon Guards (Carabiniers and Greys) and Band of the	13.00	Army Cadets
		13.15	Ray Prior Falconry
		13.45	Tomorrow's Gun Dogs

	Dragoon Guards
13.30	White Horse Kites
14.00	The Mighty Smith
14.30	Egg Throwing Competition Final
15.30	Pipes and Drums of the Royal Scots Dragoon Guards (Carabiniers and Greys) and the Band of the Dragoon Guards; The Royal British Legion and Dragoon Guards Regimental Associations; from the Royal Hospital at Chelsea, the Chelsea Pensioners. This arena event to commemorate the 60th anniversary of 'D-Day'
14.15	Van Buren – Illusionist
15.15	Parade of Historic Cars

The White Horse Show Committee are delighted to welcome visitors, exhibitors and helpers to this, the thirty-third Uffington White Horse Show. Attendance at the show now regularly exceeds 10,000 people; so this year we are sticking with our winning formula, but adding some new attractions. We therefore hope that all who attend will find something that interests them and that their attendance will be rewarded.

The White Horse Show Committee are very grateful to the Fish Brothers Group for their generous sponsorship of this year's arena events.

Police Message – We hope that you have an enjoyable time while at the show, but please try to avoid becoming a victim of crime. Opportunist thieves have struck twice in the past. A lady's purse was stolen when she put it down for a moment to admire articles on a stall, and a stallholder had goods stolen while her attention was distracted. Don't make it easy for thieves – wallets and purses left visible in pockets or on top of handbags give thieves an easy opportunity.

As always there will be a bar at this year's show. However, please remember: if you drink, don't drive.

This show produced another very remarkable success in attendances over its duration, culminating in yet another really good profit. This I feel was a very just reward for the extremely hard work that the whole committee and their helpers had put in over a long period of time. They all deserve the highest praise possible for this performance. When the balance sheet was produced for the show of 2004, it showed a profit of £26,046. I feel at this stage that I must reiterate yet again how in just five years the show has been turned round from making a loss in 1999 to this, the 2004 show, making the fantastic profit it did. When one looks at the overall picture of the last five shows, the profit margin turned in over those shows is £105,542. I am certain that the highest praise possible should be given to the committee by all the parishioners of the three villages. For what it is worth, I offer my extreme thanks to them all for a grand job well done. It is most gratifying from my point of view to think there is still the will in the locality to keep this show on the road. This shows the past members of the committee that all our hard work in the years past was not in vain.

The trustees were pleased to confirm that in 2004 £26,500 was received from the White Horse Show and to date they have distributed over £170,000. In 2004 the trustees awarded the following grants: Uffington Sports Club, £5,330; Uffington Afternoon Club, £300; St Mary's Church, Uffington, £2,400; Uffington Primary School PTA, £300; Uffington Primary School Foundation Stage Unit, £5,000; Thomas Hughes Memorial Hall, £2,000; Baulking Church, £500.

The grand total for these grants was £15,830. On being informed of these grants, the full White Horse Show Committee indicated their full support in the White Horse Show Trustees.

Trustees: Mr C P Avenell, Mr V J Boaler, Mr R D Kelsey, MBE, Mr J J Matthews, Mr W W T Mattingley, Mr W H Mitchell.

The organisation and planning was well in hand for the 2005

show, with the knowledge that this would be the sixtieth anniversary of the end of World War II. It was therefore decided that a programme of events to commemorate this would be fitting.

2005

The 2005 White Horse Show programme carried a fitting opening page as an introduction to the public, in particular for anyone who had not been a visitor to the show in the past, although I think that hardly anybody would not have heard of the show's existence by now, as publicity was one thing that seemed to have been done right over a long period of time. The introduction in the programme follows:

> A warm welcome to Uffington's thirty-fourth White Horse Show. Whether you are a visitor or an exhibitor or a performer, we are delighted to have you here and we hope you will have a very enjoyable show. In recent years attendance at the show has topped 10,000 people over the weekend. This has resulted in a big financial boost for the White Horse Show Charitable Trust, into which all the show's profits are paid, and you can read within this programme about the local charities and community organisations that have benefited. The committee therefore thank you for your support.
>
> Although the show is a fund-raising event, it can only succeed if visitors have an enjoyable day and want to return next year – with their friends! The show is run entirely by volunteers, but aims to maintain the highest professional standards. We try to offer something for all ages, combining the favourite attractions from previous years with some exciting new ones, and we are always open to suggestions for next year. You can read all about this year's entertainment in the programme, but here are a few ideas to whet your appetite.
>
> Sunday as always features the heavy horses. We are expecting a strong entry this year as our show has been designated a qualifying event for the West of England Championship. A new feature will be a riding display in the interval. On Monday the high point will be our pageant commemorating the sixtieth anniversary of the end of World War II. This spectacular event will combine on the ground: a military band, Chelsea Pensioners, cadets, the Royal British Legion and actors portraying life in

Everybody's favourite – the one and only Professor Crump, 2005
(© John Gibbons Studios)

wartime Britain. In the skies there will be a flying display by a Spitfire, a Hurricane and a Lancaster from the Battle of Britain Memorial Flight. Don't miss it!

Our Natural World marquee is a wonderful revamp of the old animal tent, which this year will include alpacas and otters that have appeared on TV. Ferret racing is also back and animal lovers will again be able to enjoy some excellent falconry and gundog displays. For those who are more interested in engines, we have a huge display of historic cars, motorcycles, tractors and stationary engines spanning most of the last century. If you want to 'do' rather than 'watch', try your hand at archery, have a go on the penalty shoot-out or enjoy all the fun of the fair. As always we have a wide range of interesting craft, trade and charity stalls. Children will find lots to enjoy, especially when they meet up with Professor Crump. And if it all gets too exciting, just relax with a drink from the beer tent, sit back and listen to the beautiful sound of Wantage Silver Band. We are particularly pleased that the band has agreed to stay on and accompany the hymns for our Songs of Praise service at 5 p.m. on Sunday.

For the last eight years Simon Stafford has done a fantastic job of producing all the artwork for our advertising and programme. We would like to thank him most sincerely for all his efforts and wish him well with his new projects, including the Farringdon Arts Festival. We are delighted, however, that Sam Green and Jem Packford have kindly agreed to take over Simon's role.

We are deeply saddened by the death of Barry Walker, who joined our committee last year. Our sincere condolences go to his widow, Linda, and all his family.

The committee would like to thank: Richard Whitfield for the hire of Fawler Farm fields as this year's showground; Sam Green and Jem Packford for designing this year's leaflets, advertisements and programme; Bailey & Sons Printers of Alfreton and Albry Design & Print of Wallingford for printing the show posters and leaflets; GE Capital for their generous donation.

The White Horse Show Committee is especially grateful to Nationwide Building Society for printing the show programmes.

Please note that, in order to facilitate servicing and to maintain a high standard of cleanliness, all the show toilets are located in one area which is marked on the showground map.

The full White Horse Show Committee for this, the thirty-fourth show, is as follows: chairman, Derek Kelsey, MBE; secretary, Ann Kelsey; treasurer, Ray Avenell; committee members, Paul Armishaw, Bill Mattingley, Mike Thomas, Eric Wyard, Clive Avenell, Christine Holley, Bernie Jones, Kerri Mack, Vern Dunkley, Brian White, Martin Bowsher, David Clarke, Ces Witchell; associates, Damian Wilson, Stephen Fisher, Viv Boaler, Lloyd Whitfield, Darren Scrivens, Simon Saunders, Steve Reed-Smith, Fran Walsh, Adrian Dunn, Chris Rayner, Mark Leahy, Christopher Holley, Cuan Ryan, Jackie Wyard, Annette Rayner; military organiser, Colonel A Bateman (ret'd).

The Battle of Britain memorial flight, 2005 (© John Gibbons Studios)

Songs of Praise – I would like to offer you a warm invitation to come and join in with our special White Horse Show Songs of Praise. This will take place in the main arena on Sunday afternoon at 5 p.m. Come along and sing some of your favourite hymns to the accompaniment of the Wantage Silver Band and the splendid fairground organ. This is the first year that we are holding a short, very informal afternoon service and we hope that White Horse Hill will resound to the sound of music! We need your help, so please do come along and sing. The service will be conducted by the Reverend Rosanna Martin, vicar of the Uffington Benefice.

On Saturday 27 August, the pony gymkhana took place in Arena 1 from 10.00 to 17.00.

The programme of events for Sunday 28 August was as follows:

Arena 1

- 10.00 Heavy Horse Show
- 13.00 Heavy Horse Riding Display
- 13.15 Parade of The Old Berks Hunt
- 13.30 White Horse Kites
- 14.00 Heavy Horse Show
- 15.30 Heavy Horse Parade
- 17.00 Songs of Praise – Rev. Rosanna Martin & Wantage Silver Band

Arena 2

- 11.00 White Horse Kites
- 11.30 Ray Prior Falconry
- 12.00 Tomorrow's Gun Dogs
- 12.30 Wax 'n' Wain
- 13.00 WTF Tae Kwon Do
- 13.30 Ray Prior Falconry
- 14.00 Tomorrow's Gun Dogs
- 14.30 Wax 'n' Wain
- 15.00 Parade of Historic Tractors
- 15.45 Parade of Historic Motorcycles

The timetable for Monday 29 August was:

Arena 1

- 11.30 White Horse Kites
- 12.45 Ray Prior Falconry
- 13.15 Danzone
- 13.45 Pageant to commemorate the sixtieth anniversary of the end of World War II. The Waterloo Band, Rifle Volunteers; The Chelsea Pensioners; The

Arena 2

- 10.45 Ray Prior Falconry
- 11.15 Tomorrow's Gun Dogs
- 11.45 Wax 'n' Wain
- 12.15 Merlin Engine
- 1.00 Tomorrow's Gun Dogs
- 1.30 Wax 'n' Wain
- 15.45 Parade of Historic Cars

Royal British Legion;
The Army Sea and Air
Training Corps Cadets;
The Battle of Britain
Memorial Flight Display
by Lancaster, Spitfire &
Hurricane

15.30 Egg Throwing
Competition Final

The White Horse Show Committee were very grateful to the Fish Brothers Group for their generous sponsorship of this year's arena events.

Churchill enters the arena, 2005 (© John Gibbons Studios)

A little more about some of our arena events in more detail; firstly, about the main event on Monday:

Vale Tribute 1939 to 1945 – This year all over the world people are remembering the end of World War II in 1945. Uffington is marking this sixtieth anniversary with a spectacular pageant, both on the ground and in the sky. The story of the 1939–45 war will be told with active and retired members of the armed services, local actors, original aeroplanes and vehicles. It will be accompanied by a first-class military band and a fascinating commentary, culminating in an act of remembrance to honour those who fell in the service of their country. We are privileged that the Waterloo Band and Bugles of the Royal Rifle Volunteers, pensioners from the Royal Hospital Chelsea, Sea, Air & Army Cadets, a contingent from RAF Brize Norton, representatives of the Royal British Legion, Burma Star Association, Royal Navy Association and RAF Association, and aircraft from the Battle of Britain Memorial Flight have all agreed to participate.

The Waterloo Band and Bugles of the Royal Rifle Volunteers – The Royal Rifle Volunteers is fortunate to have the Waterloo Band and Bugles as part of its establishment. The band is the only remaining Royal Green Jacket band, the regular bands having been amalgamated into the Light Division Band in 1998. The band was raised in 1987 but upholds traditions that can be dated back as far as 1665. Abandonment of the cumbersome drum in favour of the silver bugle enables the band to perform breathtaking displays at a speed of 140 paces to the minute. The Band and Bugles play at numerous events, both military and civilian. During this year these have so far included: Glorious Goodwood, Blenheim Palace 300th Anniversary of the Battle of Blenheim, RGJ Week, Winchester, Oxford Children's Hospital Campaign.

The musicians come from all walks of life and include managers, nurses and teachers, each of whom has enlisted in the Territorial Army. As with all bands – regular and territorial – its members have a secondary role, for example medical assistants or mortar men. The band is presently recruiting and would like to hear from brass and woodwind musicians between the ages of seventeen and thirty-two years.

The Milton Keynes Naval Cadet Corps and the Northampton Sea Cadets – These two cadet corps will stage training displays.

Army Cadets – The Shrivenham and Wantage detachment of the Oxfordshire Royal Green Jackets Battalion Army Cadet Force will be re-enacting the battle for Pegasus Bridge as part of our pageant. The cadets will also have an interesting static display with some military motorbikes. They will be happy to talk to you about the benefits of being an army cadet. The band and cadets appear by kind permission of their commanding officer, Lt. Col. M G Scott. The RAF contingent from Brize Norton is taking part by kind permission of the station commander, Group Captain Ian Elliot, OBE, ADC, BSc, FRIN, RAF.

The Battle of Britain Memorial Flight – The Battle of Britain Memorial Flight 2005 marks the sixty-fifth anniversary of the Battle of Britain and the sixtieth anniversary of the end of World War II. I foresee that the Battle of Britain Memorial Flight will be in great demand all over the country. The original purpose of the Memorial Flight was to help celebrate the Allied victory and the anniversary of the end of World War II. The Lancaster bomber, Spitfire fighter and Hurricane fighter represent the types of aircraft which played such an important parts in the final victory. The Flight is unique as a living tribute and more evocative than any static memorial. It flies in memory of those who flew. In these days of fast jets, it is a reminder of the remarkable achievements of the men who flew and maintained these historic aircraft in the heat of the great battles of the war.

Words by HRH the Duke of Edinburgh.

Chelsea Pensioners – The Royal Hospital Chelsea was founded in 1682 by King Charles II as a home for soldiers who were unfit for further duty because of injury or old age. At the start of the twenty-first century, the Royal Hospital still continues to provide a caring, comfortable and secure environment, with excellent medical facilities for some 350 old soldiers. This is carried out with a semi-military ethos and within buildings and grounds that form a significant part of the national heritage. However, the infirmary, a building put up to replace its predecessor which was destroyed in the Blitz, needs replacing, and the in-pensioners living accommodation is to be modernised to meet today's standards.

The term 'Chelsea Pensioner' has been used over the centuries to describe both 'in-' and 'out-pensioners'. An 'in-pensioner' is simply one who resides in the Royal Hospital

Chelsea. On entry, he surrenders his army pension. An 'out-pensioner' is a former soldier of the regular Army who receives a pension for long service and/or disability caused through service. The term derives from the period when the Royal Hospital was still being built.

On official occasions, Chelsea Pensioners wear the famous scarlet coats, complemented for ceremonial events by tricorne hats. Pensioners are invited and are guests of honour at many events, ceremonies and royal occasions. The White Horse Show is privileged to welcome these retired soldiers, who have served their country with distinction. We are delighted that they have come to Uffington to participate in our pageant commemorating the sixtieth anniversary of the cessation of hostilities in World War II and we thank them for their contribution.

Chelsea Pensioners, 2005 (© John Gibbons Studios)

Air Training Corps – The ATC is a uniformed, disciplined youth organisation for young people aged thirteen to twenty years. It was formed to provide pre-entry training for those wishing to serve in the RAF or Fleet Air Arm, but has changed to become one of the premier national youth organisations in the country.

The object of the corps is to promote and encourage among young people a practical interest in aviation, to provide training which will be useful in civilian or service life and, by fostering the spirit of adventure, to develop the qualities of leadership and good citizenship. 2121 (Abingdon) Squadron Air Training Corps are based at Dalton Barracks and meet every Tuesday and Thursday from 1915 hours to 2130 hours. We welcome their enthusiastic and disciplined contribution to our pageant.

Band of the Sea Cadets, 2005 (© John Gibbons Studios)

The Royal British Legion – The Royal British Legion is the leading charity looking after the welfare needs of the serving and ex-service members of the armed forces and their families. Within Berkshire, the Vale of White Horse, Oxfordshire and Wiltshire, the Royal British Legion branches in our communities are exceptionally busy, assisting with the rising demand for welfare assistance. This can range across all aspects of our work from providing powered scooters and wheelchairs to helping with bills or to offering a break in one of the Royal British Legion homes. The local communities in which we live continue their most generous support to the Poppy Appeal, which remains the main funding for all welfare assistance. In this, the sixtieth anniversary of the end of World War II, the public has shown an incredible appreciation of our ex-service community and an understanding of the challenges and dangers faced by our current armed forces. The White Horse Show is therefore very pleased to welcome representatives of the county branches of the Legion.

Exhortation, Col. (Ret'd) A J Bateman, OBE; parade marshal, Mr Ray Lancaster, MBE.

The committee would like to thank Sir Adrian Swire for generously sponsoring the pageant. During the pageant a collection will be taken; proceeds will be divided between the Royal Hospital's Infirmary Appeal and SSAFA Forces Help.

The Hurricane – The Hurricane is one of the classic fighters of all time. It was designed and built for war and it played a major part in achieving final victory in 1945. The prototype made its maiden flight on 6 November 1935 and deliveries to the RAF commenced just before Christmas 1937 (to 111 Squadron at Northolt). A remarkable total of 14,533 Hurricanes were built and the aircraft served operationally on every day throughout hostilities. It was at the forefront of Britain's defence in 1939–40. During the Battle of Britain, RAF Fighter Command fielded almost twice as many Hurricanes as Spitfires; Hurricanes similarly achieved a greater portion of kills. For the rest of the war the aircraft served in every operational theatre in many roles, and in 1945 Hurricanes were still in the front line helping to ensure final victory in the Far East.

Wax 'n' Wain – Europe's top comedy trampoline act invite you to a spectacular display of laughable aerial lunacy. The 'Dynamic Duo', Clive Brigdon and Alan Green, both international trampolinists, have made many TV appearances to quotes of 'Brilliant' and 'The best speciality act you will ever see!' Having completed three highly successful seasons at Chessington World of Adventures, leaving the crowd aghast, they went on to coordinate the new Western stunt show extravaganza, a presentation of two different twenty-minute performances, from humorous comedy to highly skilled acrobatics on skis. These Equity Stunt Register members perform both nationally and internationally, entertaining everywhere. A titanic act that always goes down well. Recent appearances include in Guernsey Diamond Liberation celebrations, marking sixty years of peace and freedom, Town Malling Day 2005 and Lions International May Fayre.

Barrow of Booze – As you walk round the showground you may meet someone pushing a wheelbarrow full of whisky, wine, bubbly, beer and other alcoholic beverages. This is not a mobile bar! (Our bar staff will be happy to serve you in the beer tent if you feel thirsty.) On show Sunday and Monday we are raffling the barrow and its contents to fund a Christmas lunch for Uffington's senior citizens. Last year's raffle (and donations) raised over £1,700 to provide a slap-up lunch – and the Barrow of Booze was won by our visiting Chelsea Pensioners! Well done everyone and thank you to all who took part. Try your luck again this year – just buy some raffle tickets from the 'pusher' – and all those lovely drinks could be yours, plus a barrow to push them home in.

Grand Funfair – The White Horse Show Committee are pleased that once again Hebborn's Grand Funfair will be at the White Horse Show. Harry Hebborn and his family have supported the White Horse Show for thirty years plus and we now have the third generation of Hebborns in attendance. No show would be complete without them. We are always delighted when Harry and his Grand Funfair arrive on the show field, as during the course of the show 'build-up' Harry is always willing to lend a hand – even if the hand belongs to one of his boys.

As always, the funfair will have lots of sideshows with great prizes to be won by luck or skill. You'll also find some fantastic rides like the Twister, and of course the Dodgems. So be sure to visit Hebborns fair while you are at the show.

Professor Crump – Step this way for fun, the over-grown professor is loose! A huge success when he made his White Horse Show debut in 1997, he has returned every year since by popular demand. The professor's been studying nonsense for years and gets up to all sorts of mischief. Old or young, you will not escape the balloon trickery, juggling, corny jokes and crazy gadgets of this manic eccentric on his giant yellow bicycle and push scooter.

His TV credits include *The Sooty Show*, *The Fumbles* and *Happy Monsters*. He has appeared in West End show *Barnum*, a 'Brum' video and the BBC's *Antiques Roadshow* to name but a varied few. A much-travelled man, the professor has appeared at

London Zoo (some say he should have stayed there) and performed as far afield as Germany, Dubai, Iceland and Malta. Recently he appeared at the VW Annual Ball in St Petersburg, Russia. The professor performed at Buckingham Palace for Her Majesty the Queen's party to celebrate the fiftieth anniversary of her coronation.

Having left the village, due to my wife Myra's health problems, in April 2003, one of the excuses of returning for a visit is to attend the White Horse Show. Needless to say, we have returned to see the three shows that have been held since we moved away from Uffington. To achieve this necessitated a round journey of 180 miles. Some people would say we must be mad to do this, but I am not slow in repudiating this. To both Myra and myself, attending a White Horse Show is well worth the effort. Over the last six shows (2000 to 2005), the only people who have been mad were the people not at the shows. They have missed all the top entertainment that the shows have engaged since the doldrums of the late 1990s. Since the year 2000, I believe that the attractions and entertainment offered at the shows have been first class. This, therefore, has got to be described as cheap, affordable entertainment within the price range of families. The argument to back this up comes in the attendance numbers at the shows over this period of time, and this reflects through to the profit margins of these shows. I will go further and state that the present chairman Derek Kelsey's style of leading from the front has proved a winner by gaining the complete backing of the whole White Horse Show Committee. On a lighter side (before she shoots me), yes, Ann, he had to have your support in particular, and we know only too well that you have never faltered from that position. I also like to think that the MBE that Derek was awarded in the Queen's Birthday Honours list of 2003 was related to the White Horse Shows.

On attending the 2005 show, we arrived quite early, so as to miss the crush to get in. In one way this was a bonus. By this I mean it gave us a chance to view quite a number of stalls in the marquees before they became too crowded. In this way it also enabled my wife Myra to gain access to these facilities on her electric scooter, which I think is yet another feather in the caps of the show committee – to hold a show of this size in fields of grass, you are in my eyes disabled-friendly. This became much more apparent as the day wore on, as I counted at least another six disabled people enjoying the show from the seat of a scooter. Besides this there were also three other people that I witnessed being pushed around in wheelchairs. As for toilet facilities for the disabled, these were well taken care of. This facility had been one of the items that was always at the forefront of the committee's thoughts when organising the showground's services.

A few of the 200-plus classic cars at the 2005 show, a popular attraction at every show since 1973

The crowd that attended was about as large as the committee could cope with without a significant increase in the amount of helpers they had. This was most obvious in the car park, where the attendants were stretched to the limit. This of course affected their ability to keep the traffic moving off the road. I am sure that, had the traffic been able to have kept on the move, the attendance would have been even greater than it was. But on the lighter side, the public queuing to gain access to the showground were at least being entertained. I thought that this was where Professor Crump really came into his own. By the expressions on the faces of the children waiting to enter, they were certainly enjoying the entertainment being dished out by the Mad Professor. The cost of employing him was good value for money.

As for the 2005 show, I thought that this was one of the best shows for a very long time. The pageant in the main arena accompanied by a military band was of excellent standard and organised to perfection. Having lived throughout the war in the village it certainly brought back vivid memories to me of what life was really like in those terrible dark days. This was certainly a tribute to those who paid the ultimate price in giving their lives to serve the King and country in those six terrible years from 1939 to 1945. I know full well that this was appreciated by the vast crowd that congregated around the arena to witness this event. One of the most moving things that I have ever seen at a White Horse Show took place when the Chelsea Pensioners marched into that arena. I am sure that every man, woman and child stood and applauded them. I could not see anyone sitting down. To me this act said everything possible; this in my mind was the ultimate appreciation of those fine, brave gentlemen.

As for the Battle of Britain Flight, to the people that heard this same sound, day in and day out, night in and night out, throughout that long dark conflict, this must have been the crowning glory of a really magnificent pageant. Seeing the bomb flaps open on the Lancaster also brought back memories; we occasionally saw this when one was returning during the war and had had its own problems over enemy territory and had to limp back home the best they could. Added to this, it was not unusual to see pieces of fuselage flapping in the wind after these brave men had been shot up during their operation and were making for the first airfield that could accept them. The Hurricane and Spitfire said everything in the manoeuvres that they performed, as a fitting tribute to 'the few'.

The whole pageant left the arena after this event and, in all the White Horse Shows that I have seen (that is the complete thirty-four so far), I have never seen the whole audience stand and applaud like that until the last person had left the arena. It was certainly a very moving spectacle of appreciation by the public and one I had never witnessed before. The appreciation of the public also showed in the collection which was taken for the benefit of the Chelsea Pensioners, the Royal British Legion and the RAF Association. This large collection was topped up by the White Horse Show Committee, then split three different ways with an equal amount to each organisation. On talking to a good cross-section of the general public after the pageant I was not surprised to learn the great popularity of the Chelsea Pensioners. It therefore did not surprise me to be told by many that they would welcome the sight of those fine gentlemen again next year.

Massed standard- bearers, 2005 (© John Gibbons Studios)

Conclusion

The attendance at the 2005 show just goes to prove that the arguments that were put forward back in the time of the doldrums were the right ones. If real 'class events' are put into the arena, as they have been over the last few years, then the crowds will flock in. I feel, therefore, that I must congratulate the present White Horse Show Committee for having the shrewdness and courage to adopt this policy. It seems to me that over the last two shows the military presence, with their very precise organisation, is a certain crowd puller. It has proved thus so many times in the past. I have personally gone up on to the commentators' platform in the past and witnessed crowds of ten to twelve deep all around the main arena when a military band has been performing. On top of this, when we were honoured with the motorcycle display team of the Royal Artillery, 'The Flying Gunners', in 1990, to get anywhere near to the main arena was an achievement in itself. If one looks back to 1988, when we were blessed with the presence of the Musical Ride of the Household Cavalry, it tended to cause very deep debate on the subject of cost in meetings leading up to that show. But at the end of the day the committee then decided to 'bite the bit' and pay for this event.

I agree that it made us all think very deeply about whether we were doing the right thing at that time or not, but we took the chance. We needed no further proof that we had in fact done the right thing when the crowds turned up for that show. After the show accounts were published it proved again that we were perfectly right in our judgement, as this was the year that we were pushed into the VAT bracket by the attendance record at that show. If the cost of the 1988 show was matched in accordance with the last show of 2005, on that basis I believe that they compare on a very similar level. Once again, at both of these shows where the military has been present, all records have been broken. I do not think this is a mere coincidence. If we look back to all the shows where we have had a military band, we never had a failure or a loss.

I recall back in the mid-1970s when the late Brigadier Harry Hopkinson announced to a show meeting that he might be able to book us a military band for the bank holiday Monday, albeit at quite a cost, and asked us whether he should book it. This had the immediate backing of the chairman at that time, the late John Little. True to John's style, he threw it open to discussion. Hardly any discussion took place; the decision was unanimous, 'get it' was the quick reply. That year we were blessed with the presence of the band of the Royal Gurkha Riffles, and what a display they put on, marching and counter-marching at 140 paces to the minute. It was certainly a spectacle to see. After the show was over and the accounts were seen, the committee never hesitated to engage a military band –until the mid-1990s, that is.

During that span of time the military bands that we were privileged to have was nearly unbelievable: nearly all of the Guards bands, including the Pipes and Drums of the Royal Scots Greys, the band of the Royal Marines, and not forgetting the band of the Royal Green Jackets. Throughout this time, not once did we make a loss. But for some unknown reason suddenly caution took over. Why? I still do not understand. The policy of the committee changed and it became apparent that a few seemed to want to predetermine the profit margin prior to the show taking place. This policy could only start things on the slippery slope to a disaster. I am therefore pleased that the present committee, under the chairmanship of Mr Derek Kelsey MBE, has pulled the show back to its old ways. The proof of this is surely highlighted in the attendances and profit margins of the 2004 and 2005 shows. These I will briefly set out in comparison to each other.

Firstly, the receipts:

	2004	2005
Gate Receipts	£43,424	£62,263
Rent from Trade Stands	£6,997	£9,296
Caterers	£4,000	£4,000
Sale of Novelties	£15	—

Programme Advertising	£1,185	£1,779
Programme Sales	£1,476	£1,460
Hebborn Fair	£1,000	£1,000
Elite Helicopters	£404	£471
Sponsorship	£1,050	£1,500
Proceeds from Beer Tent	£2,446	£4,116
Receipts from Side Shows	£1,019	£672
Fines for Litter	£15	—
Logs Sold	£100	£40
Bank Interest	£177	£195
Misc.	—	£4
Total Income	£63,308	£86,796

Secondly, the expenditure:

	2004	2005
Events – Group 1	£7,838	£8,122
Group 2	£3,319	£3,870
Village Entertainment	£500	£150
Field Costs	£18,668	£18,930
Publicity	£2,279	£2,545
Other Costs	£4,510	£4,750
Total Expenditure	£37,114	£38,367
Surplus Profit for Year	£26,194	£48,429

Just to look at the figures for the 2005 show, it can be easily seen why the committee was stretched and were saying that at their present strength they were at their limit. This is something that the community of the three villages must give serious thought to in the coming months. I believe that this hard-working and brave committee deserve the full backing of the whole community over the weekend of the White Horse Show. This backing must also include some of the thoughtless people in the village of Uffington who needlessly leave their vehicles on the roadside during the show. Surely it would not be that much trouble to park them off of the road for the duration of the show?

I have in the past indicated that the numerous beneficiaries of the show should in the future give serious consideration as to their reliance for funds from the trust for their existence. After again giving this subject careful deliberation, I yet again urge them to contact the show chairman and volunteer as much labour over the show weekend as possible. Surely it is in the interests of all of the beneficiaries from the three villages of Uffington, Baulking and Woolstone to ensure the continuance of the White Horse Show for many more years to come? The present show committee and trustees thoroughly deserve that support as the following grants must surely show:

Grants From The White Horse Show Trust

	2005	Cumulative
Uffington Sports Club		
Car Park	£3,000	
Youth Cricket Club	£200	
Fireworks	£350	£30,375
White Horse Show Committee	—	£2,342
Thomas Hughes Memorial Hall	£2,000	£20,243
Uffington Players	—	£3,106
Uffington Parish Council	—	£400
Uffington Youth Club	£250	£1,034
Tom Brown's School Museum	—	£11,495
Uffington Afternoon Club £	£400	3,600
St Mary's Church	—	£20,429
Uffington Christmas Tree Lights	£75	£1,021
Uffington Primary School PTA	—	£15,550
Thomas Saunders Foundation	—	£1,033
Uffington Primary School		
Library Project	£1,000	
John Little Award	£25	£10,025
White Horse Pre-School	—	£2,740
All Saints Church Woolstone	—	£15,050

Saint Nicholas Church Baulking	—	£13,025
Uffington, Baulking and Woolstone Minibus	—	£16,100
Playground	—	£3,900
Uffington Scouts	—	£3,605
Uffington Guides	—	£900
Uffington Short Mat Bowls	—	£575
St John Ambulance	—	£500
Uffington Day Centre	—	£900
Uffington Area Parents & Toddlers	—	£300
Uffington, Baulking and Woolstone Women's Institute	£150	£150
Red Cross	—	£1,070
Miscellaneous	—	£342
Totals	£7,450	£179,810

When the total of £179,810 is looked at and the reality of this figure is studied, this is only a part of the income that the show brings into the three villages. Also it must be born in mind that this figure has been achieved since the building of the Thomas Hughes Memorial Hall, and the changing of the charity trusts in 1983. If we add to this total the cost of the Thomas Hughes Memorial Hall, then it has to be increased by at least another £100,000. On top of this, all the local organisations attend the show each year to do their own money-raising. If we then take into consideration all the other money that has been brought into the three villages over the years since 1972, in the form of grants, as a direct result of the show, this figure must further increase to nearer the half-million pound mark. It is with this in mind that I again reiterate that it is in the interest of all the beneficiaries to take a long hard look at the amount of help that they offer to the show.

    Let's look at the potential strength of the recipients, for example the Uffington Primary School. Assuming that there are some seventy pupils attending that school, irrespective of whether they live within the three villages or not, it is certainly true that they all benefit from the show with equipment that has come from the trust. Working on the assumption that there are seventy pupils, this adds up to some 140 parents who ought to be taking a serious look at their position. Since the new trust was set up in 1983, some £26,608 has been given in grants to the Uffington C. of E. Primary School for various projects, which all the children attending have benefited by. If just one parent per child offered three hours of service to the show over the show weekend, this would equal a total of 210 hours of help to the White Horse Show Committee. I can guarantee that both the chairman and all the committee would be extremely grateful and would accept the offer with open arms.

With this in mind, the Uffington Sports and Social Club are also grateful recipients of the trust. Again I question the amount of help that they offer to the White Horse Show. The Sports and Social Club of course includes the football club, cricket club, tennis club and all the junior clubs that enjoy the facilities of the Craven Field. Also, we must not forget the White Horse Pre-school Group, with two parents per child – do they offer any assistance to the show? When a critical look is taken at the amount of help that the hard-working White Horse Show Committee receives from the villages over the period of the show it is somewhat pitiful to say the least. The White Horse Show Committee are working on the show for the full fifty-two weeks of every year, so when this wonderful hard-working bunch requests help for two or three days once a year, they are not asking for an arm or a leg. I realise that over the years the three churches have also received grants from the trust. This I believe to be right and just. For a start they are three magnificent buildings, which have graced the three villages for a great number of years. They are there to be used by all the villagers of all three villages, if they so choose. The upkeep of these buildings is extremely expensive. Then, of course, there is also the high cost of keeping the churchyards tidy with the grass cut as often as possible. Needless to say, this work does not perform itself; it has to be paid for and the cost of labour is increasing all the time. The show committee has always received the backing and support from the church wardens and the vicar over the years. I know for a fact this had not altered at the last show, as they were all there again helping with the show. This included the new vicar, the Reverend Rosanna Martin, who looked like she was really enjoying the hard work she was putting into the show.

The blessing being conducted by the Rev. Rosanna Martin, vicar of the Uffington benefice, at the altar of drums. In attendance: Col. (ret'd) A J Bateman, OBE, vice-president Royal Scots Dragoon Guards Regimental Association; Mr R Good, Col. Ser. (ret'd), Irish Guards, area organiser, Royal British Legion; Major K Mackenzie, Royal Canadian Air Force. Seated in rear: the Waterloo Band, the Royal Rifle volunteers – 2005 (© John Gibbons Studios)

The critics will be heard, as they have always have been over the last forty-six years of money-raising within the village. But my message to the committee is clear: just ignore them. In the past they have never had the courage to come forward and offer help or advice, and they certainly will not in the future. One sure fact is that they will always be conspicuous by their absence, and you will be far better off without their company.

In winding up this insight into the White Horse Show over its duration until the present time, I would like to thank the past and present members of the committee for all the pleasure they have given me over the years. Yes, we have had our differences of opinion over those years, but at the end of the day we all accepted the majority decision made at the time and supported the various chairmen to implement that decision. That in a nutshell is why the great event that is the White Horse Show is going on again in 2006. This is one thing amongst many that the creator of the show, the late John Little, always emphasised: make a majority decision then stick by it, as that was the only way forward. I believe that John's philosophy on this subject has proved to be right over the years. The proof of this is still there after thirty-four years. That this small community can field a united committee to run a show the size of the White Horse Show is a credit to all concerned.

In completing this insight, my final thanks go to the present chairman Mr Derek Kelsey, MBE and his wife Ann, who have given me all the support I could have expected from them, together with the information that I needed to complete this task. I hope also that they will not be offended when I again look back to 2003 and consider that Derek's MBE was an honour to the White Horse Show.

Finally, I still believe that the White Horse Show is a great legacy left to the village by the late John E Little, who had the foresight and courage to set it all in motion in 1972. Long may it continue.

About the Author

After attending the open meeting in the Old Village Hall in April 1960 and getting roped in to help form a committee to raise money to build a new village hall, I little realised at the time what a long and hard slog I had let myself in for. However, I always vowed that I would never give in until the task was completed.

The next twelve years were possibly the most strenuous part of the period leading to our success, with inflation grinding us to a near standstill, yet I now feel honoured and privileged to have worked over a period of forty-two and a half years to contribute some good to the village of Uffington. I have had the pleasure of working with so many dedicated villagers throughout that time and I am proud that together we have been able to replace a commodity that our forefathers left to the village after the 1914–1918 war.

Printed in the United Kingdom
by Lightning Source UK Ltd.
131423UK00001B/85-285/A